In Defense of Free Capital Markets

The Case Against a New Financial Architecture

by David F. DeRosa

In Defense
of
Free Capital
Markets

In Defense

of

Free Capital Markets

The Case Against a New International
Financial Architecture

DAVID F. DEROSA

BLOOMBERG PRESS

PRINCETON

First edition published 2001
1 3 5 7 9 10 8 6 4 2

DeRosa, David F.
    In defense of free capital markets : the case against a new international financial architecture / David F. DeRosa
        p. cm.
    Includes bibliographical references and index.
    ISBN 1-57660-036-X (alk. paper)
    1. Foreign exchange—Developing countries—Case studies. 2. Capital market— Developing countries—Case studies 3. Free enterprise—Developing countries—Case studies. 4. Deregulation—Developing countries—Case studies. I. Title.

HG3877.D47   2001
332'.042'091724—dc21   00-062090

Book Design by LAURIE LOHNE / DESIGN IT COMMUNICATIONS

To the memory of my parents,

Frank J. DeRosa, Jr. and Michelle A. DeRosa

Contents

C h a p t e r   O n e

Financial Policy and the Cycle of Regulation   1

C h a p t e r   T w o

Japan's Lost Decade of the 1990s   23

C h a p t e r   T h r e e

Exploding Foreign Exchange Regimes   55

Chapter Four

The Southeast Asian Currency Crisis of 1997   83

Chapter Five

Accounting for Contagion   113

Chapter Six

Exploding Hedge Funds   135

Illustrations

Figures

Tables

Boxes

A c k n o w l e d g m e n t s

In the course of the preparation of this book I have received assistance, advice, commentary, and have had useful intellectual discussions with many people. I would like to thank Tom Coleman, Peter Halle, Jared Kieling, Robert Laurent, Roger Lowenstein, Brian McCarthy, Phil Nehro, Robert Sinche, Aziza Starkow, Joseph Starshak, Bernard Sucher, Nassim Nicholas Taleb, and Charles Van Vleet. Over the course of the last few years I have been a thrice-weekly contributing columnist for Bloomberg News on topics relating to international finance and foreign exchange. The association has brought me in contact with Matt Winkler, Stuart Jackson, Chuck Stevens, and Lisa Wolfson, plus numerous other editors, reporters, and librarians at Bloomberg L.P., all of whom I thank for having helped me develop as a writer. I alone am responsible for any errors that might be contained herein.

Preface

BROAD-SPECTRUM REFORM of the international financial system has been recommended following the remarkable financial crisis in the 1990s, especially since the collapse of the Asian developing countries and so many other emerging market nations. This book argues the opposite, that reforms, meaning more regulations, are not needed. As its title suggests, the book is a straightforward defense of free-market economics, with the focus on the international financial system. It makes the case for allowing the international financial markets to remain largely unregulated.

When people advocate that the international financial system needs to be totally redesigned, one would hope that they are in possession of a solid understanding of what actually causes financial crisis. Usually that is not the case. Indeed, even commentary about international financial economics made by heads of state, ministers of finance, and central bankers often betrays a basic ignorance about the international capital market, down to the level of what it is and how it works. One has to wonder, on occasion, what influences shape their sense of recent economic history. And when confronted with a financial crisis, many leaders, but not all leaders, prefer to hunt for villains and indict the international financial system rather than admit to policy blunders of their own making. The first blame usually goes to the foreign exchange market and to the system that affords mobility to international capital.

The methodology of this book is one of examination of the historical economic conditions that produced financial crises in the 1990s and in some preceding periods. Also examined are the responses to crisis. Did government policies directed at these episodes of turmoil made matters better or worse? In many cases, at least in the history of the '90s, policy can be shown to have exacerbated the upheavals. What comes from this exercise is an understanding that financial crisis largely can be explained by looking at the domestic policies that ministries of finance and central banks have laid out for their own countries. In other words, the predisposing conditions for crisis are local in nature; crisis comes from within, not from the outside, and not because capital is permitted to move freely across borders or because of market-determined exchange rates.

Another revelation is that the concept of financial contagion, a notion that permeates speeches and press interviews given by the authorities, is dubious at best as a cause of financial turmoil. Financial crisis does not come right out of thin air to strike economically healthy nations and then spread like a communicable disease from one country to the next.

One lesson rings loud and clear, that a country's choice of a foreign exchange regime is one of the most important decisions that it makes. For example, fixed foreign exchange rate systems, but not floating systems, are in fact the breeding grounds for great financial crises, as will be demonstrated repeatedly in the cases that this book examines.

For this reason the dynamics of how a fixed exchange rate regime collapses are studied closely in this book. It will be shown that practically all of the episodes of financial crisis in the '90s occurred in countries that had fixed exchange rate systems, and that this is more than coincidence. This should become apparent as the book goes through the history of Mexico in 1994–1995, Southeast Asia in 1997–1998, South Korea in 1998, Hong Kong in 1998, Russia in 1998, Brazil in 1998, and several other countries as well.

Chapter 2 is spent entirely on Japan to answer the question of how the world's second-largest country managed to reverse its pattern of decades of phenomenal growth to end the century in a state of economic torpor. Though Japan does not have a fixed exchange rate regime, it will be shown that its economic disappointments are traceable in part to errors in the formulation of monetary policy. Other factors, ones deeply embedded in the Japanese economic and political system, also are to blame for that country's problems.

The later chapters of the book are concerned with alternative foreign exchange regimes, including currency boards and dollarization, and rebuttal of various suggestions for reform of the international financial architecture. Chapter 8 delves into the question of what should be the future of the International Monetary Fund and comes down on the side of those who want to greatly limit its activities, especially those pertaining to its financial crisis and rescue work.

Finally, I should say that this book is not intended to be a defense of hedge funds, foreign exchange trading, and speculation. There are no ulterior motives; the book is nothing more than what its title suggests.

Chapter One

Financial Policy and the Cycle of Regulation

T HE FINANCIALLY TURBULENT decade of the 1990s is a challenge for market-oriented economists to explain. Conservative economists, starting with Adam Smith, have professed for more than two centuries that a free-market economy, devoid of central economic planning and light on government regulation of the forces of supply and demand, is the most efficient and reliable economic system.

Yet in the 1990s, exchange rate crises, stock market crashes, and severe economic contractions plagued countries around the world. Eisuke Sakakibara, Japan's outspoken former Vice Finance Minister for International Affairs, captured the desperation of the time when he declared the existence of a "crisis of global capitalism."[1] It is no wonder that the free-market model has begun to be seen as an unworkable paradigm, in some people's minds.

In Asia, things began to go wrong precisely at the start of the decade. Only a few years earlier it had been heard that the next century, meaning the twenty-first, would be the "Asian century." Normally skeptical observers were confounded by Asia's economic reversal; seasoned professional investors were caught flat-footed in Asia's meltdown, first with Japan, then with Southeast Asia, and later with South Korea.

Japan, by the end of the 1980s, had been the world's pre-eminent economic growth model for more than thirty years. Trouble arose in January 1990, with a sudden decline in the Japanese stock market. Soon after, the Japanese real estate and banking sectors headed toward a state of near insolvency. Japan spent the entire decade of the 1990s in varying degrees of economic stagnation. It also experienced an uncharacteristic political instability; prime ministers came and went from the national stage faster than actors at a music hall variety show. As the economic predicament became progressively more severe, embittered and frustrated politicians began to put blame on exogenous foreign factors.

Financial chaos paid a visit to central Europe in the first three years of the same decade in the form of two currency crises. In 1979 members of the European Monetary Union decided to enter into a system of semifixed exchange rates called the Exchange Rate Mechanism. The ERM was to engender stability among the intra-European exchange rates and pave the way toward the long-cherished single European currency project. Instead, it spawned two spectacular currency crises (September 1992 and August 1993) and several dozen exchange rate revaluations.

In December 1994 Mexico experienced a stunning currency crisis only twenty days into the administration of its newly inaugurated President, Ernesto Zedillo. Previously Mexico had had a fixed exchange rate regime for the peso that allowed for a gradual, controlled devaluation. The peso crisis, which did tremendous damage to the Mexican economy, turns out to have been a near perfect blueprint for what happened two and one-half years later in Southeast Asia. The Southeast Asian crisis was nearly identical in its financial mechanics to what happened to the Mexican peso. Also, Mexico, in receiving emergency financial assistance from the United States in 1995, set the conceptual stage for the International Monetary Fund (IMF) to bail out Thailand, Indonesia, and South Korea later in the decade.

The Asian investment outlook that investors accepted as correct for most of the '90s was disarmingly simple. Japan's own decades of impressive economic growth would be Asia's lamp, lighting the way to prosperity for the so-called tiger countries, Thailand, Indonesia, Malaysia, and South Korea. Investors saw these countries as their chance to get rich by participating in a replay of Japan's postwar economic history, about to be repeated in Southeast Asia and South Korea. Putting money in these so-called tiger countries was seen as the next best thing to having had the foresight to have invested in Japan in the 1960s.

Economist Paul Krugman challenged this rose-tinted view of Asia in 1994 in a widely read article entitled "The Myth of the Asian Miracle." [2] Krugman, as he himself has pointed out, merely predicted a gradual slowing of Asian growth. Neither Krugman, nor anyone else to the best of the author's knowledge, foresaw that Asia would suffer a series of violent economic implosions. But he did make his point. In 1994, Asia's growth was about to become a story that would have to be told in the past tense.

In the summer of 1997, the Southeast Asian currency crisis ignited. Asian emerging market nations tumbled into economic chaos like dominos. The chain of events commenced when Thailand was forced to float the baht on July 2, 1997. Observers at the time remarked that some sort of previously unknown and highly contagious economic plague was loose in the Asian continent. It quickly spread throughout the region, with devastating consequences to the Philippines, Malaysia, and Indonesia. Thailand and Indonesia requested and received massive financial aid from the IMF.

The second round of the Asian crisis occurred in October 1997 when the stock market in Hong Kong experienced a steep drop. Rumors began to circulate that Hong Kong would soon be forced to abandon its fixed exchange rate regime for the Hong Kong dollar. Within two months, South Korea became the next casualty to experience a foreign exchange crisis complete with a stock market meltdown and a bank panic. South Korea requested and received billions of dollars in financial relief from the IMF that allowed it to narrowly avoid national bankruptcy.

Major changes in the political landscape followed quickly. New governments were elected in Thailand and South Korea. The crises also claimed the presidency of Indonesia's Suharto, who was forced from power after three decades of ironfisted rule. In Malaysia, Prime Minister Mahathir bin Mohamad managed to remain in power despite the near total collapse of his country's

BOX 1.1

Spot and Forward Foreign Exchange

THE FOREIGN EXCHANGE market is comprised of money-center banks, investment banks, and specialized brokerage firms. It is a wholesale market where an estimated one trillion dollars per day moves around the world. Most of the trading, some 90 percent, involves transactions for which the U.S. dollar is one side.

A spot foreign exchange transaction is a deal between two counterparties, usually banks, that requires the exchange of sums of foreign currency in two bank business days (referred to as the spot value date). For example, if one party buys ten million dollars against yen at the exchange rate of 125.00, it will receive $10,000,000 (in New York) and must deliver 1,250,000,000 yen (in Tokyo) in two days' time. The bulk of the trading in the foreign exchange market consists of spot dealing.

Many currencies are quoted against the dollar in terms of the number of units of foreign currency equal to one dollar. For example, $/¥ might be quoted as 120.00, meaning 120 yen are equivalent to one U.S. dollar. The euro, the pound, the Australian dollar, and the New Zealand dollar are prominent exceptions. Those currencies are quoted in dollars. For example, the value of the euro could be quoted as .9000, indicating that one euro costs ninety U.S. cents.

A second variety of foreign exchange trade is the forward transaction. This is the same as spot except that the value date falls after the spot value date. Forward transactions are routinely quoted for value in 1 week, 1 month, 3 months, 6 months, 9 months, and 1 year. The forward exchange rate for a particular value date is called the *outright*.

The difference between the outright for a particular date and the spot exchange rate is called the forward points. The forward points are linked by arbitrage to the difference between the interest rates in the two currencies. This relationship is called the covered interest parity theorem (see DeRosa 1996, 2000, and Keynes). Keeping all other things constant, the higher the foreign currency interest rate, the lower the forward dollar value of a foreign currency.

Forward foreign exchange is essential to hedgers. Consider the case of American investors who have decided to buy Japanese government bonds (JGBs). In the first instance the investors must exchange dollars to buy yen to pay for the bonds. As soon as they own the yen, they are exposed in the dimension of foreign exchange to movements in the yen. If the yen weakens, the investors will have a loss on the bonds; if the yen strengthens they will have a gain on the bonds—both deriving purely from the movements in exchange rates without any consideration of changes of the value of the bonds in yen terms.

So the investors might decide to *hedge* their foreign exchange exposure using forward foreign exchange contracts. The typical way that investors hedge is with short- and medium-term forward foreign exchange contracts, 3 or 6 months in term. (If the hedge is to be kept for longer periods of time, the investors can simply roll to a new forward contract as the existing contract matures.) In the example of the American investors with the JGB position, the hedge would consist of a forward contract to buy dollars and sell yen. No cash moves until the value date of the forward contract. If the yen rises in value, the hedge will produce a loss, but that will be balanced by the foreign-exchange-related capital gain on the Japanese bonds. Likewise, if the yen falls, the hedge will show a profit and the bonds will have a corresponding capital loss—all because of changes in the exchange rate. In practice there are many levels of complexity beyond this; interested readers may refer to DeRosa "Managing Foreign Exchange Risk." In its simplest form, however, this is how a forward hedge takes currency risk out of the investment equation.

economy, but he felt he needed to resort to extraordinary measures to hold on, including making wild accusations about an international conspiracy against his country.

In August 1998, Russia simultaneously defaulted on its maturing treasury debt and devalued the ruble. When the ruble was allowed to float, it plunged to near worthlessness. Many international investors who participated in the Russian debt market had hedged their exposure to the ruble with forward foreign exchange contracts that had Russian banks as counterparties (Box 1.1).

Unfortunately for the investors, Russian banks refused to perform on their forward ruble contracts when the government defaulted on its debt. The shock waves from the Russian default set off financial events felt as far away as Latin America. Violent movements in North American stock and bond markets ensued, climaxing with the dramatic collapse of Long-Term Capital Management (LTCM), a well-known American investment firm.

In September 1998 Malaysia's mercurial prime minister Mahathir declared with flourish that he had put an end to foreign exchange trading in the ringgit and imposed capital controls on international money flows trying to exit his country. Mahathir put the blame for the entire Southeast Asian crisis on currency speculators, and in particular, on the person of famed hedge fund manager, George Soros.

In January 1999, Brazil suffered a huge depreciation in its currency, and its financial markets nosedived after one of its states refused to make scheduled payments that it owed to the national government. Ecuador next was hit with a currency crisis of its own. Ecuador secured its place in history when it became the first nation to default on a Brady bond issue. Brady bonds are named after former U.S. Treasury Secretary Nicholas Brady who introduced them in the 1980s to reduce the debt burden facing developing nations.

These are the highlights of the low points of the '90s. The big picture for this troubled decade can be summarized as this: Parts of Europe, Asia, Russia, and Latin America experienced currency crises, stock market crashes, deflation, recession, sovereign insolvency, and political instability all rooted in economic dislocations.

Understandably, the stability of the global market economy has been called into question. However, the questions being asked are often the wrong ones.

The Analysis of Financial Policy

THIS BOOK IS LARGELY concerned with the analysis of financial policy, a term which the author narrowly defines to be the class of macroeconomic initiatives directed by heads of state, central bankers, and ministers of finance at foreign exchange and asset markets. The analysis of financial policy first requires consideration of the goals that officials set out to achieve. Some of these goals have been worthwhile. Others have been frivolous if not outright detrimental to the proper workings of economic markets.

The single most important financial policy decision that a country makes is its choice of which exchange rate regime to establish for its currency; as will be discussed at length in this book, many fixed exchange rate regimes have failed in their intended purpose of maintaining stability in the currency market. Quite the opposite of what was intended, fixed exchange rate regimes can cause violent macroeconomic fluctuations. A few fixed exchange rate regimes have been successful, but most have ended in spectacular crises, such as was experienced with the Mexican peso (1994), the Thai baht (1997), the Indonesian rupiah (1997), the Russian ruble (1998), and the Brazilian real (1998).

The unintended or indirect consequences of financial policy are more complex to judge. Financial policy can have far-reaching effects, some salutary, others harmful. In the period 1994–1995, the United States, Germany, and Japan banded together to try to stop the dollar from falling, principally against the Japanese yen but also against the German mark. This group, nicknamed the G3, expended considerable energy and funds to try to turn the dollar around. Eventually, the dollar did bottom out in April 1995. The complication was that while U.S. Treasury Secretary Robert Rubin and his partners in Germany and Japan were telling the world that a "strong dollar" was in everyone's interest, Asia was accumulating massive debts, most of which were denominated in dollars. The

Asian countries had in effect taken a very risky exposure to the potential rise in the dollar. As the dollar began to rise, the severity of the Asian dollar debt was magnified greatly, from the perspective of local currency. Foreign currency denominated debt was a major causal factor in the 1997 Southeast Asian currency selloff. Hence to the extent to which the G3's strong-dollar policy was successful in impacting exchange rates, it could be said to have contributed to the ensuing the bankruptcy of Asia.

Sometimes financial policy goes wrong in execution. Soon after becoming Secretary of the Treasury in 1995, Robert Rubin initiated a coordinated foreign exchange intervention to support the dollar. No sooner had the intervention commenced than did President Bill Clinton begin to deliver televised speeches attacking the Republicans in Congress for wanting to "explode the budget deficit." The dollar first rose against the German mark and Japanese yen but then promptly plunged as the market took in what the president was saying. The market could hardly have been expected to be enthusiastic about the dollar when the president was accusing the Congress of being fiscally irresponsible. Rubin's later interventions showed more of the considerable currency trading skills learned earlier in his career during his Wall Street days.

One of the most egregious technical errors in the execution of financial policy occurred in 1985 when the finance ministers and central bankers from G5 nations, the Group of Five Industrialized Nations that consisted of France, Germany, U.K., Japan, and the United States, hatched the Plaza Accord foreign exchange intervention to lower the value of the dollar against other principal currencies. The "Plaza intervention," as it has come to be known because the ministers met in the famous New York hotel by that name, was the first large-scale coordinated central bank attack on the foreign exchange market since exchange rates were allowed to float against the dollar in 1973. The error was that the G5 delegates failed to obtain, or maybe completely overlooked, a necessary agreement among themselves to coordinate their immediate monetary policy surrounding their planned currency intervention, as will be explained in Chapter 2. Even more serious errors in execution of financial policy occurred in the Asian currency crisis of 1997, as will be revealed in subsequent chapters.

Financial policy can also be directed at asset markets. Japan has a long-standing interest in preventing a declining trend in prices in its government bond market. At this writing, Japanese government bonds are at record low yields following a decade of economic stagnation. The authorities feel it is their duty to manage any rise in bond yields that they see forthcoming with the potential emergence of Japan from its ten-year slump. To this end, they engage in convoluted tactics to support the bond market, including the counterintuitive practice of having the government and its agencies buy their own bonds in the secondary market.

Another example of financial policy aimed at asset markets is in Hong Kong, where the authorities took the extraordinary step in August 1998 of direct intervention to support the local stock market. This policy initiative stands in direct contradiction to Hong Kong's long-standing legacy as the bastion of free-market economics.

The U.S. Federal Reserve, too, has been known to react to stock market fluctuations. This is not necessarily a bad thing. High praise was heaped on U.S. Federal Reserve Chairman Alan Greenspan for his handling of the threatening situation that surrounded the 1987 stock market plunge. Greenspan offered unlimited funds to the nation's banks to preclude their shutting off credit to the brokerage community. The intention of the Federal Reserve was to stop the stock market panic from spreading; it achieved this objective without crossing the line by directly stabilizing share prices.

The New York Federal Reserve showed less restraint when it decided to introduce itself into the dissolution of Long-Term Capital Management, an insolvent investment company, in 1998. Officials of the Federal Reserve Bank of New York encouraged, and maybe coerced, a group of commercial and investment banks that had lent money to LTCM into taking over the firm. At about the same time, the Federal Open Market Committee delivered a series of cuts to the federal funds target interest rate, totaling 75 basis points, or 0.75 percent. The LTCM crisis faded in a few months. Whether or not the Federal Reserve helped or damaged the situation is not clear. But what endures is the impression that a privately managed investment fund almost brought the international financial system to ruin but for the swift intervention of the government.

The broad study of financial policy might also involve the analysis of tangential areas of economic decision making, such as fiscal policy, including the implications of changes in a country's tax laws. Japan made a crucial error in judgment in April 1997 when it decided to raise its national sales tax. Critics of then Prime Minister Ryutaro Hashimoto believe his insistence on raising the tax was responsible for materially obstructing a nascent recovery in Japan. It didn't do Hashimoto much good politically either, because the electorate roundly hated his tax hike. His Liberal Democratic Party (LDP) garnered a miserable showing in the July 1998 parliamentary elections. Hashimoto accepted responsibility and promptly resigned as Prime Minister, but the bureaucrats at the Ministry of Finance (MOF) who pushed for the tax increase remained safe at their desks.

The Growth of Antimarket Sentiment

JOHN MAYNARD KEYNES in the 1923 preface to the French-language translation of his *Tract on Monetary Reform* wrote, "Each time the franc loses value, the Minister of Finance is convinced that the fact arises from everything but economic causes. He attributes it to the presence of foreigners in the corridors of the bourse, to unwholesome and malign forces of speculation." [3] These two brief sentences are prescient, for as Keynes surely would have predicted, the blame for the 1990s crises has been ascribed to everything but fundamental economic causes. Many prominent political leaders and economic ministers have ducked any examination of how their domestic policy blunders may have created the nightmarish economic conditions in Europe, Asia, Russia, and Latin America, and have turned instead to making the international monetary system their scapegoat. The fault it is said, is with the free-market system itself (Box 1.2).

Financial crisis has been identified as a natural outcome for an

BOX 1.2

Who Is Blaming the Market?

Here are some examples:

The United Nations report "Toward a New International Architecture" begins with this paragraph, entitled "The International Financial Crisis and the Need for Reform":

> World events since mid-1997, and its precedents in the 1980s and 1990s, have made painfully clear that the current international financial system is unable to safeguard the world economy from financial crises of high intensity and frequency and devastating real effects.[4]

South Korean President Kim Dae-Jung backed the regulation of speculative flows of capital as being necessary:

> To minimize the damage from speculative global capital flow, we should strengthen the financial system of the newly emerging market economies....Given the fact that a foreign currency crisis that began in one country of the region had global repercussions and grave effect on the neighboring countries of East Asia, there is an urgent need for closer cooperation.[5]

The most unexpected of all of the critics of the free market turned out to be none other than George Soros:

> There is an urgent need to recognize that financial markets, far from tending towards equilibrium, are inherently unstable. A boom/bust sequence can easily spiral out of control, knocking over one economy after another. Thus, in finding a remedy, "market discipline" may not be enough. There is also the need to maintain stability in the financial markets.[6]

Soros later amplified his remarks with:

> Financial markets are given to excesses and if a boom/bust sequence progresses beyond a certain point it will never revert to where it came from. . . . instead of acting more like a wrecking ball, knocking over one economy after another.[7]

economic system that permits the unrestricted flow of capital across borders. In this view, leveraged speculative trading in foreign exchange and fixed income markets is to blame, as are the dearth of regulation of capital markets and the practice of letting exchange rates float freely. Recently, calls for reform have sprung up everywhere demanding the reinvention of what is termed the "international financial architecture." That imposing phrase generally means the foreign exchange market, though it also can refer to international capital movements or by inference to the unregulated trading of large and leveraged investment funds. This crusade for reform has been blessed by at least two heads of major nations. German Chancellor Gerhard Schröder said: "Japan, Europe and the United States agree on this. We are on the eve of a new financial architecture."[8] U.S. president Bill Clinton promised: "[It is now time for the world to] take the next steps [of implementing a] new financial architecture and long-term reform of the global financial system. [This should include] steps to reduce the entire financial system's vulnerability to rapid capital flows and excess leverage."[9]

The common claim of the reformers is that changes must be made to the international monetary system to prevent the arrival of fresh waves of financial devastation. The proposals on the table, to name a few, include the regulation of capital flows, especially to emerging market nations, the imposition of a tax on foreign exchange transactions, the establishment of target zones to limit fluctuations in foreign exchange trading, and the policing of hedge funds and other trading concerns.

Yet a great deal of these claims are built on presumption. To believe what is being said is to give credence to some very dubious propositions. It would require one to embrace the belief that fluctuations in exchange rates serve no economic function in the allocation of economic resources but exist merely for the employment and enrichment of currency traders. One would also have to believe that a ruthless cartel of destructive speculators can hold the world for ransom at will. One would have to accept the premise that market economies are prone to spontaneous and unpredictable implosion simply because they are market economies.

An Alternative View of Crisis and Regulation

THERE IS AN ALTERNATIVE VIEW; the market is getting a bum rap. Financial breakdown is not a nomadic creature with the power to settle into any address of its choosing. On the contrary, crisis never arrives without having first received a hand-delivered invitation from domestic policy makers.

That said, it couldn't be denied that markets in and of themselves do at times go to extremes, sometimes swinging from wild optimism to pessimism and even panic over short periods of time. This idea seems to be readily acceptable even to the general public, as witnessed by the success of economist Robert Shiller's book *Irrational Exuberance.* Shiller's book is primarily directed at explaining the perceived overvaluation of U.S. common stocks at the end of the '90s. One can imagine a similar book about the phenomenon of investors having rushed into and then out of Southeast Asia and Russia in the purest sense of what popular psychology calls the "herd mentality."

It is factually correct that large amounts of capital flowed into every crisis nation in the year or two before its collapse. But for governments to moderate capital flows, even assuming that this is what needs to be done, would require the imposition of a rigid structure of global capital controls.

As we will see in the chapters that follow, better solutions appear once one recognizes that the problems of the 1990s were not caused by the malfunction of the international financial system, or by foreign currency traders, or by hedge funds, or by errant capital flows. The crises came not from the outside but rather from within. Disaster was homegrown and the natural consequence of wholly ruinous domestic policies. The worst of these policies was the decision by Mexico, Thailand, Indonesia, and other countries to adopt forms of fixed exchange rate regimes.

Moreover, a major part of the story is often conveniently overlooked by those seeking to reform the system: A substantial and speedy recovery has already taken place in South Korea and in most of the Southeast Asia countries that went through the crisis period, now that their currencies are floating. Seldom is this mentioned in the clamor for new regulations on international financial markets; credit is rarely given to the market forces for their work to repair the damage done by bad domestic financial policy.

A cynical but not wholly inaccurate description of the process by which new market regulation comes into existence runs as follows. First there is a notable financial catastrophe, of which the 1929 U.S. stock market crash is a good example. Next there is a call for market reforms and new regulations. This is what happened in the 1930s when the superstructure of American securities laws and regulation came into existence.

In time, the government's new role becomes cemented into the fabric of the marketplace. A veritable industry can evolve out of the need to monitor and enforce compliance with the new rules, and this furnishes steady employment to an army of lawyers, accountants, and bureaucrats.

The process always includes a concerted search for the guilty parties, because it is presumed that venal, self-interested persons must have been the cause of the calamity and possibly even profited from it. In the 1930s, the investment banks and the stock trading community took the fall. Stock market traders were accused of market manipulation, a term that quickly permeated the language of the new securities laws and regulations.

A second major U.S. stock market crash occurred in October 1987. The blame then was pinned on derivatives trading in stock index futures contracts and on a then-popular hedging strategy called portfolio insurance. Nicholas Brady, the sitting Secretary of the Treasury, reacted to this crash by creating a system of mandatory trading interruptions called "circuit breakers." Brady's trading halts were designed to limit the absolute fluctuation in stock prices in a short span of time. The idea was that if the market were in a free-fall, a break in trading would allow the panicked some time to collect their composure.

Brady's circuit breakers were also designed to obstruct arbitrage linkages between the shares and equity index derivatives markets. No substantive proof was ever given as to why this trading, called index arbitrage, is destabilizing to the market. In an index arbitrage trade, a trader buys or sells stock index futures contracts and simultaneously goes the other way in the underlying stocks that constitute the index. The motive is to capture any small mispricing in the futures relative to the stock index. However, because the arbitrageur always takes opposite positions in the stock market and in the futures, no net market impact results.

Brady was not the only finance minister to be fooled by index arbitrage. In the early 1990s Tsutomu Hata, Japan's minister of finance (he later became prime minister briefly) conducted a relentless campaign against index arbitrage trading on his country's securities exchanges. Hata, convinced that the derivatives arbitrageurs were responsible for the downturn in the stock market, installed a set of circuit breakers on futures trading on the Osaka Stock Market where Nikkei stock index futures trade. This opportunity wasn't wasted on the Singapore International Monetary Exchange. SIMEX actively promoted and subsequently enjoyed an explosion in trading in its own exchange-listed Nikkei futures contracts, all thanks to Hata's shadowboxing with the arbitrage community.

One question almost never heard when new regulations are proposed is whether the cost of administration and compliance with the new rules exceeds whatever benefits are being touted. It is far more likely to be presumed, as in the case of the U.S. securities industry, that near-absolute purity is worth whatever it costs. No less of an opinion was delivered in sanctimonious tones by Arthur Levitt, chairman of the U.S. Securities and Exchange Commission, in his blistering 1999 attack at online securities trading: "The laws regulating our markets are a product of the New Deal era. To me, their concepts are as indelible as the Constitution. They have weathered challenge after challenge, decade after decade, and are every bit as relevant and effective today as they were the day they were written." [10]

The securities and derivatives markets did get some relief in 1997 when the bandwidth of the Brady circuit breakers was expanded to cut down on the all too frequent disruptions in trading. But this only happened after a consensus was reached throughout the industry that Brady's circuit breakers, in their original design, had materially exacerbated the October 27, 1997 stock market plunge. There are still circuit breakers for the U.S. equity market but their workings are now linked to percentage moves in the market, not to absolute point fluctuations.

On occasion, hope for reversal of the onerous burden of regulation manages to sparkle through the dark of the night.

Such a rare event occurred in 1999 when the U.S. Congress repealed the depression-era Glass-Steagall Act of 1933 that artificially separated commercial banking from most forms of investment banking activities.

The ideology of the free market also got a sympathetic opinion from the President's Working Group on Financial Markets. The task force is comprised of Secretary of the Treasury, the Chairman of the Federal Reserve, the Chairman of the U.S. Securities and Exchange Commission (SEC), and the Chairman of the Commodities Futures Trading Commission (CFTC). The Group recommended in November 1999 that trading in financial derivatives by eligible swap participants (defined in various ways by the CFTC to include institutional market participants) should be excluded from the Commodities Exchange Act. The latter act is the primary legislation that governs trading in futures contracts.

The Working Group's report is a victory for the market in a subtle and more personal fashion, in that one of its members, Secretary of the Treasury Larry Summers, was a rabid foe of the derivatives markets in the years before he made the transition from Harvard to Washington. Here is what Professor Summers wrote about stock index futures in a guest editorial published in the *New York Times* on October 21, 1987:

> In the longer term, the stock index futures market should be regulated out of existence. The futures market circumvents margin requirements by enabling investors to have effective ownership of more than $150,000 of stock while putting down only $6,500. It makes possible trading strategies like portfolio insurance that increase market volatility by creating huge selling pressure following market declines. At the same time, the futures market offers no new opportunities to stable investors seeking to invest for the long term.[11]

Clearly something must have happened to Summers in Washington to improve his understanding of financial markets. Rarely does such an epiphany occur on the banks of the Potomac River. Supporters of free markets are thankful that the new Larry Summers, the supporter of deregulation, is the Summers who is seated in the Treasury, rather than the old Larry Summers, the man who wanted to bust the index futures market in 1987.

Despite these few triumphs for the free markets thesis, the process that produces new government involvement in the marketplace seldom reverses itself. Once new regulation is in place, it tends to stay in place, even after it has outlived its original reason for existing.

The decade of the 1990s afforded two opportunities for reformers to gain ground. First, as described above, there was the Southeast Asian crisis and the follow-up "contagion" in Hong Kong, Russia, and Brazil. Second, the collapse of Long-Term Capital Management in 1998 practically served up the entire hedge fund industry on a platter to the proponents of market reform. The two, occurring in such close time proximity, prompted renewed calls for reform, this time centered around trading in foreign exchange and interest rate markets and on what have come to be known as "highly leveraged" institutions, presumably because of the aforementioned leverage on the balance sheet of LTCM.

Suppose that the reformers are right and that major changes are needed to the way the financial system functions. Imagine that a sophisticated new team of architects is ushered in. What the reformers would soon find is that the market is not without its natural defenses and camouflage. It is not easy to halter and rein in a capital market. Regulating such things as the issuance of shares, trading in the secondary markets for shares, and arbitrage trading in stock index futures is a relatively simple process when compared to taking on the foreign exchange market. Foreign exchange is inherently an international market. It can make its home wherever it can find a set of good telephone connections. The same can be said of the over-the-counter (OTC) market for interest rate derivatives (e.g., swaps, swaptions, and forward rate agreements) which were the topic of the President's Working Group report.

The Demonization of the
Foreign Exchange Market

THE FOREIGN EXCHANGE MARKET, more than any other market, has been cast in a villain's role. Even heads of state have been known to visit invective upon the foreign exchange market; they hate foreign exchange traders even more. President Franklin D. Roosevelt bashed currency traders in his first inaugural address (1933): "Practices of the unscrupulous money changers stand indicted in the court of public opinion, rejected by the hearts and minds of men."[12]

This kind of animosity may come from the fact that few heads of state study economics. Pursuing a law school education is seen as better preparation for a career in politics. Few chief executives ever attain a fundamental understanding of the functioning of prices in modern economies. Prices, including exchange rates, are the agents that ration scarce resources among competing demands. They are what corrects imbalances between supply and demand in all markets, whether it be the market for food, labor, stock prices, or foreign currency. Prices do their work without anyone's even being conscious of their activity, much like the human body's autonomic nervous system that controls a person's breathing and the functioning of internal organs. This is a difficult lesson that economists like Adam Smith and his followers have struggled to inculcate. Unfortunately, the principles by which a modern market economy functions may never cross the minds of politicians like Roosevelt when they are taking the "high road" by denouncing the currency market.

Consider a famous outburst from French president Jacques Chirac who on the occasion of the June 1995 Halifax summit of the Group of Seven (G7) largest industrialized countries told reporters that foreign exchange "speculation is the AIDS of the world economy." Chirac went on to say that there were "ways and means" for dealing with speculators but did not elaborate on his threat. Of course nobody can top Malaysian Prime Minister Mahathir when it comes to insulting currency traders:

> We do not like currency traders. Do we want to see the wealth of nations built up over years be destroyed because currency traders wanted free trade?[13]

and

> It is said that the value of the currency trade is 20 times that of world trade in goods. But apart from the enrichment of the currency traders, what is there to show for this huge trade? On the other hand we are now witnessing how damaging the trading of money can be to the economies of some countries and their currencies. It can be abused as no other trade can. Whole regions can be bankrupted by just a few people whose only objective is to enrich themselves and their rich clients.[14]

Finance ministers and central bankers are supposed to know more about economics than heads of state do. Yet they, too, have an adversarial relationship with the foreign exchange market because exchange rates have a habit of making them look like dolts; the currency market has made a monkey out of many a minister. In much popular thinking the whole foreign exchange market is nothing more than a business centered on speculation. Even Roosevelt's Treasury Secretary, Henry Morgenthau, couldn't resist taking a shot at traders on the occasion of the signing of the Bretton Woods agreement in 1944. Morgenthau said that he hoped the Bretton Woods system would "drive the usurious money lenders from the temple of international finance."[15]

Possibly the worst thing anyone has ever done to the reputation of the foreign exchange market was the announcement by George Soros in September 1992 that his hedge fund had made a profit of over $1 billion by selling short the British pound. Soros—famed hedge fund manager or infamous currency speculator, depending on your perspective—has been tagged forever with the responsibility for driving sterling out of the Exchange Rate Mechanism. In Chapter 3 it will be argued that putting sterling in the ERM in October 1990 was pure folly, and that Soros or no Soros, the pound was set up for a beating. On the other side of the Soros trades was the Bank of England, which in the course of its ill-fated defense of the pound, squandered a great deal of its government's assets, possibly as much as 5 billion pounds of real taxpayers' money. The choice to defend the pound at a completely unrealistic exchange rate was made by the British government, not by Soros.

However, hostile perceptions of the market were reforged by the incident. Though the Soros trades were legal and by no means underhanded, people remain convinced that speculators can manipulate any currency and run roughshod over any central bank of their choosing. This dovetails with the long-standing presumption that the foreign exchange market is replete with fraud because it is an unregulated market, outside the purview of both the U.S. Securities and Exchange Commission and the Commodities Futures Trading Commission.

One frequently hears another assertion, that foreign exchange rates bear no relation to economic fundamentals. It is said that exchange rates, in that they can get out of whack with the economy, are destabilizing factors, as opposed to being market-clearing prices. This was certainly the opinion of Japan's Eisuke Sakakibara: "In the process of overcoming the crises of 1997–1998, one lesson we all learned was that the free movement of prices, be it exchange rates or interest rates, does not necessarily restore equilibrium."[16]

Such a statement reverberates from the foundations of Sakakibara's view on markets. He is one of the most influential advocates for government management of exchange rates. His last act before retirement from the Ministry of Finance (MOF) in the summer of 1999 was to launch an aggressive program to halt what he called a "premature" rise in the yen. No serious student of economics could give a proper definition of what constitutes a "premature" move in a price. That would take a MOF bureaucrat like Sakakibara to explain. And he is not alone. The foreign exchange market has been routinely branded with the stigma that it "overshoots" and that it displays "excessive" volatility.[17]

What is often missed in the rush to diagnose the foreign exchange market is an important, if not crucial distinction about volatility. In normally functioning markets prices move up and down in a more or less continuous manner. Parenthetically, financial theoreticians have described this with a class of models called diffusion processes, as was used to develop the celebrated Black-Scholes option model. Large moves are permitted with this class of model, yet one still can expect to find market makers willing to offer two-way buy-sell prices in derivative instruments.

A normal market can be trending down or up, it can even experience large fluctuations from time to time, and there will still be specialized economic agents willing to deal in derivative contracts. The importance of this is that derivatives are the principal tool that investors use to hedge foreign exchange risk. Among these are forward foreign exchange contracts and options on foreign exchange. Hence one can make the important generalization that investors are not put off by the possibility that a national currency will weaken over time—if that is their view, they can hedge, so long as there are dealers offering such instruments at reasonable prices. Where this breaks down is in the case of an exchange rate that is capable of making sharp, discontinuous movements. No dealer can afford to offer hedging contracts in an environment of potentially discontinuous moves in an exchange rate. Such a scenario has been known to occur with fixed exchange rate regimes, especially ones that are suspected of being about to disintegrate.

Chapter Two

Japan's Lost Decade of the 1990s

TO JUDGE BY WHAT was being said thirty years ago, the 1990s ought to have been a celebration of Japan's industrial dominance. Japan rose out of the ashes of the Second World War to become the second largest economy in the world. Some observers expected the size of Japan's economy to surpass that of the United States before the close of the twentieth century. The magic suddenly ended in the 1990s, when instead of success, Japan met with stagnation and financial ruin.

Is it an indictment of the capitalist market system when three decades of economic growth in an advanced economy such as Japan's can come to a halt? Specifically, what brought down the Japanese economy in the 1990s?

The Juggernaut

IN 1970 HERMAN KAHN published his influential book *The Emerging Japanese Superstate*[1], a work that would cement in Western minds the fear of Japan's impending economic superiority. Kahn, a physicist by training, was a pioneer in the field of *futures studies* and the founder of the Hudson Institute think tank. He had made a reputation with his forward-looking work on such diverse topics as the survivability of a nuclear war [*Thinking about the Unthinkable* (1962) and *On Thermonuclear War* (1978)] and the growing American problem of narcotics addiction. Kahn's book is a good place to begin to discuss both the success and subsequent failure of Japan.

Being eclectic in his methods, Kahn examined political, psychological, and sociological factors, ranging from demographic trends, to the Japanese school system, to his study of the "Japanese mind." Practically everything Kahn studied pointed him to a seemingly inescapable conclusion. Japan had a brilliant economic future and would enjoy decades of superlative economic growth:

> We find very persuasive our current conclusion to such an analysis—that high Japanese growth rates, rates in the neighborhood of 8-12 percent or so, are likely to continue for most or all of the 1970–1980 period and perhaps beyond. [2]

and:

> If I had to choose a best estimate, I would chose the medium one. In that scenario Japan probably passes the United States in per capita income around 1990 and probably equals the U.S. in Gross National Product by about the year 2000. [3]

The Japanese growth machine kicked into gear in the early 1950s as the nation began the Herculean task of rebuilding its war-torn infrastructure and industrial base. In retrospect, Kahn's predictions of Japanese growth were impressively accurate. Annual nominal gross domestic product (GDP) did in fact grow by double digits in the 1970s and by 5 to 10 percent in the 1980s (Figure 2.1).

The growth in real GDP, meaning adjusted for inflation, was less than the growth in nominal GDP, but it was still remarkable. The 1960s were phenomenal years of genuine economic development. Kahn's book projected that the boom would continue for at least another quarter of a century.

The big question that remained open for Kahn was whether Japan would step forward onto the world's stage to assume its logical place as a "superstate": "Many of us believe the 1970s and

FIGURE 2.1

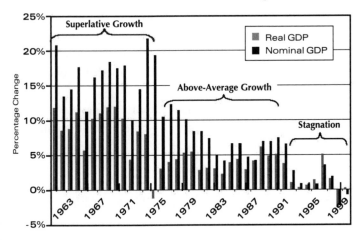

Japanese Annual Growth in Nominal and Real GDP (1990 Yen), Year-over-Year Changes

THE DESCENDING STAIRCASE. Japan's growth in the post-war era fits nicely into three periods: 1960–1973, superlative growth; 1974–1991, above-average growth; 1992–2000, stagnation. Shown here are both nominal and real (adjusted for inflation) annual changes in gross domestic product.

Source: Data from Bloomberg L.P. and Organization for Economic Cooperation and Development.

1980s will see a transition in the role of Japan in world affairs not unlike the change brought about in Europe in the 1870s by the rise of Prussia."[4]

Kahn provided dozens of reasons for projecting a continuance of Japan's success. He put heavy emphasis on the commitment that Japan made to education. Worker loyalty was a factor. He observed that Japan had a steady supply of "risk capital" that stood ready to finance whatever needed to be built. He even marveled at how some things uniquely Japanese, such as its system of lifetime employment, had worked in the national interest, despite Western reservations. Lifetime employment guarantees, he explained, allowed firms to save on capital costs by effectively borrowing money from their employees by underpaying them in their first fifteen to twenty years of service and later make it up by overpaying them in the second part of their careers.

Kahn wasn't the only analyst who was overly impressed with Japan. Eric Vogel wrote an influential book, *Japan as Number One,* its title telling all. William Ouchi wrote the bestseller *Theory Z* in which he extolled to American executives the superiority of Japanese management techniques.

Kahn believed that the single most important factor, the very mainspring of Japan growth, would be its continuing national propensity to save:

> The first and possibly most essential factor in my argument—though by itself certainly not sufficient explanation for Japanese growth rates—is Japan's high savings and investment rates, which guarantee there will continue to be, both relatively and absolutely, enormous resources available for expansion.[5]

Kahn had fallen into a basic fallacy that national savings necessarily creates economic growth. Having a high rate of savings means nothing more than that the society has chosen a Spartan intertemporal allocation of consumption. Income is socked away today, not immediately consumed on the spot, so as to provide for the promise of a higher standard of living in the future. Investment is a different matter. It is the process by which a nation attempts to catapult today's deferred consumption into the future. This can be done by either lending assets to another nation, something that Japan has done a lot of in the postwar era, or by plowing money into domestic and foreign investment projects. Japan was saving one-third of its income when Kahn wrote his book, and this money was being invested, presumably to build Japan's industrial and commercial might.

This happy picture of savings resulting in productive investment is not always the rule. A nation could save but still not grow, because it is not axiomatic that its chosen investment projects will be successful. This is the sad lesson that Saudi Arabia taught the world in the 1980s when its government poured billions of dollars into highly inefficient downstream petrochemical industries and horrendously uneconomical desert agricultural projects. Investing is one thing; getting a positive rate of return is quite another.

The analogy between Saudi Arabia and Japan is not entirely far-fetched when one considers that both economies have a core element of central planning. The Saudi Arabian government, which is controlled by the monarchy, designs and executes consecutive five-year economic plans. In Japan, planning is done by an amalgam of interests with a heavy dose of ministerial guidance.

Japan is further from a true free-market economy than one might initially think. Neither is it a command economy, as was the former Soviet Union. But the government takes a big role in economic decisions. Nothing of substance gets done in Japan without the input of the government. Richard Katz's excellent book *Japan: The System That Soured* (1998) contains the following remarkable anecdote recounted from the memoirs of Sony Chairman Akio Morita, of how the transistor came to Japan over the objection of the bureaucrats:

> It took Sony six months to convince skeptical MITI [Ministry of International Trade and Industry] officials that it wasn't wasting $25,000 by licensing the transistor. MITI officials said they didn't know why an upstart company deserved scarce foreign exchange when even the product's American inventor, Western Electric, thought it had little commercial value. MITI did ultimately give in, but it was lobbying, not the individual decisions of risk-taking entrepreneurs and investors that determined whether or not Sony got into the game in the first place.[6]

In the larger picture, what the bureaucrats wanted for Japan was a continuation of what was known as the national *industry policy*, which Katz described:

Generals, they say, are trained to fight the last war; that is why they lose the next one....The root of the problem is that Japan is still mired in the structures, policies and mental habits that prevailed it the 1950s–60s. What we have come to think of as the "Japanese economic system" was a marvelous system to help a backward Japan catch up to the West. But it turned into a terrible system once Japan had in fact caught up....In the "last war," the battle to industrialize Japan in the 1950s–60s, the "developmental state" policies that gave rise to the nickname "Japan Inc." worked brilliantly. But that was only because the country was in the "catch-up" phase of its economic evolution.[7]

Kahn gave his uncritical endorsement to ministerial oversight:

One problem with rapid growth is that often the growth rates of various portions of the economy become unbalanced, and adjustments have to be made before the imbalance gets out of control. The Japanese government by its direct pressures and its indicative planning was often able to prevent these imbalances from growing too large.[8]

Here we are left to wonder how Kahn, a man of immense intellect and scientific training, could have given so little weight to basic principles of economics. He was totally converted to the ideology professed by the Japanese bureaucrats.

Japanese officialdom sets out to manage the entire economic system as though each part were a technical problem of factory management. The ministers seemed then and seem today not to consider that the individual participants that make up the vast Japanese economy can function as self-interested agents. Taken as a whole, free economic agents constitute what Adam Smith called the "invisible hand," a collective automatic force that directs the functioning of an economy (Smith). Resolving what Kahn called "imbalances" is precisely what a market system is all about. Prices, not ministry officials, are the great equilibrators that bring the forces of supply and demand into balance.

Advocates of centrally planned economies usually get around to making the case that things ought to go smoothly when there is complete cooperation among all sectors of industry and government. If everybody is on the same plan, factories will run at minimum cost, quality will be ensured, inventory shipments will arrive on time, and workers will enjoy lifelong guaranteed employment. So it would seem that if every musician reads from the same sheet music, the band will play in sweet harmony. However, Japan's economy is infinitely more complex than a marching band. And although command economies can achieve short-run goals, what limited success they have had has never endured.

A critical defect of a centrally planned system is its inability to create an array of individual rewards that motivates efficient economic behavior by market participants. Whether such a system originates in tyranny (the former Soviet Union), or by royal decree (Saudi Arabia), or by complicity between industry and government (Japan), it will eventually fail. Sooner or later, the planners will make errors in judgment. Centrally planned economies are hit or miss propositions, with the odds favoring a miss. The only sustainable system is one in which free economic agents have the latitude to create, innovate, manage, take risks, occasionally fail, and have the freedom and responsibility to make independent economic decisions. But for Kahn,

> With government and industry firmly resolved to work together to reach the goal of economic leadership, and with the gross national product consistently growing at a rate twice that of the United States, there can be little doubt that what was a possibility—a Japanese economy of super proportions—is rapidly becoming fact.[9]

It didn't happen quite that way. What Kahn missed was that Japan's economic performance would begin to wind down in the late 1970s in the start of what we have described as a descending staircase of growth; the 1970s were better than the 1980s and the 1980s were distinctly better than the 1990s.

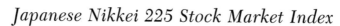

Source: Bloomberg L.P.

FIGURE 2.2

Japanese Nikkei 225 Stock Market Index

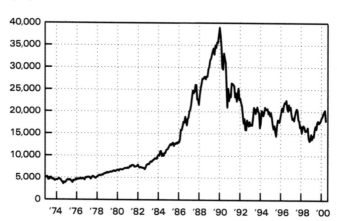

THE NIKKEI STOCK market index peaked at 38,915 on December 29, 1989. This index is a price-weighted index of 225 stocks calculated by adding the share prices and dividing by a constant called the Nikkei divisor.

On the Reefs

NEW YEAR'S DAY 2000 closed out a painful decade of economic disappointment for Japan in which its unemployment rate surpassed that of America's and its government budget surplus became a deficit. On December 29, 1989, the Nikkei stock market index had hit its all-time peak level of 38,915 (Figure 2.2). Ten years later it stood at 18,934.

The real stinger is the comparison between the Japanese market and the U.S. market. Whereas Japan's Nikkei had fallen by more than half over the decade, the American Standard and Poor's (S&P) 500 index had risen four times in value. In other words, by the end of the 1990s, the once mighty Nikkei index was worth only about 12 cents on the S&P 500 "dollar." (Figure 2.3).

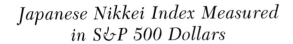

FIGURE 2.3

Japanese Nikkei Index Measured in S&P 500 Dollars

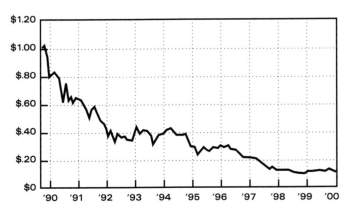

ONE WAY TO measure the fall in the Nikkei is to construct a hypothetical investment fund that costs $1.00 on December 31, 1989. The fund uses stock index futures contracts to go long $1 worth of the Nikkei stock index and short $1 worth of the S&P 500 index. On December 31, 1999, the original $1 investment would have been worth 11.7¢.

Source: Bloomberg L.P.

The prime tool that Japan has applied to its financial crisis is fiscal policy. Since 1991, Japan has tried six major stimulus packages, each ranging in size from 1.3 percent to 3.3 percent of gross domestic product.[10] Regrettably, Japan has nothing more to show for this spending than a greatly expanded level of national debt. In 1991 Japan's national government had a surplus measured at 2 percent of total potential output. The IMF, at the time of this writing, is projecting Japan to have deficit equal to 6 percent of GDP for fiscal year 1999. Gross public debt rose from about 70 percent of GDP to 120 percent between 1990 and 1998.[11]

It is not surprising that fiscal policy paid for with steadily increasing governmental budget deficits would fail to rescue Japan. To think otherwise would be to suppose that the Japanese people were fools. Obviously the money spent on public investment, the proverbial "bridge to nowhere," is going to have to be repaid some day by Japan's taxpayers. They know this is the case; moreover they realize that their government is going to have to borrow a great deal of money to balance its books, and they adjust their plans for consumption accordingly.

Nevertheless, Japan in 1996 did get some benefit from the combination of fiscal stimulus and lower interest rates. It didn't last long. The year 1997 was especially disappointing for Japan. There was the onset of the Southeast Asian crisis, an external factor totally outside of Japan's control as will be described in Chapter 4. Japan was robbed of its Asian exports markets and saw the destruction of a considerable amount of its investments in factories and financial companies in the Tiger countries.

But not all of the downturn in 1997 was caused by external factors. On April 1 of that year, as we noted in Chapter 1, Prime Minister Ryutaro Hashimoto raised the national sales tax. The jump was substantial, from 3 percent to 5 percent. The logic of such a move defies rational explanation. How could a purposive government conduct massive fiscal stimulus projects and simultaneously raise the national sales tax? Japan's growth rate slipped to nearly zero, and Hashimoto, then deservedly nicknamed "Herbert Hoover Hashimoto" by the foreign business press, resigned from office after his party's losses in the next election.

One of the most prescient observations about Japan, and also about the rest of Asia, had been made three years earlier by Paul Krugman in the *Foreign Affairs* article cited in the previous chapter. Krugman wrote: "while Japan's historical performance has indeed been remarkable, the era of miraculous Japanese growth now lies well in the past."[12]

Krugman had made a critical distinction as to the source of sustainable economic growth:

> As soon as one starts to think in terms of growth accounting,
> however, one arrives at a crucial insight about the process of

economic growth: sustained growth in a nation's per capita income can only occur if there is a rise in output per unit of input. Mere increases in inputs, without an increase in the efficiency with which those inputs are used—investing in more machinery and infrastructure—must run into diminishing returns; input-driven growth is inevitably limited.[13]

Krugman believed that Japan in the 1950s and 1960s grew both through high rates of input growth *and* through high rates of technical efficiency. When he compares Japan to the United States during that era, he finds that Japan was clearly gaining ground in a relative sense. However in more recent times:

> When one takes into account the growing evidence for at least a modest acceleration of U.S. productivity growth in the last few years, one ends up with the probable conclusion that Japanese efficiency is gaining on that of the United States at a snail's pace, if at all....In other words, Japan is not quite as overwhelming an example of economic prowess as is sometimes thought.[14]

This analysis by Krugman has to be the most disheartening of all that has been written about Japan. Krugman succeeded in doing what he had promised when he said that he intended to "throw some cold water" on the myth of Japan's economic miracle. His analysis points to a fundamental structural problem, a slowing in the rate of improvement in production efficiency. No government can fix this in the intermediate run, much less the short run.

Beyond Capitalism?

ONE SPECIFIC REASON why the bloom came off of Japan's economic rose has to do with the fact that its shareholders, as owners of firms, do not have sovereign control over their own interests. Japan is a mixed, pseudocapitalistic system.

Eisuke Sakakibara, the former official of the Ministry of Finance, wrote about this in his 1994 book *Beyond Capitalism*.

Sakakibara, known to the financial community as "Mr. Yen," was considered to be the main author of Japan's foreign exchange policy in the latter half of the 1990s. His notoriety came from his frequently being quoted on newswire services, usually delivering threats to the foreign exchange market such as "the authorities are watching the market closely" or "Japan will not hesitate to take decisive action." Over time he became the public face for the Ministry of Finance before his retirement in the summer of 1999. In 2000, Sakakibara was nominated by Japan for, but failed to be elected to, the post of managing director of the IMF which Michel Camdessus vacated.

Sakakibara wrote in his book that the Japanese people had rejected capitalism in favor of "peopleism." Japan, he told the world, had achieved a system of complete "employee sovereignty," though that must have been a surprise to the legions of salarymen who enjoy virtually no job mobility. For Sakakibara, everyone in Japan is a "stakeholder." A stakeholder can be anyone who has the political muscle to exercise an element of control over a company or an industry. That includes not only shareholders, management, and employees but also consumers, citizens, and government officials. He writes that all of them have a voice in the way Japan is managed; that's what he thinks makes the wheels of the Japanese economic machine work so smoothly.

It has always been accepted that consensus is important in Japan. But stakeholders do not make better managers than owners. Thousands of years of human behavior point to the rule that works without exception: owners take the best care of their own possessions. That includes companies, factories, banks, and all manner of other going concerns. The problem in Japan is that a stakeholder need not go to the trouble of becoming an owner. Different stakeholders have different objectives, and few of those goals are consistent with managing a company efficiently.

Sometimes being a shareholder is not enough to qualify for being a stakeholder. Witness the frustration of T. Boone Pickens who attempted to exercise some control over his investment in the Japanese company Koito Manufacturing. Pickens was denounced as a corporate raider and was handily defeated by Koito's management.

An effective obstacle to corporate raiders and takeover artists like Pickens is the practice of interlocking cross-holdings of shares between companies. This effectively reduces the total float of shares in the hands of the public and makes it nearly impossible for an outsider to buy a controlling interest in a company.

Yet one does have to thank Sakakibara for explaining why it is that so many failed companies, especially financial firms, are not afforded a respectable corporate death. The cases of the Long-Term Credit Bank of Japan and Yamaiichi Securities are notable examples of firms that existed long after they should have been put out of their earthly misery. Stakeholders never let anything die. They prefer a zombie, meaning the fictional "living dead," to the dead dead.

Contrast this with what Herman Kahn said about Japan during its period of reconstruction after the end of the Second World War: "The Japanese were willing to be astonishingly ruthless in getting rid of inefficient industries or those that were somehow not suitable."[15]

Where is that ruthless willingness to get rid of inefficient industries and companies today? Apparently it died out as stakeholder capitalism took over during the postwar period. Stakeholderitis is not something that can be cured in the near term. And speaking of Sakakibara, we have to consider the behavior of the Japanese authorities.

Curiously enough, Sakakibara's book tries to downplay the role that the powerful Japanese ministries have in planning the economy. This flies in the face of everything that has ever been heard, written, or witnessed in dealings with Japan. Every economic decision involves the input of some ministerial stakeholder. The record of the ministers is not good—to be blunt, it is terrible. Still, the ministers and their minions manage to hold on to power in a unique exception to the Japanese tradition of facing failure with resignation.

Much has been written about how the Ministry of International Trade and Industry steered Japan over a cliff through its insistence on overinvestment in heavy industry. The Ministry of Finance, Sakakibara's old shop, deserves no less blame. Its constant meddling in financial markets and exchange rates is responsible for the great financial trouble of the 1990s, as will be discussed in the final section of this chapter.

In the same vein, the late Merton Miller, the University of Chicago finance professor and 1990 economics Nobel Prize laureate, delivered this blistering attack on Japanese bureaucrats in a 1995 address that he presented in person in Japan:

> Throughout that period of spectacular growth, the Japanese economy seemed to be guided, benevolently, albeit somewhat corruptly, by what has been caricatured as Japan, Incorporated—a combination of political monopoly by the Liberal Democratic Party, the industrial policies of the Ministry of International Trade and Industry and detailed micro-management by MOF (Ministry of Finance)....In a way, therefore, the current banking and related disasters may actually be a blessing in disguise for focusing the attention of the Japanese public on matters of finance and getting them to understand that MOF and all it stands for is the *problem* not the solution.[16]

The Bubble Economy

JAPANESE ECONOMIC PROBLEMS in the 1990s can also be traced to the formation and subsequent implosion of the bubble economy of the late 1980s. What was responsible for creating the bubble economy, and why did it burst? In actual fact, a great deal of blame can be deposited at the doorstep of the Bank of Japan.

In the course of the bubble years, roughly 1986–1990, asset prices in Japan skyrocketed. Everything from stocks to land to golf club memberships doubled and tripled in value. This has been labeled a bubble because the rapid rise in asset values was followed by their collapse. The term *bubble* is a metaphor for an economy that inflates like a balloon and then suddenly deflates or bursts when it is pinpricked. In the case of Japan, the air that helped the bubble to inflate was a permissive monetary policy in the late 1980s; the pinprick was the sudden reversal of that policy

Source: Bloomberg L.P.

FIGURES 2.4A & 2.4B

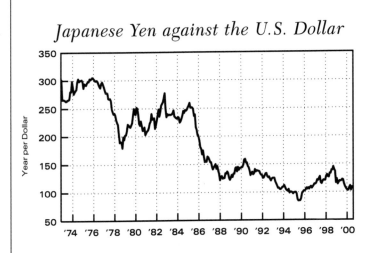

Japanese Yen against the U.S. Dollar

German Mark against the U.S. Dollar

THE U.S. DOLLAR was on a rampage in the early 1980s. President Ronald Reagan's tax cuts and Federal Reserve Chairman Paul Volcker's anti-inflation tight monetary policy pushed the dollar up against the mark and the yen. The greenback peaked in February 1985, and the Plaza Accord intervention that was designed to bring the dollar down to more reasonable levels followed in September of that year.

in the second half of 1989. In a phrase, the BOJ exercised a textbook perfect case of what economists call "stop-go" monetary policy, with the sequence of commands in Japan's case being "go" and then "stop."

The genesis of the monetary policy that fueled the bubble economy lies in Japan's response to its own participation in the secretly coordinated foreign exchange intervention, called the Plaza Accord, in September 1985, that aimed to lower the value of the dollar against the yen and the deutsche mark.[17] Figures 2.4A and 2.4B show the values of the dollar against the yen and the mark starting in 1971.

The run up in the dollar from the early 1980s is associated with the period known as "Reaganomics." Theoreticians explain the dollar's rise in terms of the peculiar mixture of monetary and fiscal policy at the time in the United States: fiscal policy was expansionary, primarily because of President Ronald Reagan's tax cuts and defense spending, and monetary policy was tight. The latter was a deliberate and successful effort by the Volcker Federal Reserve to reduce consumer price inflation. This combination, tight money accompanied by a loose fiscal stance, has been recognized by economists since Robert Mundell (1963) as a recipe for producing a higher value for the national currency.

As the dollar, thus goaded on both flanks, began to gallop ahead of the currencies of America's major trading partners, notably the yen and the deutsche mark, protectionist trade interests in the United States began to agitate. There were some attempts in 1985 by central banks, notably the Bundesbank, to stop the rise in the dollar. Finally, as was described in Chapter 1, the Reagan administration organized a united effort to lower the dollar among the members of what was then called the Group of Five Industrialized Nations or G5. The result is known as the Plaza Accord of September 22, 1985. Yoichi Funabashi (1988) has written an informative, fascinating account of the antics of the Plaza Accord ministers and their paranoid security measures, including conducting "no-paper meetings."

At the conclusion of the meetings, the ministers instructed their central banks to conduct coordinated sales of dollars for yen and for marks. A total of $10.2 billion dollars of intervention was done ($3.2 billion by the United States, $5 billion by the other four G5 countries, and $2 billion by non-G5 countries[18]). Although it appears that this may have been effective, and one has to say that the foreign exchange market was caught completely by surprise, the fact is that the dollar had begun to decline seven months earlier. That the dollar was declining is easily explained by the earlier collapse of U.S. bond yields. The yield to maturity on the 10-year bond peaked slightly below 14 percent in June 1984. By September 1986, the 10-year bond yielded only 7.25 percent. What had happened was that when the Federal Reserve relaxed its anti-inflation tight money program, the high-flying dollar came crashing down to earth.

The Plaza Accord intervention amplified the downward secular trend in the dollar, analogous to giving a man who is already falling down a flight of stairs a hard reinforcing push. The more important effect of the Plaza Accord had to do with the reaction by the Bank of Japan to what the intervention did to its balance sheet. As it participated in the intervention, the BOJ sold dollars and bought yen. This by itself was a contractionary operation because the BOJ was absorbing liquidity from Japan's banking system. Here was the catch. Funabashi (1988) reports that despite having been instructed otherwise by MOF, the BOJ sterilized its share of the Plaza intervention transactions, apparently fearing that a rise in Japanese interest rates would otherwise ensue[19] (Box 2.1).

Sterilization means that the Bank of Japan conducted open market operations to replace the liquidity drained by the Plaza Accord transactions. MOF had objected to sterilization because it correctly reasoned that the Plaza Accord dollar sales would have a larger impact if left unsterilized. A sterilized intervention has no impact on domestic money supply by definition and hence should have only limited impact, if any impact at all, on exchange rates.[20]

In essence, Japan had pulled its punches. Given its long-term aversion to a stronger yen, it is amazing that the Japanese participated at all. To the letter of the agreement, Japan sold dollars and bought yen. But the Plaza document contained a loophole. Its drafters had left the Bank of Japan a back door exit—nowhere in

---

BOX 2.1

Sterilization: A Rough Look at a Central Bank's Balance Sheet

IN ABSTRACT, ONE can think of a country's central bank as having two kinds of assets, domestic assets and foreign assets. Usually the central bank's domestic assets are bonds issued by its own government. Its foreign assets, which are sometimes called its "foreign reserves," consist of government bonds issued by other nations and foreign currency. Central banks also hold gold as an asset.

In abstract, the liability side of a central bank's balance consists of two major components. One is the amount of currency in circulation. The other central bank liability is reserve deposits that it holds on behalf of commercial banks. In most countries, commercial banks are required by law to maintain a minimum fixed proportion of their customers' deposits as reserves at the central bank.

When a central bank sells domestic government bonds in the open market, the payment it receives is reflected in a reduction in its stock of commercial bank reserve deposits, and hence a reduction in the money supply. Bonds go out of the central bank and private sector money comes in. Likewise, when a central bank buys government bonds it causes the stock of commercial bank reserves to rise, and hence the

---

the agreement did it say that Japan or the other signatories had agreed to coordinate their respective monetary policies.

A few months afterward, the BOJ, fearing that the dollar had fallen too fast, reversed itself and began to intervene to buy dollars (Cargill, Hutchison, and Ito, 1997). Buying dollars and selling yen had just the opposite effect because it supplied more yen to the banking system. Why did the BOJ reverse itself? One does not have to look too deeply into Japanese history to realize that the welfare of the Japanese export sector is viewed with paramount concern in the halls of government.

In February 1987, the BOJ agreed with the other members of

money supply to expand.

Transactions that a central bank does involving foreign reserves work the same way. In the course of a foreign exchange intervention a central bank that buys foreign currency (or equivalently, sells its own domestic currency) acquires foreign reserves. This is reflected on the liability side of the central bank's balance sheet as an increase in the stock of commercial bank reserves, and hence the money supply rises.

The central bank might choose to sterilize its foreign exchange intervention. This term means that the central bank offsets the domestic effects of the intervention with transactions in domestic government bonds.

In September 1985, the Bank of Japan participated in the Plaza Accord intervention to sell dollars (and buy yen). This act by itself reduced the Japanese money supply. Simultaneously, the BOJ decided to sterilize its part of the intervention. The BOJ purchased government bonds to add back money supply to the banking system.

There is a legitimate question among economists as to whether a sterilized intervention can have any lasting effect on the foreign exchange market.

the G7 council that the drop in the dollar should be halted. This became known as the Louvre Accord because the meeting was in Paris. This time the Bank of Japan openly and gladly bought dollars for yen, and this time with little sterilization.[21]

The activities of the BOJ in this period appear to have been designed to do two things. First, the Bank wanted to correct any residue of tight monetary policy left by its participation in the Plaza intervention. Second, it wanted to brake the rise in the yen. When it saw that it could not achieve the latter, it resorted to massively expansionary monetary policy to correct for the impact of the stronger currency. Cargill, Hutchison, and Ito (1997) write:

FIGURE 2.5

Japanese Nikkei Index and Japan's Official Discount Rate

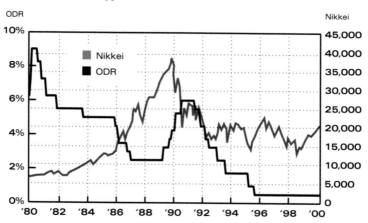

THE BANK OF Japan executed one of the most effective tightenings in central bank history in late 1989, though it later wished it had not done so. Note the coincident peaking of the stock market with the hikes in the Official Discount Rate (ODR).

Source: Bloomberg L.P.

During the period 1986–1988 Japan's foreign-exchange reserves jumped more than fourfold, from $22 billion to $90 billion. This jump was accompanied by an increase in monetary-base growth from 5 percent to nearly 15 percent. The discount rate was lowered several times during 1986 and again in February 1987. The 2.5 percent discount rate set in February 1987 was maintained until the middle of 1989.[22]

Nobody really knows what causes asset bubbles to form, but there is some consensus that they are rooted in monetary phenomena. The most comprehensive survey of asset bubbles is

Source: Data from Bloomberg L.P. and Organization for Economic Co-operation and Development.

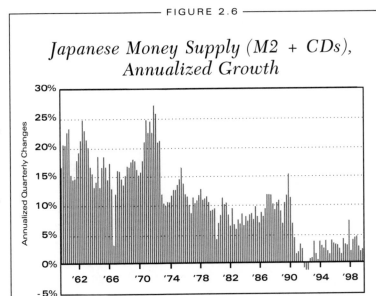

FIGURE 2.6

Japanese Money Supply (M2 + CDs), Annualized Growth

M2 + CDs (see Box 2.2) could easily be confused with the graph of annual changes in GDP (Figure 2.1). Like GDP, it breaks into three identifiable periods: 1960–1974, 1975–1990, and 1990–2000. No better case for the destructive power of bad monetary policy has been made since the Great Depression of the 1930s in the United States.

Charles Kindleberger's popular book *Manias, Panics, and Crashes: A History of Financial Crises.* Kindleberger tells us that "financial crisis [is] a hardy perennial." It starts with some disturbance or event that appears to offer a get-rich-quick opportunity. Suddenly, everyone is buying stocks or real estate, or even tulip bulbs (seventeenth-century Holland). Yet even Kindleberger comes up short on the question of what truly causes bubbles, at one point writing that a bubble can only be defined by its "bursting."

Did the Bank of Japan incite the bubble economy? At a minimum, the BOJ could be taken to task for pursuing procyclical monetary policy when the bubble began to form in the mid-1980s,

———— BOX 2.2 ————

Components of the Money Supply and the Basics of Monetary Aggregates

STUDENTS OF MONETARY theory, or "monetarists," define the monetary base (sometimes called high-powered money) as all outstanding currency in circulation plus commercial bank reserves held at the central bank. The central bank has direct control over the monetary base. The central bank can change the size of the monetary base by acquiring or selling assets. When the central bank sells assets, such as government securities, it accepts payment from the banking system, which makes the nation's monetary base contract. Alternatively, when the central bank buys securities it causes the monetary base to expand.

Another measure of the money supply is the broad-based aggregate called M2. M2 is defined as the sum of currency in circulation plus checking accounts plus time deposits. Economists usually add certificates of deposit to arrive at the most watched aggregate for Japan, M2 + CDs. This monetary aggregate depends on the size of the monetary base and the flow of bank lending activity. It is also affected by the reserve requirement, which dictates the fraction of deposits that must be held at the central bank. Overall, the decline in the rate of growth of Japan's M2 + CDs aggregate reflects declines in both the growth of the monetary base and in the bank lending.

By either measure, the bottom line is that the central bank had allowed the rate of growth in the money supply to shrivel to dangerously low levels. That is immediately evident in Figure 2.6. Japan has given the monetarists their best evidence that money matters since the Great Depression in the United States.

as its behavior after the Plaza Accord intervention shows. Instead of restraining the bubble it exacerbated the situation by adding a steady supply of excess liquidity to the economy. In its efforts to blunt the effects of a seemingly ever-strengthening yen, the BOJ fueled one of the greatest episodes of speculation in modern times. Soon ordinary Japanese citizens became stock market players and real estate market operators. Even something as trivial as a golf club membership could make someone real estate wealthy.

All of this came to a screeching halt in mid-1989 when the Bank of Japan abruptly changed course and began to raise interest rates. The discount rate was raised in steps from 2.5 percent to 4.25 percent by the end of 1989 (Figure 2.5). At the same time the BOJ allowed for a precipitous decline in the growth of monetary aggregates (Figure 2.6). The Ministry of Finance did its part in bringing the economy up short by raising the capital gains taxes on land speculation. The rest, as they say, is history. The first catastrophe was the stock market. Then the crisis spread to real estate. Next the banking system began to freeze up, and soon Japan was locked into its ten-year slide to zero growth.

A Critique of Japanese Monetary Policy

WHAT HAS MADE things seriously worse since the collapse of the bubble economy in 1990 is that the Bank of Japan has pursued a policy that seems almost designed to prevent an economic recovery. Sometime in 1991, the BOJ began to realize the extent of the damage that was occurring to the Japanese economy with the collapse of the asset bubble. Thereupon it began to reduce interest rates in a series of moves that eventually took the discount rate to practically zero in 1995. The policy of the BOJ since then has been to leave a sufficient supply of liquidity, no more and no less, in the banking system to keep the short-term rate pegged at a minimal level, and even zero since early 1999.[23] Bank of Japan Governor Masuru Hayami repeatedly declared throughout 1999 and 2000 that this policy by itself would be sufficient to bring Japan out of its economic slump.

On the surface of things it would look as though the BOJ was executing expansionary monetary policy, as would be appropriate for the depressed state of the Japanese economy. However, whatever it was doing, it wasn't working. By the year 2000 Japan had had nearly five years of record low interest rates, but economic growth continued to slow in every year. The case of Japan points to the error of trying to judge the degree of ease or tightness in monetary policy by looking at market rates of interest.

Two crucial factors were missing in the BOJ's logic. One was a recognition that though the observed market interest rate was zero, the real interest rate was positive. Economic agents respond to the real interest rate because it is the anticipated actual cost of funds adjusted for the expected appreciation or depreciation of the consumer price level. Because consumer prices in Japan were falling, meaning that the country was experiencing deflation, the real interest rate could be positive even though the nominal rate was zero. In other words, the BOJ was watching the wrong rate of interest by concentrating in maintaining a zero market rate of interest. Falling consumer prices themselves can be a significant economic danger. Theoretically, Japan could go into a downward deflationary spiral. This was explained, but not predicted, in a 1998 IMF report: "If a protracted cyclical downturn ultimately led to expectations of deflation, real interest rates would rise, further depressing output and inflation expectations in a self-reinforcing manner." [24]

The second element that was missing from the BOJ's consideration was the declining rate of growth in the money supply. The most widely examined measure of the Japanese money supply is called M2 + CDs (the sum of currency in circulation, checking accounts, time deposits, and certificates of deposit—see Box 2.2). Annual percentage growth in this measure is shown in Figure 2.6.

The disturbing thing about Japan in the 1990s was that so many graphs looked alike. Money supply growth, GDP growth, and the stock market all looked like descending staircases. This was ominously reminiscent of the case that Milton Friedman and Anna Schwartz (1963) made for monetary policy having been a major determinant of the Great Depression in the United States in the 1930s. The latter was more severe than anything experienced to date in Japan—and no wonder, because as Friedman and Schwartz wrote, "From the cyclical peak in August 1929 to the cyclical trough in March 1933, the stock of money fell by over a third.... The contraction is in fact a tragic testimonial to the importance of monetary forces."[25]

Friedman addressed the case of Japan in a December 17, 1997 guest editorial in the *Wall Street Journal* entitled "Rx for Japan: Back to the Future":

> The surest road to a healthy economic recovery is to increase the rate of monetary growth, to shift from tight money to easier money....Defenders of the Bank of Japan will say, "How? The Bank has already cut its discount rate to 0.5%. What more can it do to increase the quantity of money?" The answer is straightforward: The Bank of Japan can buy government bonds on the open market, paying for them with either currency or deposits at the Bank of Japan, what economists call high-powered money. Most of the proceeds will end up in commercial banks, adding to their reserves and enabling them to expand their liabilities by loans and open market purchases. But whether they do so or not, the money supply will increase.[26]

What Friedman was suggesting was that the BOJ *monetize* some portion of the Japanese bond market, meaning that it should initiate a regular program to buy up some portion of the national debt. When the BOJ would enter the bond market to buy up government paper it would pay for the bonds by writing a check to the seller. In the process, the supply of bank deposit reserves would have to rise, and hence the money supply too would rise.

Krugman (1998) offers a different take on Japan's macroeconomic condition. He concludes that Japan has entered into a liquidity trap, which is an old macroeconomic concept that dates back to J. R. Hicks (1937). Krugman assets that Japan's well-known propensity to save, coupled with a decline in domestic investment opportunities, has driven the equilibrium full-employment real interest rate below zero. But the actual real interest rate is positive because of the Bank of Japan's reputation as an inflation fighter. What is more, consumer prices are falling at a time when the Bank of Japan is keeping the short-term nominal interest at zero. Hence Japan is stuck in the predicament of having excess savings—or said another way, insufficient consumption—to achieve full employment. If the real interest rate were to fall, people would save less, consume more, and the economy would expand.

Traditional monetarists dispute the existence of Krugman's liquidity trap yet they generally agree with his recommendation that the Bank of Japan ought to initiate a steady and credible program to raise the rate of expansion of the money supply. Krugman believes that this should be accompanied by an announcement that the Bank of Japan is targeting some minimal rate of inflation so as to drive down the real rate of interest.

The argument that the BOJ advanced against this, what it called a "quantitative easing," was that because bank lending activity was lethargic, and that since there was already a surplus of liquidity in the banking system, adding more reserves to the system would have no impact on the economy.

What is wrong with this argument is that money is money. It would be preferable for the new bank reserves, originating from the central bank's bond purchases, to be lent out to consumers and industry. But even if that does not happen, at least immediately, the new reserves are still money that has been injected into the economy, even if they only end up sloshing around in the banking system as unlent funds. Eventually the increase in the money supply would have to have an impact on the falling consumer price index. Reinforcement could come from announcing that the BOJ was targeting some mild rate of inflation, perhaps on the order of 1 or 2 percent per year.

Such a policy could break the expectation of falling consumer prices and prevent the possibility of a deflationary spiral. It would also lead to a lower real interest rate. Another thing it would do is lower the value of the yen, something that Japanese officials have been trying to accomplish since the currency was first allowed to float against the dollar in 1973.

Calls for quantitative easing by the BOJ were heard around the world in 1999. They came from economists and from senior officials at the IMF, like Stanley Fischer and Michael Mussa. Even MOF began to champion the cause for a quantitative easing. MOF had finally woken up to what was going on but could do nothing because the BOJ had been granted its independence under the new "Bank of Japan Law" of April 1, 1998.

Unfortunately, BOJ governor Hayami dug in his heels at what he regarded as a breach of the Bank's newly acquired independence. When MOF demanded in 1999 that the Bank of Japan not sterilize its interventions that were aimed at stopping the rise of the yen, the BOJ resisted. It promptly sterilized every one of MOF's yen interventions, thereby effectively passing up a free opportunity to stop the downward spiral of consumer prices and put a halt to economic stagnation.

Ministerial Diversions

JAPANESE BUREAUCRATS AND politicians have a remarkable ability to achieve a state of national focus away from the real causes of their nation's economic maladies. No ministry is more accomplished at this than MOF. Over the decade MOF has blamed Japan's economic woes on a variety of factors, none of which was actually a material cause for concern.

Early in the '90s, MOF began to get interested in the equity derivatives market. Nikkei index futures contracts were listed on the Osaka exchange and the Tokyo Price Index (TOPIX) futures were listed on the Tokyo Stock Exchange. The Nikkei 225 is a price-weighted index of 225 stocks; TOPIX is a broad-based capitalization-weighted index of Japanese stocks. Index arbitrage had become a profitable activity for the American and British securities firms in Japan, but the local Japanese securities firms were slow to catch on to how the game worked.

A stock index futures contract is a cash-settled, exchange-listed derivative that mimics the behavior of the underlying stock index adjusted for interest costs and dividends. There is a relatively simple, mechanical formula that alerts traders when the futures contract has run sufficiently ahead or behind of the underlying cash market to make an arbitrage trade profitable. The term cash market refers to the underlying stocks that can be grouped together in a portfolio (or "basket") to replicate the index. When futures are sufficiently above cash, the arbitrageur sells futures and "buys cash"— that is, acquires the actual stocks that make up the index—and holds both positions until it is worthwhile to unwind the trade. When futures are sufficiently below cash, the opposite happens, meaning that the arbitrageur buys the futures contract and "sells cash."

In the early 1990s, stock index futures traded significantly above the cash market for periods of time. This meant that the arbitrage community was predominantly long stocks and short futures. The size of the aggregate arbitrage position across the whole brokerage community had begun to get large relative to the amount of trading done purely in stocks. MOF began to get worried, though exactly what MOF was worried about has never been clear. Officially, MOF's representatives railed against the arbitrageurs and blamed them for having brought about the fall in the stock market.

The arbitrageurs defended themselves by explaining that they were both long (via baskets of stocks) and short (meaning the futures)—in other words, their stock and futures positions canceled each other. What MOF never conceded was that an index arbitrage trade is a market neutral event. To MOF, the only thing that mattered was that the arbitrageurs were in possession of a lot of shares of common stock that they might someday want to sell. The officials began to fret that the arbitrage community might try to sell their shares and cause a market crash. That of course could never happen. To unwind their trades, the arbitrageurs would have to sell stock and buy futures simultaneously. Net of everything the liquidation of an index arbitrage trading position could not lead to a selloff in the stock market.

Nevertheless, MOF decided to lean on the Osaka Stock Exchange where the Nikkei futures contracts were traded. Soon all kinds of disruptive features were installed to foil the arbitrageurs. Osaka raised its margin requirements on Nikkei futures contracts and put in Brady-style circuit breakers. But the arbitrage community had the last laugh because the Singapore International Monetary Exchange (SIMEX) happened to have its own version of the Nikkei Index futures contract. Soon trading in stock index futures began to bleed out of Osaka, and also Tokyo, in the direction of SIMEX. And try though they did, there was nothing that MOF could do to convince SIMEX to delist its newly popular Nikkei contract.

In the end, MOF's war on the arbitrage community accomplished nothing in the way of halting the downward plunge in the Japanese stock market. Moreover, it seems that MOF never did realize that the index arbitrageurs were doing Japan a service. Markets function better when there is a close association between the cash market and the futures market. This is because as a matter of simple economic efficiency, it is better to have one and only one price in the market at a moment in time for the index. It was in Japan's own economic interest to have any meaningful discrepancies between cash and futures arbitraged out of the market.

MOF has a similar blind spot when it comes to the dollar/yen exchange rate. Foreign exchange is the area where Japan decks itself out in full battle dress. Virtually no day passes in the foreign exchange market without some directive from a Japanese official. If the yen has made an unwanted move, a direct threat is issued, usually something like "Japan will not tolerate excessive strength in the yen." Once in a while, this jawboning catches the market off-guard and there is a pop in the exchange rate. But most of the time it does little more than introduce noise and extra volatility into the market. The official interest in managing exchange rates may have started with the Plaza and the Louvre interventions. Since that time, MOF has been on top of the foreign exchange market like a hawk.

One thing that we know from observing MOF's behavior is that it abhors large movements in exchange rates. Whenever there is a big move, a MOF spokesman steps forward to declare that volatility, too, is "undesirable." But the question of why the big move occurred is never addressed because MOF tacitly assumes that the foreign exchange market is a private club run by undesirable elements. MOF thinks of exchange rates as being toys for speculators more than as being economic prices. The minister and his staff believe their responsibility is to guide the exchange rate to what they regard as fundamentally acceptable levels and to keep all movements in exchange rates small in magnitude. But what about economics? Exchange rates are prices, not playthings. When they move, by a lot or by a little, it is for the purpose of achieving equilibrium between supply and demand.

In 1998, MOF made a lot of commotion in the foreign exchange world saying it wanted to stop the yen from strengthening "prematurely." Like most things that MOF is worried about, this fixation with not having a strong yen exposes a deep-seated official prejudice towards the interests of one group, the exporters, over those of another group, foreign investors who had committed funds to Japan.

In 1999, Japan saw a brief respite from its troubled decade when the Nikkei index rose on foreign investor buying. The problem, if it was a problem, was that these same foreign investors had to buy yen to buy Japanese stocks. When in 1999 this began to happen in large amounts, the yen appreciated against the dollar and even more so against the euro. The MOF's response was to intervene directly in the currency markets to buy dollars and sell yen on twelve different occasions for a total of $64 billion in 1999 alone. This might have made a dent in the movement of the yen except for the fact that MOF ran directly into the iron wall of the Bank of Japan. The BOJ, as was described above, asserted its independence and stubbornly sterilized MOF's yen sales. Not surprisingly, the MOF's interventions accomplished little or nothing beyond adding an unnecessary element of volatility into the currency market.

The Japanese government bond market is another preoccupation of MOF. By 2000, after a decade of malaise, Japanese government bonds were trading at record low yields. What MOF seemed to fear was that yields might skyrocket upward once a real economic recovery became apparent. That this could happen in theory was correct, especially if the BOJ ever succeeded in halting the downward march of consumer prices. The national budget was in deficit and there was talk of additional fiscal stimulus programs, two more factors that gave the authorities concern for the bond market.

MOF's answer to this "problem" was to conduct a public relations campaign to assure Japanese citizens that Japanese government bonds (JGBs) were completely safe investments. The minister of finance himself, Kiichi Miyazawa, was heard lecturing investors that JGBs were totally safe investments because the bondholder was assured of getting paid coupons and principal on time. At no time did he warn them that they might suffer substantial capital losses if the Japanese government yield curve were to shift upward.

MOF had an even more potent trick to keep the bond market guessing. As it turned out, the government of Japan was the biggest buyer of Japanese government bonds. By carefully manipulating announcements about when the various parts of the government would be in the market, the MOF was able to keep short-sellers of bonds on the sidelines. As in the case of Japanese stocks, MOF was out to get anyone who took a short position.

But with bond yields as well as with the yen, economics uniformly tells us that there is no such thing as Sakakibara's "premature" move in a price, or a yield, or an exchange rate. To speak of a premature move in any price is to evince ignorance of economics. As Merton Miller once eloquently spoke, the laws of economics do work for Japan: "No uniquely Japanese (or American) economics exists, any more than a Japanese physics or Japanese chemistry. The fundamental laws of economics apply everywhere."[27]

At the start of this chapter the question was asked what was responsible for Japan's sorry performance in the 1990s. The logical next question is what can be done to bring Japan back to prosperity and growth.

The Future of Japan's Economy

UNFORTUNATELY MANY BUT not all of the factors that brought Japan low in the 1990s cannot be changed in the near term. There are a variety of institutional impediments in Japan that limit the flexibility of economic agents in their decision making. For one thing, the heavy hand of ministerial oversight is at work throughout the system. Also, property rights are abridged by what Sakakibara proudly dubbed his theory of "peopleism." Under this notion, the rights of the so-called stakeholders include being able to overrule corporate owners. These factors are responsible for misdirecting the nation's monstrously large domestic savings into poor economic projects and for impeding the process of restructuring the economy following the bubble period. The most obvious need is for shareholders to be empowered and nonshareholder stakeholders to be disenfranchised.

One thing that could change in the near term is the policy of the Bank of Japan. The BOJ has managed to cramp any chance of economic recovery by throttling the rate of growth in Japan's money supply. This is something that could be altered in an instant by the BOJ's adopting a program of absorbing a portion of the outstanding Japanese government bonds. The resultant swelling of the BOJ's balance sheet and expansion of the money supply might avoid the further disaster of a deflationary downward spiral in consumer prices.

The entire role of the Ministry of Finance, as well as the other ministries, needs to be seriously refocused. MOF should get out of the business of trying to micromanage world exchange rates, Japanese government bonds yields, and stock market prices. This, along with a massive reduction in the ministerial input into the planning of the economy, would go a long way toward the successful rehabilitation of Japan.

The greatest asset in any country is its human capital. Japan is rich in that regard, having a well-educated population and a highly dedicated workforce. For this reason alone, the Japanese people should be optimistic about their future but cautious about the role that its government has mapped out for itself.

Chapter 3 *Three*

Exploding Foreign Exchange Regimes

T HE CURRENCY CRISES that were prevalent in the 1990s contributed in no small part to the economic dislocations that plagued the decade. Yet the origins of exchange rate crises are widely misunderstood, with the most popular explanation being that speculators are to blame. And some observers point to international capital flows as being the cause. They claim that money can move "too freely" between markets for the well-being of the international financial system. Neither the speculator hypothesis nor the capital mobility explanation is satisfactory.

Any currency, even one that is freely floating, can experience a sharp depreciation as part of a general macroeconomic reversal. Stock market crashes, political crises, natural disasters, or the economic collapse of an important trading partner country, to name a few examples, all can induce the value of a currency to plummet.

Although all exchange rate regimes, be they fixed or floating, can be brought low as part of a general economic meltdown, only fixed exchange rate regimes can explode essentially of their own accord. This insight is usually lacking in discussions about the currency crises of the 1990s where there needs to be acknowledgment that the common denominator that exists for nearly all of these chaotic episodes is a fixed exchange rate regime.

An *exchange rate regime crisis*, or simply, a *currency crisis*, comes about when market pressure forces a country to devalue its currency or abandon its fixed exchange rate regime altogether. This phenomenon is always rooted in the distortions that fixed foreign exchange regimes create by giving artificial stability to the currency.

This chapter and the next review the fixed exchange rate crises of the 1990s, meaning the European Exchange Rate Mechanism (ERM) (1992 and 1993), Mexico (1994), and Southeast Asia (1997).

Distortions Arising from Fixed Exchange Rates

AT THE ONSET, WHEN A country decides to fix its exchange rate, it must instruct its central bank to stand ready to buy or sell its currency at an established exchange rate. The object of this exercise is to peg the value of its currency, called the domestic currency, to that of another country's currency, the latter being called the reserve currency. To facilitate this, the central bank must hold foreign reserves, meaning bonds and foreign currency issued by the reserve currency's government.

When the central bank buys the domestic currency to prevent it from falling in value, it must sell some of its foreign reserves. The success of any fixed exchange rate regime requires the central bank to be willing to deplete its stock of foreign reserves in order for it to conduct interventions into the currency market.

If the central bank comes to realize that it cannot preserve the fixed exchange rate, it may decide to try to devalue the domestic currency. *Devaluation* by definition occurs when the central bank lowers the fixed rate for the domestic currency, thereby making it less valuable against the reserve currency; *revaluation* means just the opposite, that the bank raises the fixed rate of its currency. In extreme cases the central bank may be forced to abandon the fixed exchange rate regime altogether and go to a floating exchange rate regime.

In theory, the interest rate associated with a fixed exchange rate currency should exactly equal the interest rate on the reserve currency. In reality, it rarely does. The domestic interest rate usually exceeds that of the reserve currency because there is a risk that the exchange rate regime might fail. Even in cases in which the market has great confidence that the regime can endure, there can be a risk premium on the domestic currency interest rate, though it might be small. But if the confidence in the regime erodes, the spread between the domestic and reserve currency interest rates can become enormous.

Whatever is the level of the domestic currency interest rate, it is artificial, of course, because it is a function of the reserve currency interest rate and having the exchange rate fixed. The apparent stability in the exchange rate is totally unnatural. These distortions in the interest rate and the exchange rate are the underlying causes of what can turn into an exchange rate explosion.

Consider the case of a foreign investor who is interested in putting money into a country that has a fixed exchange rate system. The investment decision will be determined in part by whether the investor believes that the currency regime is stable. If confidence exists that the system can hold, the investor's preference would be tilted toward investing in assets denominated in the domestic currency and the investor will not consider hedging foreign currency exposure. This is because the domestic currency offers a higher interest rate than the reserve currency. Moreover, as a practical matter, the higher the domestic interest rate relative to the reserve currency interest rate, the greater the cost of doing currency hedging. Hence foreign investors will tend to accumulate positions that are long the local currency (Box 3.1).

There is another group, investment managers, hedge funds, and bank currency traders, who also will be attracted to fixed exchange rate currencies if they believe that the regime will persist. They have no interest in investing in the country, per se. They are solely motivated by a desire to capture the interest rate differential between the two currencies. They express this in a number of trading strategies that go long the domestic currency and short the reserve currency. Though the size of this differential may seem small, the potential profits are enormous when leverage is used. Investment strategies of this nature are generically called *carry trades*. They can be found practically anywhere there is a fixed exchange regime.

BOX 3.1

The Mechanics of Currency Hedging

INVESTING ABROAD CAN involve taking foreign exchange risk. This is readily apparent in the case of buying a foreign government's bond that is denominated in that country's own currency. Real estate and investments in foreign common stocks also have degrees of exposure to foreign exchange risk.

Most institutional currency hedging is done using forward foreign exchange contracts. Forward contracts are used instead of spot contracts to avoid having to make immediate physical delivery of foreign currency.

If an investor has acquired a bond denominated in a foreign currency, then his trade to hedge the currency risk associated with the bond is to sell the foreign currency forward to some value date, such as 3 or 6 months. As the value date approaches, the investor must roll the forward hedge for an additional period of time. Each time the contract is rolled, the profit or loss on the hedge must be settled with the dealer.

Currency hedges constructed with forward contracts can be removed any time the foreign exchange market is open by doing a matching trade in opposite direction. In the example given, such a trade would be to buy the foreign currency in the form of a second forward contract that has the same value date as the outstanding hedging contract. DeRosa *Managing Foreign Exchange Risk* has extensive discussion of hedging foreign exchange risk.

The most famous carry trade in recent history germinated within the European Exchange Rate Mechanism (ERM), the complex program for exchange rate stabilization operated by the European Monetary System from March 1979 until January 1999. Known as the *convergence play*, this carry trade was expressed with long positions in high-yielding Italian and Spanish debt hedged with short positions in the lower-yielding German mark. The idea was to profit from the high yields on Italian and Spanish paper while using the German mark to hedge the currency risk of the lire and peseta. The German mark, which was the anchor currency in the ERM program, happened to have a relatively low interest rate compared to other European currencies. As long as the ERM held together, meaning no substantial devaluations of the lire or peseta, the trade made money. It was like getting free interest. An IMF report explained this trade as follows:

> For example, a U.S. investor purchasing an Italian Government bond could hedge this exposure with a forward contract in lire. However, if he chose to bet on convergence, without taking an open position in the dollar-deutsche mark exchange rate, he could hedge the latter exposure by selling deutsche mark forward; if the lira stayed within the existing exchange rate bands, this would yield higher returns. Obviously, the proxy hedge actually leaves the investor's position exposed to realignments of the deutsche mark-lire rate.[1]

But the bottom line was that for investors to participate in this trade it meant having to take exposure to the cross-exchange rate between the lire and peseta against the German mark. When the lire and peseta were sharply devalued, as were the ERM currencies during the crises of 1992 and 1993, investors found themselves on the receiving end of some gargantuan exchange-rate induced capital losses. It was only then that the true risk of the convergence trade became widely appreciated.

In the case of Mexico, dollar investors became positively addicted to a carry trade involving peso-denominated short-term government debt issues, known locally as *Cetes*. These instruments offered a nice step-up from U.S. dollar interest rates with no apparent currency risk. During the early '90s, the peso was pegged to the dollar, though a very gradual depreciation was allowed before the December 1994 float.

Thailand's carry trade was the famous "Thai baht basket trade." Prior to July 1997, the Bank of Thailand pegged the baht to a basket of currencies comprised of dollars, marks, and yen. In its most simple incarnation, the baht basket trade consisted of borrowing in dollars, marks, and yen, in the prescribed proportions, to finance investments in Thai baht bonds or baht bank deposits. When the baht was floated, it plunged, and investors took the full hit for the devaluation and were left owing debts in hard currency, dollars, marks, and yen. On a more sophisticated level, the trade consisted of a long position in the Thai baht that was hedged with forward contracts in the basket currencies.

Indonesia managed the rupiah by pegging it to the dollar with an allowance for gradual and controlled depreciation in the currency. This incubated still another Asian carry trade. Investors found ingenious ways go long rupiahs, thinking that they were earning a preferred rate of interest while enjoying the safety of a supposedly bulletproof fixed foreign exchange.

Significant amounts of leverage have been used by aggressive investors who wanted to accumulate enormous positions in carry trades. But carry trades are strange animals indeed. They appear to earn steady profits for long periods of time with little or no exposure to risk. Economists have come to call this phenomenon the *peso problem*. Peso problem trades seem to defy the basic economic principle that there can be no profit without some risk exposure. The IMF described the peso problem in a report on the September 1992 ERM crisis and the convergence play:

> In some way, the convergence play is another version of the "peso problem." In the mid-1970s the Mexican peso had exchanged for the U.S. dollar at the same rate for two decades. The Mexican interest rate was significantly higher than dollar interest rates, year after year. This phenomenon was dubbed the "peso problem."... The interpretation in 1975, which is now commonplace, was that the probability of a large devaluation was low because empirically the event had not occurred in a long run of data. The devaluation, once it occurred, would be large because of the large

divergence in interest rates. The game for any market participant was to time the conversion of funds back to dollars before the devaluation and obtain higher than the market return on dollars.[2]

History provides many examples of carry trades that have met their days of reckoning. When a fixed exchange rate regime appears to be in trouble, the carry traders see financial disaster staring them in the face. They become desperate to get out of their positions, even if it means having to pay exorbitant prices to eliminate their exposure to the domestic currency. This adds colossal pressure to the already weakened fixed exchange rate regime. The losses on a carry trade can end up being substantial. Ironically, what can be lost in an instant of panicked trading can easily erase all the profits from years of being in the carry trade. The joke among traders after the 1992 ERM crisis was that the convergence trade was like "bending over to pick up pennies while being in the path of an advancing steamroller."

So we have the nonhedged foreign investors and we have the carry traders. And then what of the role of the local residents? Their incentives point the same way as the foreign investors. They are enticed to structure their borrowings in the reserve currency because they want to borrow as cheaply as possible and their own domestic interest rate exceeds the reserve currency rate. Yet this is a bomb in the making because of the risk of the domestic currency experiencing a devaluation. If the domestic currency were to be devalued, the reserve currency indebtedness would be magnified upward in local currency terms. Hence it can be seen that local residents too, when they borrow in reserve currency terms, have a de facto foreign exchange exposure that is long the local currency and short the reserve currency.

The key point is that everyone—the foreign investor and the local investor—is long the domestic currency. Everybody will try to sell the domestic currency or hedge their exposure if they come to suspect that devaluation or an abandonment of the regime is in the cards. The cumulative long position in the domestic currency, which may have taken years to accumulate, will be put up for sale

BOX 3.2

The Nuts and Bolts of Currency Speculation

TO UNDERSTAND THE role of speculators, we must follow the mechanics of going short the domestic currency. Going short means that individuals sell a currency that they do not own. This is done in the hope of being able to buy it back at a cheaper price at a later time. It is similar to selling short shares of common stock. With stocks the short seller must borrow shares to make delivery to the buyer. There is a lending fee that must be paid by the short seller to obtain the loan of the shares. In foreign exchange a short sale is accomplished by selling the currency in a forward transaction. As was explained above, a forward foreign exchange transaction has its value date further out on the settlement calendar than spot, the latter being a trade for nearly immediate settlement. To stay with the analogy of the short sale of stock, the forward sale of a currency involves paying a "lending fee" of sorts that is based on the spread between the interest rate on the currency being sold and the currency being bought. But this "lending rate," rather than being explicitly stated, is folded into the forward exchange rate. The amount by which the forward exchange rate diverges from the spot exchange rate, called the *forward points*, determines the cost of going short the currency.

at once in a block if the fixed exchange rate regime begins to crumble. The magnitude of these positions accounts for the ferocity of fixed exchange rate currency firestorms.

Once a currency crisis begins, a fourth group, who could legitimately be called currency speculators, arrives on the scene trying to get in on the action. They, too, attempt to sell short by taking a forward position (long the reserve currency and short the domestic currency). They hope to be able to close out their positions with vast profits once the currency regime has cracked and the exchange rate for the local currency has plummeted. But their trading is perilous because they are usually too late and because they

Herein lies a basic principle of currency trading: The higher the domestic interest rate, the more expensive it is to maintain a short position in that currency.

One widespread misperception is that the foreign exchange market is rife with situations that are riskless "one-way bets." Practically speaking, these almost never exist. One has to take into account the cost of carrying a speculative position. Seasoned currency traders know to balance the probable gains from devaluation against the cost of maintaining a short position in the currency.

This is why a central bank may choose to hike its short-term interest rate to defend its currency in the face of market pressure. The idea is to try to muscle speculators out of the market by raising the cost of their going short or staying short the domestic currency. But in so doing, the bank must accept that it is damaging its own economy. Higher interest rates may lead to bankruptcies and higher rates of unemployment. That damage can be catastrophic, as has been evident in the history of emerging-market nations where bank loans are typically based on floating interest rates.

have to pay enormous costs to finance their short positions in domestic currency.[3] While it often appears that they have huge sway over the market in a crisis, they actually are never really large position-wise relative to the other groups that have been mentioned. The positions accumulated by the local residents and foreign investors that must be liquidated always dwarf those of the speculators (Box 3.2).

The balance of history in the 1990s is not on the side of the central banks when it comes to managing currency crises. Although there have been successful defenses of fixed exchange rate regimes, a good number of central banks were broken. When the situation became critical, they faced having to choose between keeping what was left of their foreign reserves and maintaining their exchange rate regimes. Many were forced to devalue their currencies. Others decided in the end to let their currencies float, having abandoned their fixed exchange rate regimes.

Many central banks have compounded their situations by attempting to defend their fixed exchange rate systems with direct intervention in the foreign exchange market. This is the sad record of the Banks of England, France, Germany, Mexico, Thailand, Indonesia, and Malaysia, to name a few. These, and many other central banks, have squandered billions of dollars of reserves trying to defend doomed fixed exchange rate regimes.

The European Exchange Rate Mechanism Crises: 1992 and 1993

THE TREATY OF ROME in 1957 called for the creation of the European Economic Community. This started the process of European economic unification that led to the establishment of the European Economic and Monetary System (EMS) in March 1979 and the most ambitious experiments in fixed exchange rates since Bretton Woods.

At the start, the EMS called for the creation of a new currency, the European currency unit (ECU). The ECU was originally a gross domestic product (GDP)–weighted average of the EMS currencies in 1979. Periodically its composition was supposed to be modified to reflect changes in the relative GDP of member nations. The composition of the ECU did change when new currencies were admitted to the EMS. In November 1994, the composition of the ECU, then comprised of eleven currencies, was permanently fixed. The largest components of the ECU were the German mark (30.1 percent), the French franc (19.0 percent), and the British pound (13.0 percent).[4]

To some extent the ECU did trade for a while as though it were a real currency. Some European governments even issued debt instruments denominated in the ECU, but ECU notes and coins were never put into circulation. The ECU was replaced by the euro on January 1, 1999, but not before it played an important role in the operation of the Exchange Rate Mechanism (ERM), a complicated exchange rate stabilization program operated by the member EMU countries.

The ERM was supposed to work as follows. Each of the ERM participating currencies was assigned a targeted exchange rate with respect to the ECU called its *ECU central rate*. The ratio of any two ECU central rates was defined as the *bilateral central rate* between two participating currencies. All of the bilateral central rates taken together formed the *ERM parity grid*. Each participating country was responsible for maintaining its currency's position within the grid within a tolerance of a predetermined band. The bandwidth applicable for most participating currencies was equal to plus or minus 2.25 percent, but some currencies were allowed to travel within a wider bandwidth equal to plus or minus 6 percent. To make this work, the member countries were supposed to coordinate monetary and fiscal policy and carry out an orderly implementation of structural economic reforms. They also agreed to make direct intervention into the foreign exchange market to maintain their currencies' ERM positions.

The intended purpose of the ERM was to dampen the volatility of European exchange rates in the period leading up to the launch of the euro. Full interest rate convergence was seen as a necessary precondition to the debut of the single currency. Logically speaking, if exchange rates could be fixed within narrow trading zones, then interest rates in the respective currencies naturally would have to converge on a common level.

But the ERM was anything but a stabilizing influence. The ERM, which was a fine example of financial engineering run a-mok, actually induced record levels of volatility in European exchange rates. From the time of its inception in March 1979 until the creation of the euro at the start of 1999, the ERM suffered a total of eighteen realignments affecting fifty-six central rates. It also spawned two spectacular currency crises.

September 16, 1992, the day of the sterling ERM crisis, is a day that lives in traders' minds as one of the most chaotic times in modern foreign exchange history. Not only was the foreign exchange market in chaos, but stock and bond markets in all of Europe were also in a complete uproar. Massive selling of sterling took place as it became apparent that the U.K. had made a massive error in joining the ERM.

This crisis featured the famous episode in which George Soros reportedly earned $1 billion from a short sterling/mark position. The Soros trading in the ERM currency and debt markets, trading that actually netted him about $2 billion, was a singularly brilliant piece of speculation. There never has been anything like it, before or since. Soros quickly became known as "the man who broke the Bank of England."

Soon afterward Soros spoke about his ERM trading in an interview with London *Times* journalist Anatole Kaletsky:

> We did a lot of sterling and we did make a lot of money, because our funds are so large. We must have been the biggest single factor in the market in the days before the ERM fell apart. Our total position on Black Monday had to be worth almost $10 billion. We planned to sell more than that. In fact when [Chancellor of the Exchequer] Norman Lamont said just before the devaluation that he would borrow nearly $15 billion to defend sterling, we were amused because that was about how much we wanted to sell. But things moved faster than we expected, and we didn't manage to build up the full position. So a billion is about right as an estimate of the profit, though dollars, not pounds.[5]

In the same interview, Soros revealed to Kaletsky that he had other positions across the ERM:

> Mr. Soros sold lire and bought German bonds. He took big long positions in British, German and French interest rate futures. And he bought the London stock market, hedging this with sales of German and French shares. The week after the British devaluation, Mr. Soros made further gains

by siding with the French authorities against speculators who were attacking the franc. In all the funds made about $2 billion.[6]

Soros's astounding trading acumen was revealed in the above passage when he spoke of his having reversed gears to defend the French franc against attacks by other speculators as the crisis subsided. But as was mentioned above, the Soros trading in sterling and related markets forever changed the way that the general public views hedge funds, if not the entire foreign exchange market. Soros made it look to the man on the street, and daresay many politicians and central bankers, as though he or any of his imitators could obliterate any exchange rate regime of their choosing. Is this really true or did the Europeans, particularly the British, set themselves up for a fall?

The most relevant thing about the September 1992 ERM crisis is that it originated from a form of a fixed exchange rate regime. All of the conditions identified above that make for a potentially explosive foreign exchange regime were present. None of them relies on the existence of a superstar currency speculator.

The first factor was the formation in the years leading up to September 1992 of a massive carry trade known as the *convergence play*. The ERM created serious distortions in European capital markets. Despite apparent exchange rate stability, European currencies featured widely disparate interest rates (Figure 3.1).

The IMF wrote of the resultant capital flows into the ERM countries:

> One of the important factors motivating these inflows was the growing perception by international investors that the member countries of the EMS were on a continuous convergence path toward European Monetary Union (EMU), under which interest rate differentials in favor of the high-yielding ERM currencies would increasingly overestimate the actual risk of exchange rate depreciation. As one portfolio manager recalled the prevailing view, "why settle for

Source: Data Resources, Inc. Reprinted by permission of the International Monetary Fund.

FIGURE 3.1

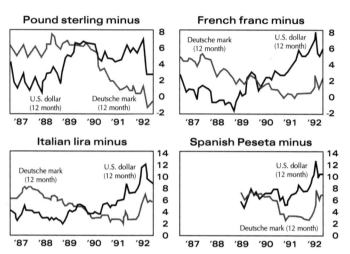

The Convergence Play

INTEREST RATE DIFFERENTIALS among the ERM participants created the famous "convergence trade." Traders and investment managers were free to invest in the highest-yielding currencies among the ERM countries with no fear of exchange rate risk because currencies were stabilized inside of Europe. These graphs show the size of the interest rate spreads against the German mark and U.S. dollar for the pound sterling, French franc, Italian lire, and Spanish peseta.

the yield on a deutsche mark bond when you can get a higher yield on a peseta or lira bond without a compensating risk?"... In yet another reflection of the fixed exchange rate assumption, the exchange risks of positions against non-ERM currencies was frequently "proxy-hedged," for example, a hedge of a deutsche mark position against the U.S. dollar was emplaced when lira securities were acquired.[7]

Source: Data from International Monetary Fund, *World Economic Outlook*, May 1993, Table A15 and International Monetary Fund, *World Economic Outlook*, October 1999, Table 1.4.

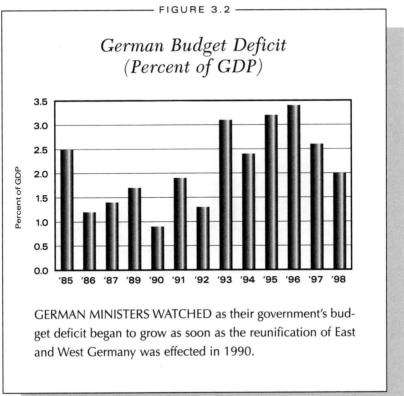

FIGURE 3.2

German Budget Deficit
(Percent of GDP)

GERMAN MINISTERS WATCHED as their government's budget deficit began to grow as soon as the reunification of East and West Germany was effected in 1990.

The attraction to the convergence play was virtually universal. According to one portfolio manager it amounted to having "government-sponsored arbitrage." The ERM was the catalyst for the surprising growth in popularity of a new class of money market mutual funds that specialized in the short-term securities of foreign governments with high interest rates. Morningstar, Inc., estimates that over $20 billion dollars of investor money flowed into these funds between 1989 and 1992. The main engine of portfolio performance for these funds was the convergence play.

As for the overall size of the market's position, the IMF reported that "without pretending too much precision, estimates suggest that the total of such convergence plays could have been as high as $300 billion."[8] Whatever were its true dimensions, the position associated with the convergence play that was unwound in Sep-

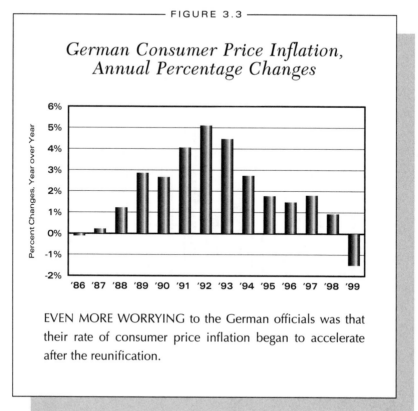

FIGURE 3.3

German Consumer Price Inflation, Annual Percentage Changes

EVEN MORE WORRYING to the German officials was that their rate of consumer price inflation began to accelerate after the reunification.

Source: Data from Bloomberg L.P. and OECD.

tember 1992 was larger by multiples than anything either the Bank of England or Soros was attempting to move in the market.

The second factor that caused the September 1992 ERM crisis was the exceptional and deliberate contractionary monetary policy conducted by the German central bank, the Bundesbank, in the period leading up to the events. Certainly, the designers of the ERM could not have foreseen that East Germany would achieve its liberation from the East Bloc amid the chaos surrounding the imminent disintegration of the Soviet Union. This process started with the fall of the Berlin Wall on November 9, 1989. German Chancellor Helmut Kohl, not wanting to miss this historic opportunity, called for a fast vote on reunification by referendum on July 1, 1990. On October 3, 1990, East and West Germany became one country.

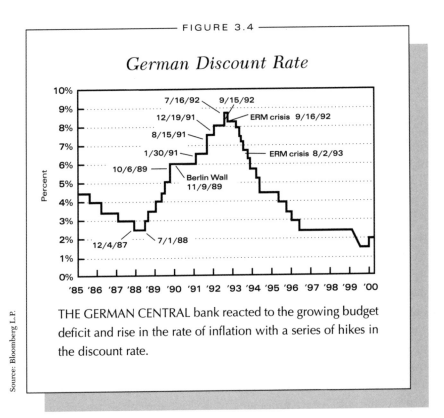

FIGURE 3.4

German Discount Rate

THE GERMAN CENTRAL bank reacted to the growing budget deficit and rise in the rate of inflation with a series of hikes in the discount rate.

Source: Bloomberg L.P.

It was not until the tumultuous celebration began to wind down that the immensity of the cost of reunification became apparent to the German government. As government spending soared, the once-proud German Finance Ministry found itself with a large and growing budget deficit, at least by its normal standards (Figure 3.2).

Moreover, the rate of inflation began to pick up immediately (Figure 3.3).

Germany had the most conservative central bank in Europe, if not in the world. Not unexpectedly, the response of the Bundesbank was to hike the short-term interest rate repeatedly. From the time of the fall of the Berlin Wall to July 16, 1992, a period of eighteen months, the Bundesbank raised the discount rate four times, starting from 6 percent and reaching 8.75 percent (Figure 3.4).

The Bundesbank was the anchor central bank of the EMS, yet

it was raising interest rates during the time when the other ERM central banks were hoping to guide their interest rates to common lower levels. The Bundesbank, in so doing, put the interests of the German economy ahead of the European Union.

The third factor that led to the September 1992 crisis was the inclusion of the pound sterling in the ERM twenty-three months earlier. The bilateral central rate for sterling against the German mark was 2.95 when it entered the ERM on October 8, 1990. Economist John Williamson estimates that sterling's Fundamental Equilibrium Exchange Rate (FEER) was 2.24 for the mark.[9] The FEER for a currency is an econometric estimate of its long-run real value, a concept that Williamson introduced.

The first indication that something might be horribly wrong with the ERM structure occurred on June 3, 1992 when a market panic in the currency and European bond market ensued following the defeat of a Danish referendum on the Maastricht treaty. Investors were seriously concerned that the entire single currency project might be doomed. The Danes had called for a vote on the treaty, which twelve member nations had signed on February 7, 1992. The Maastricht treaty contained a set of common provisions that defined the new European Union. The aim of the treaty was to transform the European Common Market into a monetary union, and as such, it set out a timetable for the launch of the new single currency, the euro.

On September 16, 1992, the day that George Soros was referring to in the London *Times* interview as "Black Monday," the full crisis erupted, two months after the final Bundesbank rate hike of July 16, 1992 (Figure 3.4). In the course of the day, the Bank of England would raise short-term interest rates from 10 percent to 12 percent and then announce that it would raise rates again to 15 percent on the next day, all in defense of the pound. The U.K. fought the market tooth and nail, buying large blocks of its own currency against the mark.

It didn't work. The *Financial Times* would later proclaim that "Sterling was being sold like water running out of a tap."[10] Sterling was down and later completely out of the ERM. On the afternoon of September 16, when it became apparent to everyone that the battle was lost, the Bank of England (BOE) rescinded both interest rate hikes. The crisis forced Great Britain, Italy, and Finland to withdraw from the ERM. Sterling had started the day at the bottom of its ERM band equal to 2.7780 against the mark. Sterling continued to plunge against the mark, reaching as low as 2.32 by February 1993.

Also annihilated that day were practically all of the players who had staked their careers and fortunes in the convergence play.[11] It was likewise the beginning of the end for many of the aforementioned short-term international money market funds, practically all of which disappeared almost as quickly as they had appeared on the investment scene. The full cost to the British Exchequer has never been disclosed to British taxpayers, but one has to imagine that it was many billions of pounds.

Eleven months later, in August 1993, a second ERM crisis occurred, but this time the primary targets were the French franc and the Italian lire. The EMS was compelled to widen the intervention bands to plus or minus 15 percent, an act that nearly converted the ERM to floating exchange rates. Even with these measures, Spain and Portugal, two countries whose currencies were devalued numerous times earlier in the ERM period, were forced to devalue one last time on March 6, 1995.

Eventually the European currencies did stabilize and convergence was achieved. But this happened after the August 2, 1993 widening of the ERM trading bands to plus or minus 15 percent, so the question that the Eurocrats face is whether it was truly in their interest to have created the ERM. The fact is that convergence was achieved not through manipulation of exchange rates but as a natural result of improved economic conditions in their respective economies.

Neither of the ERM crises would have occurred had the EMS not insisted on trying to limit the fluctuations in exchange rates inside Europe. The whole episode should have argued an open-and-shut case for the economic incompetence of the European ministers who designed the ERM. Yet instead, the ERM crises have served to convict the foreign exchange market in the court of public opinion.

BOX 3.3

What Is a Current Account Deficit?

THE TERM *CURRENT ACCOUNT* refers to the net difference between what a country exports and what it imports in the way of goods and services over a given period of time. A country that exports more than it imports, as is the case for Japan, is said to be in a current account surplus position. If a country imports more than it exports, as did most of Southeast Asia before the summer of 1997, then the country is said to be in a current account deficit position.

For the national books of account to balance, a country with a current account deficit must import investment capital. This is the basic identity that underlies the organization of national income accounting.

Current account deficit countries to some extent get by on the good will of their foreign creditors and investors. The position of the United States among current account deficit nations is special because the dollar is the principal reserve currency of the world. Smaller countries, especially emerging market countries, have not been so lucky trying to sustain their current account deficits.

Foreign Exchange Crises in Emerging-Market Economies

MANY FOREIGN EXCHANGE crises in the 1990s occurred in the emerging-market countries previously heralded for stupendous rates of growth. Several had forms of fixed exchange rate regimes, and all ran persistent and large current account deficits right up to the start of their crises (Box 3.3).

Mexico and most of Southeast Asia were running huge current account deficits, exceptional in size by any standard, at the onset of their crises. But this was generally overlooked at the time, because the argument was made that these fast growing economies required large inflows of foreign capital. Some analysts rationalized away the risk of a currency crisis by concluding that the Bank of Mexico and the central banks of Asia were sufficiently stocked with foreign reserves to hold off an attack on their fixed exchange rate systems. Yet when crisis struck, the size of their reserves proved woefully inadequate, something that could have been deduced from what had happened to the much larger European central banks in the ERM crises of 1992 and 1993.

Analysis quickly exposes the implausibility of an emerging market nation's running a sustained, large current account deficit while trying to maintain a fixed exchange rate regime. The capital that flows in from abroad, which sustains the current account deficit, can stop or even reverse direction in an instant if there is even a whisper that devaluation is being considered.

The most crisis-prone environment of all combines a fixed exchange rate system, a history of current account deficits, and an investment environment where confidence is rapidly decaying. That in fact was the combination of factors, the perfect witch's brew, that brought down Mexico and most of Southeast Asia in the 1990s.

The Mexican Peso Crisis: 1994–1995

THROUGHOUT MOST OF the twentieth century, Mexico was a relatively poor country that happened to be located to the south of the United States, a very rich country. The prospects for Mexico started to improve in the 1970s. By the 1980s, Mexico had transformed its economy into a respectable emerging market success story.

A succession of Mexican presidents—Jose Lopez Portillo, Miguel de la Madrid, and Carlos Salinas, all of the Institutional Revolutionary Party (PRI)—built the image of the "new" Mexico over the period 1976–1994. The favorable outlook was enhanced when the United States, Mexico, and Canada entered into the North American Free Trade Agreement (NAFTA) which became effective on January 1, 1994.

In December 1994, the Mexican peso suddenly was the target of tremendous selling pressure. In a matter of days the peso declined to less than half of its previous value against the dollar. A massive macroeconomic contraction ensued, bankruptcy spread like wildfire, and the Mexican people began to experience great economic suffering.

What went wrong in Mexico? Francisco Gil-Díaz and Agustín Carstens, both economists with the Bank of Mexico, studied the crisis and stated: "We find clear evidence that Mexico experienced a politically triggered speculative attack, not a crisis based on the misalignment of real phenomena."[12]

Basic economic analysis argues differently. The fall of the peso was actually due to real economic forces, as will now be demonstrated. A proper *postmortem* must begin with Mexico's fixed exchange rate regime.

Mexico's "crawling peg" fixed exchange rate regime worked as follows. Starting on November 11, 1991, the Bank of Mexico fixed the value of the peso to the dollar within a formal intervention band. The peso was capped at an upper level equal to 3.0520 to the dollar. The floor was expanded at a rate of 0.0002 pesos per day, meaning that a gradual depreciation in the peso was theoretically allowed. This daily change in the floor was increased to 0.0004 pesos per day on October 21, 1992.[13]

In spite of the peso stabilization program, which required that the government stand ready to buy pesos at the pegged rate, a substantial spread remained between interest rates in Mexico and the United States. In January 1994, the spread between the Cetes interest rate and comparable U.S. dollar rates was 6.22 percent, annualized. Cetes are short-term peso-denominated treasury bills issued by the Mexican government. By July the spread between the Cetes rate and the U.S. dollar rates had risen to 9.94 percent. The spread closed somewhat to around 7 percent in early December before the crisis.[14]

Yet a substantial incentive remained for foreign investors to hold pesos as long as they believed that the fixed exchange rate regime could be preserved. The peso floor was allowed to drop by a mere 0.0004 pesos per day, which equates to a theoretical maximum annualized rate of depreciation in the currency of 4.8 percent.

Capital literally poured into Mexico in the early 1990s. The IMF estimated $91 billion of foreign capital was absorbed between 1990 and 1993, with $30 billion in 1993 alone. The risk of a forced devaluation seemed remote, given the appearance of massive economic progress. But what was really happening was that Mexico was creating a first-class "peso problem" for itself.

After the fact, it is amazing that foreign investors never realized that there was the possibility that huge blocks of the capital that were stampeding into Mexico might someday turn around and try to leave *en masse*. There was remarkable complacency about the fact that Mexico's current account deficit had steadily risen from $3.8 billion in 1988 to $29.5 billion in 1994.[15] Many sophisticated and professional investors ignored the warning signs of impeding disaster because they were convinced that their commitments to Mexico were nothing short of owning a gold mine.

The authorities reinforced their misjudgment. In a display of boldfaced spin doctoring, Pedro Aspe, the former Minister of Finance, dismissed his country's current account position with the following remarkable logic in 1993:

> Some macroeconomic indicators have changed meaning since I was a student. A large current account deficit signals these days not a profligate government but a strong expansion of private investment financed by capital repatriation or direct flows from foreign investment.[16]

Aspe's remarks amount to a treacherous economic fallacy that was often heard in emerging markets in the 1990s. The fact that capital happens to be flowing into a country does not necessarily mean that the country is growing or even prospering. Rather, as in the case of Mexico, it may be nothing more than a sign that an economic distortion, here being the peso stabilization regime, is pulling in foreign capital. This money could be going right down a rat hole, so to speak, for all the investors care. Their entire incentive for investing in the country rests on the preservation of the artificially stable exchange rate, rather than on carefully scrutiniz-ed real economic opportunities.

Given the importance that investors attached to the apparent stability of the exchange rate, surprisingly little attention was given to the very real possibility that the peso might have been massive-ly overvalued prior to the crisis, as economist Rudiger Dornbusch believes:

> By 1993, Mexican producer prices had risen in dollars by over 45 percent since the late 1980s compared with prices in the United States. An overvaluation of at least 25 percent could be discerned. Growth slowed down (except for elec-tion year spending), real interest rates were extremely high when measured by rates on commercial bank loans, and the external balance shifted towards a massive [capital account] surplus. All the symptoms of a troubled financial situation were in place.[17]

One external factor that exacerbated Mexico's problems was a shift in the U.S. Federal Reserve monetary policy toward tighten-ing in early 1994. Practically speaking, this could not have come at a worse time, with Mexico in such a precarious position. It is an example of how a policy of a large country can have disastrous indi-rect and unintended consequences for a smaller neighbor.

On February 4, 1994, fearing that inflationary pressures were building in the rapidly expanding U.S. economy, the Federal Open Market Committee raised its target for the federal funds rate by 25 basis points. This was Federal Reserve Chairman Alan Green-span's warning shot, so to speak. Over the next nine months, the Fed raised the Fed Funds target six more times. In the course of the year, the Fed hiked short-term interest rates by a cumulative total of 300 basis points. The final rate hike, of 75 basis points, occurred on November 15.

How much of the peso crisis ought to be assigned to the actions of the Fed?[18] The answer is that the Fed rate hikes were material in that they added yet more pressure on the peso, since the peso was pegged to the dollar. But there were a great number of other ruinous influences unique to Mexico at work at the time.

Chief among these internal factors was an acute loss of confidence in the political stability of Mexico that began to build in 1994, as Gil-Díaz and Carstens mentioned. Long-standing discontent in the southern province of Chiapas turned into violent disruptions in January 1994. More damaging was the assassination of PRI presidential candidate Donaldo Colosio on March 23, 1994. The political situation stabilized over the course of the summer when Ernesto Zedillo, who received the PRI's nomination after Colosio's death, was elected president. Zedillo was sworn into office on December 1 and trouble arrived at his doorstep immediately. On December 19, violence again erupted in Chiapas.

In an attempt to boost investor confidence, the Salinas administration (that preceded Zedillo's) decided to reconfigure the structure of the government debt by introducing a new form of government bond called *tesobonos* in April 1994. Tesobonos were short-term debt securities that paid in pesos but were indexed to the U.S. dollar. In issuing the tesobonos, the Mexican government effectively issued U.S. dollar denominated debt. Equivalently, the lower the value of the peso relative to the dollar, the more pesos the government would owe to the tesobono holders to preserve the dollar value of the debt. By November, 50 percent of the government debt (or $24 billion) was in the form of tesobonos. By December, tesobonos represented two-thirds of the government debt.

Financial crises often have their unique signature policy initiatives that go wrong with disastrous consequences. With Mexico, it was the decision to issue the tesobonos. These bonds, being dollar-linked, effectively created a financial doomsday machine in the basement of the state treasury. As the crisis progressed, the deterioration in the value of the peso was matched by an upward revaluation of the domestic currency value of the government's debt. The feedback loop was that as the peso weakened, the government's tesobono debt increased, which in turn put more downward pressure on the peso.

When the turmoil struck on December 20, 1994, the government's initial reaction was to try to defend the peso. Froot and McBrady report that the Bank of Mexico lost $4 billion intervening to support the peso between December 20 and 22. On December 22, Mexico announced that the peso would be devalued by 15 percent. It was too little, too late.

Two days later, the selling pressure on the peso was so massive that the government was forced to abandon outright the fixed exchange rate regime and let the peso float. As recounted by the IMF,

> Reflecting continuous pressure during the next two days, and a steep decline in reserves, the peso was allowed to float on December 22, after which Mexican financial markets experienced heavy selling pressures. These pressures were exacerbated by two factors. First, the value of Mexico's dollar-linked tesobono debt increased sharply as the peso depreciated. Second, the depreciation of the peso and the associated rapid rise in domestic interest rates increased the amount of nonperforming loans in the Mexican banking system, in part because most loans in Mexico have floating interest rates that quickly reflect market rates.[19]

The damage done by the peso crisis did not confine itself to Mexico alone. There were some spillover effects, largely confined to Argentina and Brazil. The Argentine stock market fell 14 percent from December 19 to December 27. The Brazilian market fell by 17 percent over the same period.[20] Other countries in the region were less affected and some, like Chile and Colombia, saw their stock markets rally during that week.

Brady bond spreads in the region shot up in response to Mexico, with Argentina's and Brazil's rising 389 basis points and 207 basis points, respectively.[21] But the largest, and most ominous of the so-called spillover effects to hit Argentina and Brazil came in the foreign exchange markets.

Argentina operated a fixed exchange rate regime that will be further discussed in Chapter 5 and Chapter 7. On December 28, one week after the Mexican float, the central banks of Argentina sold $353 million of its reserves. Over the course of the next three months, one-third of the central bank's reserves were expended to preserve the fixed exchange rate regime.[22]

Brazil had a similar experience with having to expend considerable reserves to keep its currency above the central bank's objective floor of R$0.85 to the dollar. On March 6, 1995, the authorities switched exchange rate regimes to a system of adjustable exchange rate bands.

Another kind of damage resulted from the method by which the developed countries tried to deal with the Mexican crisis. Mexico ushered in the era of the great supranational crisis bailout program.

On January 2, 1995, Robert Rubin, the newly installed Secretary of the Treasury, announced an $18 billion international credit package for Mexico.[23] Later that month, President Clinton announced a multilateral assistance package for Mexico that totaled nearly $50 billion. The funding came from the United States ($20 billion), the IMF ($17.9 billion), the Bank for International Settlements ($10 billion), and various Latin American governments and Canada ($2 billion). At the time this qualified as the largest financial bailout in history,[24] a dubious honor that would soon be conceded to Southeast Asian nations.

A number of serious questions are raised by the Mexican bailout. For starters, who exactly got bailed out? Critics say that the holders of the tesobonos, many being foreign investors and non-Mexican banks, got relief while the ordinary citizens of Mexico were left to suffer economic recession.

A far bigger question surrounds the larger concept of *moral hazard*. This term is thought to have originated from the insurance industry where it refers to cases in which losses are attributable to the moral character or derelict behavior of the insured. Economists use the term to cover instances in which investors participate in high-risk ventures, maybe even ones that are inherently deficient in the economic or social sense, only because of the existence of an actual or implied government guarantee of return of principal.

The case for having free markets rests on the premise that there be a connection between choices and outcomes. Investors need to enjoy the rewards from having taken risks and having made intelligent, informed decisions. Symmetrically speaking it is also necessary that they suffer disappointment when their choices turn out to be mistakes. Otherwise capital will be allocated to unwise investment projects.

Government-sponsored bailouts of failed projects or even of failed economies represent merely another form of market distortion. When investors come to expect that they can fall back on the U.S. Treasury or the IMF to come to their rescue, they stop trying to make careful judgments.

In this way, the Mexican peso crisis bailout of 1995 only accelerated the flow of international capital into the economies of Southeast Asia.

C h a p t e r *F o u r*

The Southeast Asian Currency Crisis of 1997

THAT THAILAND, THE Philippines, Indonesia, and Malaysia, four of the so-called Southeast Asian tiger nations, managed to weather the immediate consequences of the collapse of Japan's bubble economy is remarkable. One might suppose that the sinking of so large a ship would have sucked down in its wake the far smaller tiger economies. But the tigers managed to prosper, at least superficially, for most of the 1990s (Table 4.1).

Southeast Asia met its Waterloo in the summer of 1997. A tremendous currency crisis erupted in Thailand and quickly spread to the Philippines, Malaysia, and Indonesia. The initial manifestation was violent selling of the local currencies. Thereupon stock and real estate prices plunged and widespread financial insolvency followed (Table 4.2).

The cumulative magnitude of the dislocation to these economies can be seen in the dramatic reversals in GDP growth (Table 4.1). The greatest damage occurred in Indonesia, the fourth most populous nation in the world. The IMF estimates that Indonesia will have lost 82 percent of its four-year potential output in the period dating from the summer of 1997. The figures for Korea, Malaysia, and Thailand are 27 percent, 39 percent, and 57 percent, respectively.[1]

The Asian authorities quickly placed the blame on currency and stock market speculators. The most vocal attacks came from

TABLE 4.1

Real GDP Growth, Current Account, and External Debt: Indonesia, Malaysia, Philippines, and Thailand, 1990–1998

		1990	1991
INDONESIA	Real GDP Growth*	9.0%	8.9%
	Current Account Balance (% GDP)**	-2.8%	-3.4%
	Total External Debt % GDP in U.S. Dollars**	63.4%	63.8%
	Percentage of External Debt Denominated in Dollars**	45.0%	46.2%
MALAYSIA	Real GDP Growth*	9.6%	8.6%
	Current Account Balance (% GDP)**	-2.1%	-8.8%
	Total External Debt % GDP in U.S. Dollars**	50.3%	51.7%
	Percentage of External Debt Denominated in Dollars**	62.8%	62.8%
PHILIPPINES	Real GDP Growth*	3.0%	-0.6%
	Current Account Balance (% GDP)**	-6.1%	-2.3%
	Total External Debt % GDP in U.S. Dollars**	72.8%	74.3%
	Percentage of External Debt Denominated in Dollars**	52.7%	46.6%
THAILAND	Real GDP Growth*	11.6%	8.1%
	Current Account Balance (% GDP)**	-8.3%	-7.7%
	Total External Debt % GDP in U.S. Dollars**	34.6%	38.3%
	Percentage of External Debt Denominated in Dollars**	64.1%	65.4%

*Source: Data from International Monetary Fund, *World Economic Outlook*, October 1999, Tables 1.2, 6; and International Monetary Fund, *World Economic Outlook*, December 1997, Table A1.

Malaysian Prime Minister Mahathir who went into ad hominem tirades against George Soros on a number of occasions. He called Soros "criminal" and "an idiot." And Mahathir didn't stop there. He also stated that Soros had conducted his alleged attacks on currencies as part of a "Jewish agenda" against Southeast Asia.

Mahathir found company in denouncing Soros in Martin Peretz of the *New Republic*, who claimed that Soros "...benefited

1992	1993	1994	1995	1996	1997	1998
7.2%	7.3%	7.5%	8.2%	8.0%	4.7%	-13.7%
-2.2%	-1.5%	-1.7%	-3.3%	-3.3%	-1.8%	4.0%
61.1%	58.0%	60.1%	59.6%	58.5%	63.4%	150.9%
45.4%	45.5%	44.5%	45.0%	48.4%	47.8%	45.5%
7.8%	8.3%	9.3%	9.4%	8.6%	7.7%	-6.7%
-3.8%	-4.8%	-7.8%	-10.0%	-4.9%	-5.1%	12.9%
49.8%	59.0%	47.9%	40.7%	39.2%	45.8%	53.2%
62.9%	60.8%	60.5%	60.7%	63.5%	64.6%	64.8%
0.3%	2.1%	4.4%	4.7%	5.8%	5.2%	-0.5%
-1.6%	-5.5%	-4.6%	-4.4%	-4.7%	-5.3%	2.0%
64.3%	68.4%	65.2%	60.4%	60.6%	61.5%	82.5%
55.4%	53.0%	49.4%	52.0%	56.6%	56.5%	54.0%
8.2%	8.5%	8.6%	8.8%	5.5%	-1.3%	-9.4%
-5.6%	-5.0%	-5.6%	-8.0%	-7.9%	-2.0%	12.8%
38.7%	43.1%	47.2%	53.4%	54.9%	62.2%	80.7%
61.7%	66.0%	68.1%	70.2%	71.1%	67.5%	63.1%

**Source: Data from Institute of International Finance, Inc., *Comparative Statistics for Emerging Market Economies*, December 1998 and April 2000, Tables D102, D610.

handsomely by whipping the currencies and markets of poorer counties, then returned to some of those countries to offer his philanthropy." [2]

Indonesian President Suharto also claimed that currency speculators were to blame for his country's crisis: "There are parties trying to engineer the fall of the rupiah to the 20,000-level against the dollar." [3]

TABLE 4.2

Exchange Rate and Stock Market Movements In Southeast Asia, 1996–1998

Peak-to-Trough Percentage Changes*

SOUTHEAST ASIA'S CURRENCIES and stock markets were obliterated in 1997–1998 crises.

CURRENCY		STOCK MARKET	
THAILAND			
Thai baht /U.S. dollar		Thailand Stock Exchange Index	
May 14, 1997	26.15	July 28, 1997	685.69
January 9, 1998	55.68	September 3, 1998	206.73
Change	-53.04%	Change	-69.85%
PHILIPPINES			
Philippine peso/U.S. dollar		Philippines Composite Index	
May 14, 1997	26.5400	July 1, 1997	2,815.54
January 8, 1998	45.0400	September 11, 1998	1,082.18
Change	-41.07%	Change	-61.56%
INDONESIA			
Indonesia rupiah/U.S. dollar		Jakarta Composite Index	
May 14, 1997	2,569.33	July 8, 1997	740.88
January 9, 1998	16,756.94	September 21, 1998	256.83
Change	-84.67%	Change	-65.33%
MALAYSIA			
Malaysian ringgit/U.S. dollar		Kuala Lumpur Composite Index	
May 14, 1997	2.5326	July 2, 1997	1,086.24
January 8, 1998	4.7249	September 1, 1998	262.70
Change	-46.40%	Change	-75.82%

Source: Bloomberg LP.

*Foreign exchange depreciation measured from May 14, 1997 when Thailand imposed capital controls; stock market depreciation as percentage change in index measured from a high level in July 1997.

Officials in Thailand also put forward speculation as the explanation for their currency's violent decline. On June 24, Bloomberg News quoted a Thai central banker as saying that the attack on the baht in May was Soros's doing: "Soros was the main guy. When a currency is attacked, it's expected that he be involved."[4]

Yet there is scant evidence for any of these claims, at least as concerns the hedge funds. Hedge funds are thought to be the largest single class of currency speculator along with commercial and investment bank trading operations. Two extensive studies have appeared to address the role of hedge funds in the crisis. One study done by the IMF entitled "The Asian Crisis: Capital Markets Dynamics and Spillover" that appeared in the September 1998 edition of *International Capital Markets* was prepared by a team of economists who scoured the Asian nations in 1997 and 1998, holding discussions with a wide range of market participants. Their findings are of extreme importance to any understanding of what happened in Southeast Asia in 1997:

> The hedge funds have been singled out as having played an important role in the onset of the Southeast Asian currency crises. It would appear, however, that they were only one among the group of investors in the broader dynamic that unfolded and do not appear to have played a critical role, either as leaders or by cornering the markets. While several hedge funds together took positions against the baht, the majority of these positions appear to have been taken when other major investor groups had already begun to get out of the baht, and they did not, therefore, appear to have led the speculative attack on the baht. Moreover, while they together took a quantitatively important position against the baht, the majority of those positions appear to have been taken when the Bank of Thailand began offering large positions against the currency. It would otherwise have been difficult for the hedge funds to build up substantial positions.
>
> The one other simultaneous buildup of hedge fund positions appears to have been on the Indonesian rupiah. These positions were, however, taken after its initial depre-

ciation and were long positions, reflecting the view that the rupiah had overshot, and the expectation that it would appreciate.

It appears that only a few of the hedge funds took modest positions for short periods, at differing points in time, on the Malaysian ringgit.[5]

These findings were corroborated in an academic paper written by Brown, Goetzmann, and Park (1998) entitled *Hedge Funds and the Asian Currency Crisis of 1997*. The authors test the hypothesis that hedge funds were responsible for the crash of the Asian currencies in late 1997. Their methodology comes from Sharpe (1992) which introduced an econometric technique called "style analysis." This approach infers the composition of an investment portfolio from its historical performance over time. The authors ran their tests using data on the ten largest hedge funds, including Soros's Quantum Fund. Their conclusions were as follows for hedge fund positioning in the Malaysian ringgit:

> The estimated net positions of the major funds were not unusual during the crash period, nor were the profits of the funds during the crisis. In sum we find no empirical evidence to support the hypothesis that George Soros, or any other hedge fund manager was responsible for the crisis.[6]

Brown, Goetzmann, and Park also tested for hedge fund exposure to a basket of Asian currencies over the period of 1993–1997. The basket was comprised of the currencies of the Philippines, Taiwan, Thailand, Japan, Malaysia, Singapore, China, and Indonesia. Their findings were:

> As we observed with monthly data, the bets on Asia are occasionally quite strong—sometimes long and sometimes short. As with the monthly data, however, it appears that the exposures in late 1997 were modest, and unrelated to the steep drop in the currency basket. Again, no evidence that these representative managers were culprits in the crash.[7]

Eisuke Sakakibara, Japan's vice minister of finance for international affairs, would later come to have second thoughts about assertions he once made of hedge fund culpability:

> It was wrong to name them as the sole villains, but there is no question that there were attacks from hedge funds in Thailand, and attacks by copy funds from February 1997.[8]

The copy funds to which Sakakibara refers are supposedly investment funds operated by investment banking firms that try to mimic the investment strategies of hedge funds. He was right; the hedge funds were active in the attack on the baht but what he did not reveal is why it was that Thailand alone became their target.

If hedge fund currency speculation did not break Southeast Asia, what did? One factor working against the tiger countries was the fact that China devalued its currency by 50 percent in 1994 in preparation for its development of export industries. More important in the case of China were the structural reforms that took place in the 1990s that arguably improved that nation's competitive position in Asia.[9] A far bigger external contributing factor was the strong-dollar policy pursued by the United States, Germany, and Japan in the early 1990s.

The Consequences of the Strong-Dollar Doctrine

THE U.S. DOLLAR CAME under significant selling pressure in the first term of the Clinton administration. In part the negative sentiment derived from the new president's entanglement in the Arkansas Whitewater real estate scandal. Geographic association with the Mexican peso's crisis and growing skepticism about Canada's fiscal difficulties further damaged the dollar.

The dollar also got mixed up in the Clinton trade initiative with Japan. A significant element of the Clinton administration's foreign trade policy was directed at reversing the enormous trade disparity with Japan. U.S. Trade Representative Mickey Kantor's hammering of Japan to open its markets to foreign goods produced little in the way of concrete results for the United States. Parenthetically, Kantor's opponent, Ryutaro Hashimoto, made his political career on his efforts to keep Japan safe from America's demands on trade. Hashimoto was seen in Japan as having outmaneuvered the Americans, and a grateful nation elected him Prime Minister in January 1996.

By 1993, the foreign exchange market had come to believe that Clinton's aides wanted the dollar to fall against the yen to redress the aforementioned issue of Japan's massive exports to the United States. That suspicion was confirmed when treasury secretary Lloyd Bentsen replied in the affirmative to a reporter's question about whether the administration was seeking a weaker dollar. Additional confirmation came from Secretary of Commerce Ron Brown who stated unambiguously that the dollar was a legitimate "trade weapon."

But soon the rapid fall of the dollar began to be seen as something that could jeopardize its status as a reserve currency. Bentsen decided that it was in the best interest of the country for him to try to reverse the direction of the dollar. His preferred instrument was coordinated intervention with dozens of central banks participating by buying dollars against yen and marks.

Bentsen put together an intervention as if he were organizing the closing ceremony of the Olympic games. In rapid succession, countries all over the world announced to the news media that their central bank was buying dollars. The idea was to create an impression that central banks everywhere were standing behind a strong dollar. This fooled nobody. Traders knew that the smaller central banks were participating in name only. The failure of the Bentsen interventions to stop the dollar's slide added to the anti–dollar market sentiment.

Bentsen unexpectedly announced his retirement in November 1994. Clinton nominated Robert Rubin, a presidential aide and former cochairman of Goldman, Sachs & Company, to the post. Rubin was sworn in as Treasury Secretary in January 1995. The hallmark of the Rubin foreign exchange policy was a single-sentence mantra that he repeated every time he was in front of the media: "A strong dollar is in the best interest of the United States."

Rubin avowed that the dollar was artificially undervalued and decided on further central bank intervention. He formed an exclusive partnership with Germany and Japan, correctly reasoning that the size and might of the participants would be what mattered, not their numbers. The trio, dubbed the G3, conducted massive coordinated interventions to try to prop up the dollar.

Japan, of course, loved Rubin's idea of braking the fall in the dollar. Japan has always been on the side of any policy initiative to weaken the yen, a currency that has been in secular strength since the end of the Bretton Woods system in the early 1970s.

Germany's case was more complex. Chancellor Helmut Kohl was finding it difficult to convince his electorate of the wisdom of his pursuing a monetary union with their Mediterranean neighbors. The Rubin dollar plan interested the Germans because they needed to see immediate improvement in their own economy and in those of the other European Union states to meet the Maastricht treaty criteria that they themselves had imposed on the European Union. A surge in European exports did later occur, so it could be said that in some part, Europe had effectively devalued its way to monetary union.

The dollar finally hit rock bottom on April 18, 1995 when dollar/yen traded at 79.70 and dollar/mark at 1.3534. Thereupon, the dollar rose in a spectacular fashion against all currencies.

How much of the dollar's recovery can be credited to the Rubin interventions? Although it is not clear that the G3 managed to brake the fall of the dollar, it is easy to believe that it accelerated its rise in 1995 and 1996.

The significance of the strong-dollar doctrine for Southeast Asia was not immediately realized. In the course of the 1990s, Southeast Asia steadily took on large amounts of debt, most denominated in dollars. This reflected a widely held but erroneous belief that the dollar would continue to depreciate against the other major currencies. If one had to borrow, better to borrow in a currency that would lose value, as the dollar was projected to do, than to borrow in a currency that would add value, as the yen and mark were expected to do. Moreover, at least for the fixed

exchange rate regime countries, the dollar offered lower borrowing costs than local debt, via the same mechanisms that were described in the previous chapter.

Thus a gigantic stock of dollar-based indebtedness massed in
Thailand, Malaysia, and Indonesia in the years leading up to the
crisis of 1997, putting the region in a very dangerous position.
Effectively, the balance sheet of the tiger countries was long their
domestic currency and short dollars, all based on a wing and
prayer that their fixed exchange rate regimes would endure.

The strong-dollar policy also damaged the Asian tigers in
respect to trade. The rise in the dollar was a de facto depreciation
of the yen, which meant that they lost a competitive advantage to
the Japanese exporters. The total effect of the strong-dollar policy
was the foreign exchange equivalent of a pincer movement, in that
a stronger dollar and a weaker yen together put the squeeze on
Southeast Asia.

Several years later, Eisuke Sakakibara reflected on this aspect
of the G3 (United States, Germany, and Japan) dollar policy:

> I don't think that a weak yen provoked the Asian currency
> crisis (in 1997), although it's true that Asian currencies
> strengthened (against the dollar in 1997) on the course of
> the yen's weakening, because Asian currencies had been
> pegged to the dollar back then. And the weaker yen, by giv-
> ing Japan's exports a price advantage on world markets,
> undermined the competitiveness of its Asian competitors.[10]

Thailand Kicks It All Off

THE SOUTHEAST ASIAN currency crisis of 1997 originated in
Thailand, but there were ample conditions present in other nations to have had the crisis erupt elsewhere in the region.

In the case of Thailand, the central bank established a fixed
exchange rate regime under the auspices of the Exchange Equalization Fund in November 1984.[11] The baht was pegged to a basket
of currencies composed of dollars, yen, and marks. Although the
Bank of Thailand never announced the exact composition of the

basket, regression analysis using data from February 1997 estimates that the dollar accounted for about 84 percent; the yen, 9 percent; and the mark, 7 percent.

Pressure started to build on the Bank of Thailand in December 1996 to devalue the baht. The bank later described this as a time of "deteriorating fundamentals, looming problems in the financial sector, and widespread rumor of currency devaluation."[12] Substantial capital outflows ensued, but Thailand managed to convince foreign investors to return by promising large budget cuts. The bank dates the baht crisis as having commenced in February 1997 when economic data showed a sharp slowdown in the country's exports. The bank again managed to hold the line, this time by conducting large interventions in the foreign exchange market to support the baht.

On May 7 finance minister Amnuay Viravan announced that Thailand would not be able to achieve a balanced budget for the year as was earlier promised. The market took the news hard. The bank was immediately confronted with ferocious selling of the baht and their stocks.

At the time it was estimated that the total foreign exchange reserves of Thailand were equal to $38 billion. It was known in professional circles that the net reserves might be substantially lower because the bank reported its position on an accrual basis. Some astute individuals put the story together—the Bank of Thailand was not including its forward transactions when it totaled up its foreign reserves.

The Bank of Thailand responded to the pressure on the baht with more intervention, this time in massive size, given the size of the bank's balance sheet. When this failed, it resorted to a form of capital controls on May 14 that the bank itself described thus:

Toward the end of May 1997, currency defense took on an additional dimension. An informal capital control was imposed to deny the market of baht supply. Foreign exchange transactions with, and lending to, non-residents were limited only to those with genuine underlying commercial or investment activities. This measure effectively created a 2-tier foreign market where there was normal supply of baht and the offshore where baht was scarce. So much so that immediately following imposition of the control, offshore Thai baht overnight interest rates rose to over 1,000 percent.[13]

The Bank had effectively choked off the supply of forward swap deals that traders and speculators would need to roll short baht positions. A more colorful way of saying this came from Soros Quantum Fund portfolio manager Stanley Druckenmiller: "They kicked our butts and they've taken a lot of profit we might have had. They did a masterful job of squeezing us out."[14]

The Bank of Thailand had won the battle, but it was soon going to lose the war. After the initial shock about what the Bank had done faded, attention began to turn to whether the new two-tier market was stable. The present author won no friends in Asia but did manage to capture the mood correctly when he was quoted in the *Wall Street Journal* on May 22: "It still may go [the speculator's] way; it is not over.... All these emerging market catastrophe trades are attempts by the market to probe whether there's another Mexico out there."[15]

On June 19, Finance Minister Amnuay resigned. On June 30, Prime Minister Chavalit Yongchaiyudh assured the nation in a televised address that the baht would not be devalued. The Bank of Thailand described what happened next:

> Domestic confidence returned for a while until mid-June when the then Finance Minister resigned under political pressure. The demand from panicked local corporations to buy US dollars to hedge their foreign exchange exposure resulted in a heavy loss of reserves through the EEF [Exchange Equalization Fund] window....The crisis of confidence on the part of domestic residents showed no sign of abating and was beyond the Bank's control. The peg was abandoned on July 2, 1997. The exchange rate was then left to market forces.[16]

In the next six months the baht dropped from its previously pegged rate of about 26 to the dollar to 55, and the Asian crisis showed signs of spreading throughout the region. Thailand circa 1997 indeed had turned into Mexico circa 1994.

All of the same causal factors that had brought down Mexico were in evidence in Thailand now, plus a few special forces unique to Thailand. Like Mexico, Thailand had been in a period of enormous economic growth in the period preceding the crash—growth in real gross domestic product (GDP) exceeding 8 percent in every year from 1990 to 1995 (Table 4.1). This helped Thailand pull in enormous amounts of foreign capital commensurate with its large current account deficits.

Another common factor was the degree to which local Thai companies had indebted themselves to lenders in foreign countries. Because the baht interest rate chronically exceeded the dollar interest rate, Thai companies found borrowing in dollars attractive, as was discussed above.

Making this worse still was the predilection of Thai companies to borrow on a short-term basis. At its peak in 1995 the outstanding short-term Thai debt totaled $45 billion out of the $90 billion of total external debt[17]. The Bank of Thailand reported that this practice could be attributed to there having been an upward sloping U.S. interest rate curve. If true, then Thai companies fell for one of the oldest illusions in finance, the mistaken belief that borrowing for relatively short-term maturities represents bargain financing. Though the cost of borrowing may sometimes be cheap, debtors can end up unable to arrange new financing at a reasonable cost when their loans mature. In the Thai crisis, some borrowers found it impossible to obtain new financing at any price. And this occurred precisely at the time that their revenues were plunging. Financial companies that were in a shaky condition even before the crisis were staggered by the double punch of rising funding costs and collapsing collateral values.

The Bank of Thailand freely admits to the poor state of the Thai financial sector in 1996 but attributes it to the process of financial liberalization that began in the early 1990s. Its report on the crisis which was cited above is rife with accusations that shareholders pushed banks to make risky loans and that the general investing public had "let its guard down."

What is missing is an admission of responsibility for how badly the bank and the government as a whole had neglected its duties to regulate but not overregulate the financial sector. A prime example is the government's creation of the Bangkok International Bank Facility (known as the BIBF) and Provincial International Banking Facility (PIBF) which institutionalized and subsidized short-term borrowings from abroad.[18]

Also overlooked in the bank's analysis was the role that the baht carry trade played in the buildup to the crisis. Massive baht positions had accumulated solely because of the presumption that the bank's peg for the currency would endure. In February 1997, the spread between Thai baht interest rates and the Bank of Thailand's basket (dollars, yen, and marks) ranged between 500 and 600 basis points. The Thai baht carry trade, in all of its variations, involved being long the baht and short dollars, yen, and marks. Sophisticated carry traders executed directly in the interbank market. But the baht carry trade went very high up the investment food chain, and even to unsophisticated investors, as prime investment banking firms competed to create structured notes, total return swaps, and other derivative transactions whose very existence depended on the carry trade.[19]

But the truly remarkable aspect of the Thai crisis was how poor the response by the Bank of Thailand was. The outcome for Thailand would have been much improved if the bank had simply ignored the crisis and done nothing more than letting the baht float. It also can be argued that the fixed exchange rate for the baht might even have survived had the response from the bank not magnified the severity of the crisis.

In the first two weeks of May 1997, the Bank of Thailand decided to switch its intervention from spot foreign exchange transactions to forward transactions, buying baht against dollars for value in three and six months. Given that these trades were not for immediate settlement, as spot foreign exchange trades would have been, the bank chose to ignore the implications for its balance sheet. Yet there is no mistaking the fact that the BOT was massively exposed to the fate of its own currency. Moreover, the bank negotiated these forward contracts at off-market forward exchange rates, fearing that its own presence in the foreign exchange market otherwise would drive up Thai baht interest rates. Speculators thereby effectively received a subsidy from the bank to take short positions in the baht. Thanks to its own central bank, the baht turned into a true "one-way" bet for short sellers.[20] According to the IMF:

> Market participants estimated the Bank of Thailand's forward book at $26 billion at the end of June 1997, of which the macro hedge funds accounted for some $7 billion, "other" offshore counterparties for $8 billion, onshore foreign banks for $9 billion, and onshore domestic banks for $2 billion.[21]

From another angle, it would have been practically impossible for the short-sellers to accumulate such an enormous short position in the baht had it not been for the sales that the Bank of Thailand made. The exact parallel here is to the blunder made by the Central Bank of Mexico in issuing the dollar-linked tesobono bonds discussed in Chapter 3. Like the tesobonos, the Thai Bank's forward contracts constituted a financial bomb that the bank itself had planted underneath the state treasury.

In its report on the crisis, the Bank of Thailand was unable, or unwilling, to own up to the enormity of the damage it did, as can be seen by the following defense of its policy:

> Cynics, however, have compared the BOT's swaps to giving speculators the ammunition. This is useless analogy. Since money is fungible and the central bank is the sole issuer of local currency, therefore—by definition—all local currency held or sold by anyone must be supplied ultimately by the central bank. What matters is the monetary policy decision on the appropriate interest rate at which the central bank would supply local currency to the financial system.[22]

The fact that central banks are the issuers of money is irrelevant. Nothing can excuse the Bank of Thailand's having committed the financial blunder of the decade in supplying all comers with massively cheap financing on short baht positions.

The next nation to feel the immediate heat of the Thai baht's meltdown was the Philippines. The Philippine peso seemed to catch a piece of every punch thrown at the baht. Like the baht, the peso was subject to a fixed exchange rate regime, but unlike the baht, the peso was pegged exclusively to the U.S. dollar. The Philippines, like Thailand, had enjoyed substantial economic growth in the earlier part of the decade. Following suit, the Philippines' current account deficits had been on the order of 5 percent of GDP before the crisis.

Pressure began to build against the peso immediately after May 14 when the Thai central bank imposed its ill-fated capital controls. The immediate response of the central bank, Bangko Sentral ng Pilipinas (BSP), was to raise the overnight deposit rate by 1.75 percent to 13 percent and to sell dollars against the peso. Over the course of the next months, the BSP would raise overnight lending rates in steps from 13 percent to 32 percent.

When the Bank of Thailand finally floated the baht on July 2, tremendous selling hit the Philippine peso. The BSP attempted to hold the peg by intervening to sell dollars and buy pesos. Between July 2 and July 10 the BSP is estimated to have lost more than $1.5 billion of its reserves.[23]

On July 11 the BSP raised the white flag of surrender by allowing the peso to move in a wider range to the dollar. Three days later, on July 14, the IMF offered the Philippines $1.1 billion under fast-track regulations that had been drawn up after the Mexican peso crisis in 1994–1995.

Additional patterns of spillover effects, which traders since the Mexican peso crisis of 1994–1995 had started to refer to as *tequila effects*, rippled through emerging market nations as far away as Brazil, where the equity market fell 15 percent during the week of July 11 to 18.

One month later, on August 11, the IMF announced a rescue package for Thailand totaling $16 billion in loans from the fund and from other nations. The Mexican paradigm, meaning crisis followed by supranational bailout, had begun to play in Southeast Asia. In the words of Thai Prime Minister Chuan Leekpai, "Confidence and optimism are out, and uncertainty and gloom are in." [24]

Indonesia Follows

INDONESIA IS THE FOURTH MOST populous nation in the world. It emerged from Dutch colonial control and Japanese occupation after the Second World War to become subject to the rule of the iron-fisted dictator, General Sukarno, who once declared himself president for life. Sukarno was overthrown in 1966, making way for the next political strongman, General Suharto. Suharto ruled the country for over three decades, and it can easily be argued that he would still be in power were it not for the economic crisis that gripped the country in 1997.

Indonesia in the Suharto years is popularly but not inaccurately viewed today as a kleptocracy that was operated for the private welfare of the family and friends of the president. Suharto promoted his own private label of crony capitalism under the guise of redressing presumed wrongs done to the indigenous Javanese population by the ethnic Chinese business class.

Visitors to Indonesia were quick to note the obvious, that everything valuable was funneled into the president's circle. Suharto and his six children, collectively known "Suharto Incorporated," controlled vast parts of the Indonesian economy:

> The Suharto children are all reputed to have become multimillionaires by trading on their direct line to the presidential palace, involved everything from clove cigarettes to toll roads, from petrochemical plants to automobile manufacturing. So pervasive is the first family's reach into the Indonesian economy that a long-running joke here is that the corruption begins as soon as you arrive at Jakarta's international airport: You can buy a pack of cigarettes, hop in a taxi, take a toll road to the city and check into a hotel, putting money into a Suharto family member's pocket with each step.[25]

Moreover, Suharto's children controlled many of the top banks in the nation, a fact that precluded any notion of independent financial supervision by the central bank. One stunning piece of anecdotal evidence noted by observers at the time was the common practice among upper-class families of purchasing banking licenses as university graduation gifts.

Against these dark realities, it has to be said that wealth did trickle down to the lowest levels of Indonesian society in the Suharto years. But while there is little doubt that Suharto Incorporated managed to siphon off great wealth, the greater damage that it did to Indonesia was from how badly it ran the country. What is important for the immediate purposes is not so much to put out an indictment of the greed of the Suharto regime but rather to lay a foundation for why that nation's financial system could degenerate so quickly into a state of total collapse.

Indonesia for a short while seemed to defy common sense by appearing to have withstood any contagion from Thailand and the Philippines. Forward swap points on the Indonesian rupiah hardly budged until things started to heat up in Indonesia, and this did not occur until the middle of August. It is surprising how many smart people were fooled into believing that Indonesia had somehow escaped the crisis. As stated above, there is evidence (Brown, Goetzmann, and Park, 1998) that some of the large hedge funds were actually long the rupiah, apparently having been convinced that the worst was over for Indonesia.

As can be seen from Table 4.1, Indonesia went into the crisis following years of impressive economic growth in the general economy. Indonesia did have a current account deficit, but not nearly as large as the ones in Thailand and Malaysia.

The central bank had kept the rupiah on a crawling pegged regime since 1987, under which the currency was allowed to depreciate within a fixed bandwidth relative to the dollar. As with the baht, the rupiah carried an interest rate premium to the dollar, and a substantial carry traded existed.

Selling pressure began to accumulate on the rupiah in mid-July. On July 11 the Bank of Indonesia decided to widen the band to 12 percent from 8 percent, but that was to no avail. Finally, on August

Source: Bloomberg L.P.

—— FIGURE 4.1 ——

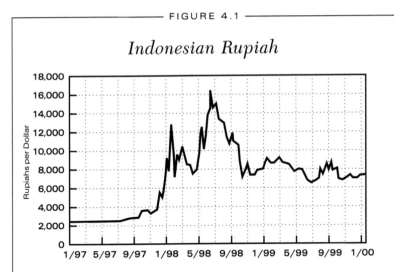

Indonesian Rupiah

INDONESIA'S RUPIAH PEGGED to the dollar with slippage allowed at a controlled rate before August 1997. Note that the rupiah did not immediately respond to the floatation of the Thai baht on July 2, 1997. The fireworks came weeks later. The rupiah became a floating currency on August 14, 1997.

14, the Bank abolished the managed exchange rate regime and let the rupiah float; it immediately began to plunge. The dollar/rupiah exchange rate rose from its pegged level of about 2,500 to the 13,000 level in four months (Figure 4.1).

At the start of 1998, things began to stabilize and the unit returned to levels below 10,000. Then, in May 1998 the rupiah began to drop again, and by the middle of the summer dollar/rupiah was trading above 16,000—a loss equal to 85 percent from its pegged level.

On October 8, 1997, Indonesia formally requested assistance from the IMF. When the IMF revealed the terms of its $40 billion bailout, Indonesia was horrified. The Fund insisted on commitments to wide-ranging reforms as a precondition of Indonesia's receiving any money.

These included cancellation of the national automobile manufacturing project, reduction of government subsidies, and a drastic
restructuring of the banking system over a short period of time.
Eisuke Sakakibara, the Japanese vice finance minister for international affairs at the time, gave a first-person account of his dealings
with Indonesia:

> He [Suharto] flatly stated that he would agree with the IMF
> plan, but had no intention of observing the conditions....
> The president, his family and cronies began to realize that
> the structural reform plan initiated by the IMF and tech-
> nocrats might shake the foundations of the Suharto admin-
> istration.[26]

Suharto agreed to the IMF's terms, began to receive its money,
and then went on his way merrily ignoring, even reversing, the
actions that he promised to fulfill. In one instance, banks that were
controlled by the Suharto family were supposed to have been
closed for reasons of insolvency. The banks were closed, as promised, but only to be immediately reopened under different names.
As Sakakibara described:

> On November 2, two days after the IMF and Indonesia
> agreed on the assistance package, 15 of the large national
> projects slated to be canceled according to the terms of the
> IMF agreement were revived. Two electric power genera-
> tion projects controlled by Suharto's eldest and second
> daughters were given the go-ahead immediately.[27]

A surrealistic drama was being acted out in which the main plot
was Suharto's regime outwitting the Fund by evading the prescribed reforms.

Far worse things were in the works, as Sakakibara described:

> The IMF reform plan has several fatal drawbacks as it was
> hastily mapped out without taking its economic and social
> impact into consideration. The plan could have completely

destroyed Indonesia's financial system as it called for the shutdown of 16 banks without providing a safety net, such as deposit insurance.... A run on banks took place after 16 Indonesian banks were closed, causing a panic on the financial and foreign exchange markets from late November through December. The value of the rupiah plunged as a result.[28]

Sakakibara was correct in his description of the events in Indonesia. Following the run on the banks, the IMF agreed to a second bailout package on January 15, 1998.

A complication arose sometime around the start of 1998, when Professor Steve Hanke, a Johns Hopkins University economist who specializes in exchange rate regimes, was appointed as a special adviser to Suharto. Hanke advised Suharto that the rupiah problem could be immediately cured if the country would adopt a currency board. It appeared to Suharto that Hanke had a painless cure for Indonesia's ailments.

A currency board is an extreme form of a fixed exchange rate regime. The term *board* is antiquated and does not refer to a group of directors, but rather to an agency of the government charged with exclusive control of the country's money supply and its exchange rate policies. The board can function in parallel to the central bank, or it can be operated as part of the central bank. The concept of a currency board goes back in time to the days of the British Empire. Britain gave certain of its colonies permission to issue their own currency, provided that the new currency be pegged to the pound and that the colony agree to exchange its currency for pounds upon demand. An essential further requirement of this arrangement, which became known as a currency board, was that the colony had to have on hand sufficient reserves, in pounds, to cover the entire outstanding amount of the colonial currency. In modern times, a currency board would need to have a large enough quantity of foreign reserves to cover the base money supply (currency in circulation plus commercial bank reserves held at the central bank). Hong Kong and Argentina operate currency board exchange rate systems with a degree of success.

The concept of having a currency board is not without its imperfections, however, principal among which is the fact that the currency board's foreign exchange transactions represent automatic, unsterilized adjustments to the national money supply. From a theoretical point of view, Hanke's plan was not totally objectionable though there are some issues with his concept to be explored in Chapters 5 and 7. Hanke never got to see his ideas for Indonesia put into place.

On February 10, 1998, Dow Jones newswires reported that Hanke, in a working paper prepared for Suharto, had recommended that the targeted exchange rate for the rupiah should be 5,500 to the dollar.[29] That announcement sunk any chance that the Indonesian currency board had. The rupiah was trading well above 10,000 at the time. Market participants and pundits quickly concluded that the Suharto family was planning to loot the central bank's reserves by converting rupiahs for dollars at a massively preferential rate of exchange, meaning that they would have first dibs on the central bank's dwindling foreign reserves.

Hanke objected to this vociferously, stating that no such working paper had ever been written by him and that he had no recommended target for the rupiah. He later wrote "the [*Wall Street*] *Journal* finally fessed up in a belated and muddled correction."[30]

Yet the exact level at which the rupiah would be pegged was never disclosed, and it is not improbable that preference would have been given to Suharto Incorporated. It should be noted that Hanke himself was never acting in anything but good faith. He was an unpaid, and probably unthanked, adviser to Indonesia and was hardly part of a conspiracy to loot the central bank. All things considered, it is hard to imagine that his currency board project, if properly implemented, could have done more damage to Indonesia than what the IMF programs did to the financial sector.

Operatively, it was the IMF, with the support of the World Bank and the Clinton administration, that stopped the currency board project dead in its tracks. In their defense, it could be argued that they had grave concerns over the possibility of monumental fraud in the setting of the exchange rate for the rupiah. But it is more likely that the IMF simply preferred its own programs for Indonesia. On April 10, 1998, a third IMF agreement was signed. This time the IMF was determined not be euchred by false promises of reforms.

With the issue of the currency board scuttled, market participants turned to the question of whether Suharto himself could survive the crisis. By May 1998, Suharto, the absolute ruler of Indonesia for more than three decades, was forced to resign.

Michel Camdessus, Managing Director of the IMF, would later reflect on the fund's ambitious reform efforts in Indonesia and Suharto's fate: "We created the conditions that obliged President Suharto to leave his job. That was not our intention."[31]

Suharto's handpicked successor, vice president and adopted son, B. J. Habibie, became president. Habibie lost the October 1999 presidential election to Abdurrahman Wahid (popularly known as "Gus Dur").

Indonesia was the greatest victim of the Southeast Asian crisis. The damage to the economy and to the society surpassed everything that happened in the neighboring countries. This was made all the worse because Indonesia is such a heavily populated country. Next in our discussion is Indonesia's neighbor to the north, Malaysia.

Malaysia Pulls a Fast One

MALAYSIA FELT THE consequences of Thailand's distress almost immediately after the Bank of Thailand enacted capital controls on May 14, 1997. Both the ringgit and the Malaysian stock market went into steep dives. The ringgit had been trading around 2.5 to the dollar in May (Figure 4.1). At its worst point, in January 1998, it had fallen to 4.72 to the dollar, which equates to a drop of 47 percent. The Malaysian stock market fell by 75 percent, from July to its nadir in September 1998.

The ringgit was in deep trouble by the time the Bank of Thailand floated the baht on July 2, 1997. The central bank, Bank Negara Malaysia, initially put up a struggle by intervening into the foreign exchange market. It abandoned its efforts to save the ringgit on July 14.

Malaysia's case differs in one important respect from those of Thailand, Indonesia, and to go back further in time, Mexico. Malaysia, unlike these other countries, operated a more or less floating exchange rate for the ringgit. As a consequence, the ringgit was not subjected to the buildup of a large carry trade the way the baht, rupiah, and Mexican peso were.

Malaysia's exchange rate regime was a *dirty float*, a term that distinguishes it from a pure hands-off exchange rate regime governed exclusively by supply and demand. There is, of course, no such thing as perfectly clean float because every central bank at some time or another has tried to meddle in the market for its currency. What makes Malaysia stand out is the intensity with which its central bank attacked the foreign exchange market, or to be precise, the foreign exchange traders.

In the early part of the 1990s, Bank Negara was on a campaign to weaken the ringgit. It feared that the massive flow of capital into Malaysia would strengthen the ringgit and damage the country's export industries. Negara waged a ferocious war against speculation in the ringgit, complete with numerous episodes of intervention. It also had an early experience with imposing capital controls on the foreign exchange market in 1994, something that neither Negara nor the entire foreign exchange community would forget.

In part, that explains why the ringgit came crashing down in the summer of 1997 with all the appearances of a fixed exchange rate currency that had just been unpegged. Everyone who was exposed to the ringgit, either through owning Malaysian investments or by having loans denominated in ringgits, had one thought and only one thought in July—when will Malaysia's irascible Prime Minister Mahathir Mohamad impose capital controls or some form of restriction on the movement of money? This expectation, which was subsequently justified, created panicked selling of the ringgit. The German language has a word for this, *Torschlusspanik*, which literally means "the fear of the door slamming shut."

Still the ringgit's plunge is more fundamentally linked to the condition of Malaysia's overall economy, which was entering a state of severe turmoil. The currency's slide in Malaysia's case was not so much a causal factor in the reversal of the economy as it was a result of problems that derived from the underlying economy.

Thailand's crisis triggered a reevaluation in the minds of investors of the Southeast Asian tigers, including Malaysia. An acute
reversal of confidence in Malaysia followed, in the minds of both
domestic citizens and foreign investors. In spite of Malaysia's having ameliorating factors, such as a high national savings rate, the
country was damned to crisis for reasons that go deep into its economic and political fabric.

Foremost among these was that the Malaysian economy was
dominated by the government's central planning. Economic decisions were made at the highest levels in the government of Prime
Minister Mahathir, who came to power in 1981. He, his ministerial flunkies, and his cronies ran the country from top to bottom.
Early on they made a decision to invest substantial amounts of the
national resources in low-cost manufacturing plants to make computer and electronic components. The bet paid off, but the downside was that success emboldened Mahathir to dream of yet
greater glory.

What followed was something a psychiatrist, more than an
economist, could explain. Mahathir went out of his way to prove
that Malaysia was the best in the world at anything it touched. In
the course of his megalomaniacal and despotic rule, tiny Malaysia,
with a total land area of only 127,000 square miles and a small
population of 18 million, would build the tallest buildings in the
world (Petronis Towers), the longest building in the world
("Linear City"), an airport with the tallest control tower in the
world, and even a hotel with the tallest flagpole in the world.
Malayan economist Jomo Kwame Sundaram summed it up, brave-
ly, as this: "Mahathir has a pharonic side to him. These are modern pyramids." [32]

Mahathir's inner circle was responsible for a national automobile company. Proton was declared a huge national success and its
cars were dubbed "the pride of Malaysia." The company looked
profitable but, in truth, car sales owed more to a massive import
tax that was imposed on foreign-built cars than to Malaysian auto-
motive engineering. In the study of development economics this
ruse is called the "infant industry" argument. Industries that other-

wise would not be financially feasible are endowed from birth with local monopoly rights over domestic consumers. What is not reflected in the statements of profit and loss for the new companies is the welfare loss inflicted on citizens who are blocked from buying the foreign goods of their choice.

In 1995, Mahathir promised his country's inhabitants a 7 percent annual real growth for the foreseeable future. His delusions of grandeur were spelled out in "Vision 2020," a sweeping blueprint for Malaysia's next quarter-century. This plan was intended to make Malaysia into a fully industrialized and technologically cutting-edge civilization by the second decade of the twenty-first century.[33] Two years later Malaysians would realize, but dare not say openly, that Vision 2020 was blind as a bat.

As part of the plan, Mahathir dreamed of a broad challenge to California's Silicon Valley with the construction of his $20 billion Multimedia Super Corridor. His new economy needed a new capital, perhaps his ultimate memorial, so he planned for a $8 billion new city, Putrajaya, that would house 250,000 people. All of this required new sources of energy, so plans were developed to make a $5.5 billion hydroelectric generating plant in the heart of Borneo, with connections to Malaysia by a 400-mile underwater cable. When environmentalists protested that the project would destroy thousands of acres of primeval rainforest, Mahathir angrily denounced them as "enemies of the state."

In sum, Malaysia could have given Japan a run for its money when it came to the worst excesses of central planning. It could also compete with Indonesia for the title of the Asian capital of crony capitalism. Indonesia had Suharto Incorporated but Malaysia had Mahathir Incorporated.

Meantime, Malaysia had developed a pattern of running large current account deficits (Table 4.1). Mahathir,[34] stung by comparison of his country's condition to Mexico of the early 1990s (pre–peso crisis), defended the capital inflows as being necessary to support its rapid growth. He insisted that Malaysia's capital inflows were going to worthwhile investment projects, not to consumption. Negara's chief economist expressed the party line as follows:

Our current account deficit isn't being financed by short-term capital flows, which would be unhealthy, but by longer-term inflows.... Imports of capital and intermediate goods create the potential for production and exports.[35]

What Mahathir and his economist didn't say was that these supposedly worthwhile undertakings, the recipients of the foreign investments, were actually economic losers.

Earlier in this chapter there was discussion of how Thailand's problems in 1997 stemmed in part from its dependence on short-term financing. The trap that Malaysia fell into was thinking that it would be safe to run a massive current account deficit so long as financing was not short-term. This of course leads to another dangerous belief. Long-term lenders may not be able to call for immediate repayment in a crisis but they are not going to sit on their hands. For one thing, they will immediately attempt to hedge their exposure to the local currency. No matter how they go about this, whether it is through the use of forward contracts or other derivative instruments, selling of the local currency will occur. They may even resort to fashioning a crude but effective hedge by going short the stock market to offset losses on their illiquid, long-term investments.

Few analysts did more than note the fact that Malaysia was running what could someday become an unsustainable external balance. No one questioned where all of the foreign investment was going. Mahathir did at times make superficial gestures aimed at reducing the size of the current account deficit, mostly after 1996 when the deficit was projected at more than 8 percent of GDP. What Mahathir really wanted to do was to rearrange the economy so that there was room to import the raw materials that were needed to build Proton cars and construct more trophy real estate projects. If that could be done while at the same time squeezing foreign-made goods out, all the better.

The heavy hand of Malaysia's government was felt in all areas of economic life. Consider these words from Bank Negara's annual report in 1996:

Despite this positive outlook, there is no room for complacency.... A major challenge for macroeconomic management is therefore to ensure that investments are directed
toward strategic sectors that add to productive capacity and
promote higher value added while, at the same time, ensure
that such activities do not aggravate the balance of payments
position. In this regard, priority should be given to projects
with the highest economic rate of return, particularly those
with low import content and high export potential.[36]

Such a pronouncement can only come from a government
agency of a centrally planned economy. In Malaysia the extent of
the influence of government planning went well beyond anything
experienced in noncommunist Asia.

In the end, it all came for naught when the roof caved in during 1997. Malaysia of the 1990s represented the quintessential
case of confusing capital inflows with true economic growth.

When the game stopped in the summer of 1997, Mahathir
reached out for scapegoats. At first he lashed out at currency
traders and at George Soros, in person. On September 20
Mahathir lectured delegates to an IMF/World Bank conference in
Hong Kong that currency trading is immoral and should be
stopped. He began to assert that the Western nations had "invent-
ed" currency trading to preserve emerging market nations like
Malaysia in their state of underdevelopment.

There was an element of blatant hypocrisy in his accusations.
The fact is that in the late 1980s and early 1990s, Mahathir's own
central bank, Bank Negara, operated like a hedge fund.
Appropriate for a country that was fixated on having the world's
largest everything, Bank Negara may have been the world's largest
currency speculator. Though it chose to refer to these activities as
"active reserve management," Bank Negara was openly trading
speculative positions of enormous size in currencies based on its
directional views on the future moves in exchange rates. This only
stopped when the cumulative losses were too steep to stomach.
Bank Negara then bowed out of the market.

As things began to get worse, Mahathir took to framing his own handpicked successor, Anwar Ibrahim, with preposterous accusations of immorality. Anwar was removed from his posts of Deputy Prime Minister and Minister of Finance, put on trial, found guilty of sexual crimes, and sentenced to a long prison term. In destroying Anwar, Mahathir eliminated a political rival and silenced critics of his economic policies.

Next Mahathir began to rail against the IMF, rejecting local calls that he should follow the Philippines, Thailand, and Indonesia in calling for emergency funding.

In his most daring move, Mahathir on September 1, 1998, declared a complete halt to foreign exchange trading. He froze the greatly depreciated ringgit at 3.80 to the dollar and impounded all foreign investor capital to keep it from leaving the country. The success or failure of these extraordinary measures, which produced outrage in investment communities all around the world, will be considered in Chapter 8.

Chapter Five

Accounting for Contagion

E VERY COUNTRY AFFLICTED with financial crisis would like to believe that its troubles have been imported from some other place. When financial distress strikes neighboring countries in rapid succession, the notion can gain acceptance that financial trouble is capable of spreading like a contagious disease.

Is financial crisis catching? Contagion is a term that derives from medical science. It conjures up the image of an epidemic where a virulent disease spreads uncontrollably through a healthy population. To make medical references to economics invites further comparisons. Influenza can spread in epidemic fashion. But not all diseases are epidemic in nature. If over-weight men with high blood pressure, high cholesterol counts, and chest pains start showing up in hospital emergency rooms, it does not mean that heart attacks are contagious but rather that all of the men have the predisposing conditions for coronary artery disease. The heart attack model, more than the influenza model, fits financial crisis.

Respected economist Anna J. Schwartz wrote:

The question is whether an individual country that has mis-managed its affairs will precipitate an international finan-cial crisis.... One myth is that the individual country's loss of creditworthiness has a tequila effect. The supposed tequila effect is that other countries without the problems of the troubled country are unfairly tarnished as also subject to these problems. In this way, it is said contagion spreads the crisis from its initial source to other innocent victims.[1]

For some people, the appearance of contagion is proof that speculators can have their way with any market. The idea is that malevolent traders can line up emerging market countries against a wall and shoot them, one by one. Joseph Yam, the chief executive of the Hong Kong Monetary Authority, echoed this when he wrote that: "We face a world crisis. If Hong Kong, with its sound fundamentals and prudent financial management, can be brought to the brink of systemic breakdown by aggressive cross-border speculation, then something must be wrong with the world financial order."[2]

I define *contagion* as the hypothesis that financial crisis can spread from one country to the next of its own accord. True contagion, if it exists, should be able to bring down even nations that are in perfect economic health. Speculation is supposed to be linked up with this, playing the role of what pathologists call the vector of a disease, meaning the mechanism responsible for transmission of the financial epidemic to new victim nations.

Good economists like Schwartz don't hold contagion theory in high regard. We have already covered two suspected instances of contagion. The first was the spread of financial distress throughout Latin American following the Mexican peso crisis of 1994–95 that was discussed in Chapter 3.

The most famous suspected case of contagion is the crisis that ran through Southeast Asia in the summer of 1997. But the argument for pure contagion does not hold up well under examination of Southeast Asia's crisis. Did the crisis really spread spontaneously from Thailand to the "innocent" bystander economies of the Philippines, Malaysia, and Indonesia? A better explanation, as was described in the previous chapter, is that these countries shared preconditions that made them all ripe for failure. As Schwartz described it:

Glib references to spillovers from disturbances that origi-
nate elsewhere are common in the current literature on
international financial crises. The truth is that it is not necessary to invoke spillovers to account for multicountry
financial disturbances. Capital flight from countries with
similar unsustainable policies is not evidence of contagion.[3]

The appearance of contagion can simply be created by errors
in financial policy that are duplicated across countries in response
to common random economic disturbances. An example is the
practice of central banks to try to defend pegged exchange rate
regimes that have come under market pressure. Thailand, the
Philippines, and Indonesia (and also Malaysia) wasted billions of
dollars of their foreign reserves this way.

A second explanation for suspected contagion has to do with
the apparent indiscriminant withdrawal of capital from countries
and markets that bear only casual resemblance. Contagion advocates once were impressed by the fact that the Philippine peso
came under selling pressure in the midst of the Mexican peso crisis in 1994–1995. The dubious explanation given was that all currencies having the misfortune of being called "peso" had fallen out
of favor. A more realistic explanation was that both countries had
shaky fixed exchange rate regimes.

Still it is not unreasonable to wonder if elements of the institutional structure of the investment industry might be responsible
for panic spreading from country to country. For example, the
American mutual fund industry has enjoyed considerable success
in gathering money through the packaging of investment products
sold as country and sector funds. Bad news about an individual
Thai company, for example, could cause investors to sell "Thailand" by redeeming their shares in a country fund or even sell
"Southeast Asia" by pulling out of a Southeast Asian regional fund.
If this happens fast enough and on a big enough scale it could
cause a drop in the local stock markets and have adverse implications for the local currencies as well.

But if the institutional structure of the mutual fund industry is

TABLE 5.1

Real GDP Growth, Current Account, and External Debt: Hong Kong, Korea, Singapore, and Brazil, 1990–1998

		1990	1991
HONG KONG	Real GDP Growth*	3.4%	5.1%
	Current Account Balance (% GDP)*	8.9%	7.1%
KOREA	Real GDP Growth*	9.5%	9.2%
	Current Account Balance (% GDP)*	-0.9%	-2.8%
	Total External Debt % GDP in U.S. Dollars**	19.5%	20.0%
	Percentage of External Debt Denominated in Dollars**	65.6%	62.6%
SINGAPORE	Real GDP Growth*	9.0%	7.1%
	Current Account Balance (% GDP)*	8.3%	11.4%
BRAZIL	Real GDP Growth**	-2.9%	0.3%
	Current Account Balance (% GDP)**	-0.9%	-0.3%
	Total External Debt % GDP in U.S. Dollars**	34.8%	33.9%
	Percentage of External Debt Denominated in Dollars**	61.9%	63.0%

SINGAPORE WEATHERED THE Southeast Asian storm with comparatively little economic dislocation.

---

the root cause, then contagion shouldn't create anything more than a very short-lived phenomenon. There are other classes of investors, perhaps more sophisticated than people who buy country funds, who would pounce on the chance to buy the cheap shares.

The most famous example of alleged contagion to hit the U.S. asset markets occurred in October 1997 when the monetary crisis in Hong Kong caused a record downdraft in the American stock market. There were also serious signs of contagion effects in Brazil and Korea. These episodes are discussed later in this chapter.

1992	1993	1994	1995	1996	1997	1998
6.3%	6.1%	5.4%	3.9%	4.9%	5.3%	-0.1%
5.7%	7.4%	1.6%	-3.9%	-1.0%	-3.2%	0.7%
5.4%	5.5%	8.3%	8.9%	6.8%	5.0%	-5.8%
-1.3%	0.3%	-1.0%	-1.7%	-4.4%	-1.7%	12.5%
20.7%	21.6%	24.3%	26.1%	31.7%	34.6%	46.1%
48.5%	61.0%	67.2%	69.2%	70.0%	64.5%	63.2%
6.6%	12.8%	11.4%	8.2%	7.5%	9.0%	0.3%
12.1%	7.3%	16.3%	17.3%	15.9%	15.7%	20.9%
-0.5%	4.9%	5.9%	4.2%	2.8%	3.0%	0.1%
1.4%	-0.1%	-0.3%	-2.5%	-3.1%	-4.2%	-4.7%
34.8%	38.5%	31.4%	26.9%	27.4%	27.5%	32.7%
62.6%	63.2%	56.5%	58.5%	60.6%	61.1%	74.4%

* Source: Data from International Monetary Fund, *World Economic Outlook*, October 1999, Tables 1.2, 6, and International Monetary Fund, *World Economic Outlook*, December 1997, Table A1.
** Source: Data from Institute of International Finance, Inc., *Comparative Statistics for Emerging Market Economies*, December 1998 and April 2000, Tables D102, D610.

Singapore Weathers the Storm

THE CASE OF SINGAPORE is one of the strongest arguments against contagion theory. Singapore had to be the most likely case of a country vulnerable to contagion. This small country in the center of Southeast Asia has essentially an open economy that is highly exposed to external economic shocks. The crisis of the summer of 1997 ought to have obliterated Singapore. Yet Singapore rode out the storm with remarkably little damage.

Singapore's growth rate in real gross domestic product for 1997 was 9.0 percent, measured annually. In 1998 Singaporean real

GDP rose by 0.3 percent, the lowest rate in the decade of the 1990s (Table 5.1).

Yet compared to its neighbors, Singapore gave a great performance in 1998. Indonesia's GDP fell in 1998 by 13.7 percent, Malaysia's fell by 6.7 percent, and Thailand's by 9.4 percent (Table 4.1). How did Singapore manage?

Singapore, unlike Thailand, the Philippines, Malaysia, and Indonesia, had a relatively stable financial sector, was running a current account surplus, and was not immensely indebted. Moreover, Singapore had a floating exchange rate. By comparison with its neighbors' currencies, the Singapore dollar fared rather well, falling only 20 percent over the eighteen months from July 1997 when Thailand abandoned its fixed foreign exchange regime.

Singapore does share some similarities with Malaysia in the sense that there is a business culture of collective decision making with heavy government involvement. Singapore's government is famous for its own brand of heavy-handed paternalism. Yet in contrast to Malaysia, where the government drove the country to pursue uneconomical development projects, Singapore's government was circumspect in its designs for economic growth.

Singapore demonstrates the importance of understanding the underlying conditions that predispose financial instability. What damage Singapore suffered was due to the real economic decline in the region, not to the spread of an Asian financial flu.

The IMF recognized this in a laudatory report published in April 1999 entitled "Fundamentals, Timely Policy Measures Help Singapore Weather the Asian Crisis." The report mentioned as Singapore's "roots of resilience" that

> Singapore's favorable performance reflects, first, strong fundamentals. The country's fiscal policy is guided mainly by medium-term considerations, and the budget typically has been in surplus (averaging 5 percent of DGP during fiscal years 1990-98) at moderate levels of expenditure and taxation. These surpluses have produced a substantial level of fiscal reserves. Monetary policy has been anchored by the exchange rate and directed at price stability, and that has

helped limit inflation to an average of about 2 percent during 1990-98. Generally flexible labor markets and polices have led to skill development and higher value-added activities; the trade regime is very open, and Singapore has a high degree of capital mobility. Finally, the banking system is well supervised and has a strong capital base.[4]

At least one other thing helped Singapore—superior leadership by comparison to the other Southeast Asia countries. While Suharto and his family were trying to hold on to power and wealth and while Mahathir was ratcheting up his invective against imaginary enemies of his state, Singapore's prime minister, Goh Chok Tong, was preparing his people for an economic struggle. He explained the crisis and outlined what the government's response would be. This directness and transparency prevented a full panic.

It is true that most Westerners would chafe at the nagging that Singapore's citizens receive from their government on a regular basis (don't chew gum, flush public toilets, speak more Mandarin, get married and produce trophy children). Yet the government of tiny Singapore proved its mettle at the moment of truth.

Hong Kong Chooses Crisis

AT MIDNIGHT ON JUNE 30, 1997 the former British Crown Colony of Hong Kong became part of the sovereign territory of the People's Republic of China. The period leading up to the reversion was marked by tremendous optimism for both Hong Kong and China. Investors took heart at the rising stock markets in Hong Kong and Shanghai. There was also circumstantial evidence of a stable future for Hong Kong as a special administrative region of China in the fact that hotels were solidly booked for months into the second part of 1997.

The timing of the hand-over was hardly auspicious because of the events that had transpired in Thailand. Two days after China took over, the Thai baht broke loose from its peg and the Southeast Asian crisis went into full bloom. Yet the Southeast Asian crisis seemed to deflect off of Hong Kong with no observable damage.

Amazingly, Hong Kong's Hang Seng stock index actually rose during the month of July 1997.

In October, things were drastically different when Hong Kong became engulfed in a full-blown market turmoil of its own. The trigger occurred on October 20 when the central Bank of Taiwan abandoned its support for the New Taiwan dollar which immediately fell by 9 percent.

Although the political and economic connection between Taiwan and Hong Kong is tenuous, the fate of the New Taiwan dollar proved critical. Asian countries not part of Southeast Asia suddenly looked susceptible to a fall. The Central Bank of Taiwan had massive foreign reserves amounting to multiples of what the Southeast Asian countries possessed going into the summer of 1997, but still lost its battle with the foreign exchange market. If that could happen to Taiwan, why could it not happen to Hong Kong?

Hong Kong itself was in possession of some odd $96 billion of foreign reserves that it used to operate its famous currency board. As will be explained in Chapter 7, a currency board is a particularly extreme form of fixed exchange rate regime. In Hong Kong's case, the board pegged the Hong Kong dollar to the U.S. dollar at a fixed rate, 7.8000, by offering to buy or sell out of its stash of foreign reserves.

Despite their appearance, currency boards are not bulletproof foreign exchange regimes. For one thing, the continued operation of the board under conditions of duress is a function of the country's willingness to sacrifice hard currency reserves. At some time or other, the country might decide that enough is enough and that keeping its foreign reserves is more important than maintaining its currency peg.

Meantime, whenever the board buys or sells currency it creates an unsterilized adjustment to the nation's money supply. In effect, the currency board makes the domestic money supply into a yo-yo. Money supply rises and falls with the state of confidence in the currency, all the while inducing potentially gut-wrenching adjustments in the real economy.

Another disadvantage with having a currency board is that the country relinquishes control of its monetary policy. The monetary

policy of the central bank in the reserve currency country effectively takes over the show because domestic currency has a hard
peg to the reserve currency. But that does not mean that the interest rates for credit in the local currency will be the same as those
for credit in the reserve currency, especially in the midst of a crisis. That gets to the roots of what happened to Hong Kong in
October 1997.

According to the IMF, selling pressure intensified on the Hong
Kong dollar on October 21 and 22 with rumors that Hong Kong
was going to abandon its currency board regime following the
monetary turmoil in Taiwan. Local residents and foreigners began
to sell both the Hong Kong dollar and Hong Kong stocks. The
IMF concludes that most of this selling was in small lots that could
be characterized as hedging rather than speculation. The report
then reveals:

> As domestic banks' sales of Hong Kong dollars collectively
> exceed what they could settle by using their credit balances
> in settlement accounts with the Hong Kong Monetary
> Authority, they bid aggressively for funds on the interbank
> market, and interbank interest rates shot up to 280 percent
> by noon on October 23. On that day the Hang Seng Index
> fell by more than 10 percent. The sell-off in equity markets
> appears to have been due also in part to deleveraging by
> some large local retail investors—a small number of whom
> reportedly account for a substantial component of the retail
> market—in response to tightening margin requirements
> and the increase in interest rates. Foreign institutional in-
> vestors (mutual funds and pension funds) also contributed.[5]

What seems to have happened is that the massive selling of
Hong Kong dollars created what currency dealers call a *tom/next
squeeze*. The local foreign exchange market had so large a short
position in the Hong Kong dollar that it became nearly impossible
to obtain short-term credit in order to roll positions from "tomorrow" to the "next" value date. The world, and, more importantly,
everyone in Hong Kong, wanted to borrow Hong Kong dollars to

create short positions in that currency to hedge anything and everything that was denominated in Hong Kong dollars, or to go outright short the currency as a speculative play. Consequently the short-term interest rate popped up.

Whatever happened that day to lift interest rates to nearly 300 percent, the question that should be put to the Hong Kong Monetary Authority is why it didn't do what any responsible central bank would have done. Why didn't it stabilize the market by supplying emergency liquidity to the banking system to prevent what started out as a panic in the foreign exchange market from spreading, as it did, to the stock market?

For example, the HKMA could have conducted purchase/re-purchase operations with the banks on an overnight or weekly term, all the while continuing to operate its currency board system as promised, buying and selling the HKD at the established peg.

Admittedly, this would have interrupted the pure functioning of the currency board in the sense that it would have created additional money supply beyond what the normal workings of the board would have naturally afforded. But what is the ultimate purpose of the currency board? If job number one is to maintain an iron-clad peg for the currency then there is no reason why going the extra step to stabilize the short-term interest rate market in the course of a market panic cannot be appended to the original program of buying and selling Hong Kong dollars in the spot market. And it should be noted that the Hong Kong Monetary Authority has the resources to do so.

In one sense, all that a currency board consists of is a promise to defend the value of the domestic currency using an ample stock of foreign reserves. A currency board is the most interventionist of all foreign exchange regimes—intervention is conducted on continuous, automatic basis. When people want to sell the local currency, the board is there to buy from them. Likewise, when people buy, the board sells. If extraordinary circumstances develop, why should secondary steps not be implemented to stabilize short-term interest rates and defend the currency peg?

Actually, Hong Kong Monetary Authority CEO Joseph Yam himself attempts to do practically the same thing, only with words, when he periodically mentions that he is considering dollarization for Hong Kong (see Chapter 7). What Yam effectively does is put a scare into short-sellers and hedgers by suggesting that the Hong Kong dollar and U.S. dollar interest rates might completely converge because of dollarization.

What is being suggested here does get away from the pure workings of the theoretical currency board and there is no guarantee that interest rate stabilization would be effective. It should be remembered that the problem of defending a fixed exchange rate regime has been shown in numerous instances to have been insurmountable. Moreover, the program to stabilize the short-term interest rate must be short-term in nature itself or the peg will require adjustment or have to be outright abandoned sooner or later.

Instead, the HKMA chose to watch its markets melt down. Later there would be accusations that hedge fund speculators had pounced on yet another country, this time Hong Kong. The authorities became seriously distracted with the idea that speculators were trying to make a "double play"[6] in Hong Kong by going short the currency and the stock market at the same time. The idea put forth was that speculators were selling short the currency to put pressure on interest rates to rise and that this, in turn, would take equity prices lower. The problem with this explanation, at least according to the IMF, is that "There does not appear to be any evidence of a concerted strategy by any groups of investors to simultaneously short the Hong Kong dollar and the equity markets."[7]

The Hong Kong authorities to this day blame speculators for the October 1997 problems. Regrettably, the new government of Hong Kong has begun to think about markets in ways not unlike Malaysia's Prime Minister Mahathir.

Panicked Selling of U.S. Equities

THE HONG KONG episode was the first time that the Asian crises touched the shores of the United States. American investors had watched with a certain sense of wonder at the humbling of the tiger nations. The American stock market seemed to steam through it all with immunity. That delusion of isolation was shattered on October 27, 1997.

The predicament of Hong Kong in October 1997 somehow mattered more to the U.S. equity market than had the sudden collapse of the Southeast Asian countries earlier that year. One rationalization for this was that Hong Kong was operating a hard peg to the dollar by virtue of its currency board. Thailand, the Philippines, and Indonesia, though also dollar-pegged, were not under the auspices of a currency board.

When the turmoil hit Hong Kong, investors began to suspect that if Hong Kong did devalue its dollar, China might feel obliged to respond by devaluing its currency, the yuan,[8] to preserve the viability of its young export industries. The fear was that if both China and Hong Kong were to devalue, a new round of turmoil might result, with second helpings of trouble for all of Asia.

A general sense of panic in U.S. markets emerged on October 27 as investors began to dump their shares in frenzied selling. At that time, the New York Stock Exchange had circuit breakers in place, as was described in Chapter 1. By 2:20 P.M., the market had dropped 350 Dow Jones Industrial Average points whereupon the first trading halt was called for a period of thirty minutes.

The market reopened at 3:05 P.M. and promptly fell another 200 points, tripping the day-limit price-move circuit breaker. Hence trading was halted for the day before the end of regular trading hours for the first time in the Exchange's history. The total decline in the Dow Jones Industrial Average for the day was 554 index points (from 7715.41 on Friday, October 20 to 7161.15 at the close on October 27) or 7.2 percent. The drop in the S&P 500 index on October 27 was 64.5 points (from 941.64 on October 24 to 876.99) or by 6.8 percent. Trading was also halted in the Standard and Poor's 500 index futures contracts on the Chicago Mercantile Exchange.[9]

New York investors had begun to fear that the Asian crisis had mutated into a new and frightening global pathogen. The market opened the next morning to the downside. Yet a few hours later, the market began to recover, rapidly. In less than a month, the equity market had fully recovered and was back to trading at the levels seen before October 24.

Was the October 27 stock market plunge caused by contagion, or not? That investors in New York temporarily panicked over some events in Hong Kong is itself not evidence for the contagion theory. It is in the nature of markets to be prone short-term episodes of irrational, even hysterical investor behavior. The fact that the market could make a full recovery in short order with little or no damage to the other sectors of the U.S. economy is actually powerful evidence against contagion having spread discord to America.

The October 1997 market disruption illustrated better the damage that can be done by circuit breakers rather than any harm coming from contagion. The final 200 Dow point plunge in the last twenty-five minutes of trading on October 27 was simply a rush to sell before the final circuit breaker tripped, the one that would shut down the exchange for the day. As with Malaysia in the previous summer when investors rushed to get their money out of the country before capital controls were imposed, New York investors were scrambling to sell before circuit breakers closed down the market.

Merton Miller, the Nobel laureate at the Graduate School of Business of the University of Chicago and a well-known critic of circuit breakers, expressed this succinctly: "It lasted ten years, the illusion that this [circuit breakers] would keep the market from crashing. The notion behind circuit breakers is that it is a 'cooling off' period. You give investors time to think about the situation...they think...and then they panic."[10]

Brazil Squeaks Through

HONG KONG'S OCTOBER 1997 episode had more devastating effects in Latin America than in the United States. The nation that was hit hardest was Brazil. According to the IMF,

The prices of Brazilian Brady bonds fell by 18 percent in the week following October 24th, the BOVESPA stock market index fell by 22 percent, and the real came under severe pressure, both on the currency futures market on the Bolsa de Mercadorias e Futuros and on the spot market, with market participants reporting central bank reserve losses of $10 billion in a matters of hours at the peak of the attack.[11]

Before this episode, Brazil had been enjoying respectable economic growth. The economy had responded well to the "real plan," a radical master plan for the Brazilian economy introduced in March 1994. The real plan was a fixed exchange rate system wherein the currency of Brazil, the real, was pegged to the U.S. dollar with allowances for a gradual devaluation.

On the surface of things, it looked like an enormous success. Its biggest achievement was that it curbed the chronic hyperinflation in consumer goods prices that had plagued the country for years. Inflation in 1996 was an astonishingly low 5 percent, whereas in previous years it has been running in thousands of percent. Investors began to feel confident that Brazil had a bright future. Inflation had been contained and the new currency looked to be stable, all this stood in stark contrast to the economic disappointments of the 1980s, "Brazil's lost decade."

As international investors moved their money into Brazil the current account deficit began to grow steadily from 0.3 percent of GDP in 1994 to 4.2 percent in 1997 (Table 5.1). Not surprisingly, Brazil began to pile up a lot of foreign debts, about two-thirds of which were denominated in U.S. dollars by 1997.

Investor sentiment about Brazil turned cautious after the Southeast Asian crisis. Investors began to wonder about the stability of the real plan and the sustainability of the current account deficit. Economists declared that the real was overvalued, perhaps by as much as 20 percent, against the dollar. That amount of overvaluation would require the real to depreciate steadily for three years at the officially allowed rate of devaluation equal to 0.6 percent per month.

By some thinking, Brazil in 1997 began to appear less like a growth miracle and more like Thailand and Indonesia. But the goings on in Asia in the summer of 1997 seemed not to inflict tremendous damage on Brazil. But then in October 1997, with Hong Kong in dire straits, the Brazilian stock market sold off violently. Everywhere one heard how investors had started to focus on the fact that the same predisposing symptoms of impending financial collapse that brought Southeast Asia low were present in Brazil.

Somehow, the authorities in Brazil managed to defend their fixed exchange rate regime in October 1997. The key factor that allowed the Brazilian response to the attack on the real in October 1997 to succeed was the willingness of the Banco Central do Brazil to raise interest rates to extreme levels but only on a temporary basis. The bank doubled the short-term interest rate on October 30 from 1.58 to 3.05 percent a month, equivalent to 43.4 percent annually. This made it very costly to take a short position in the real. More importantly, the bank immediately discussed its plan to lower the interest rate as soon as was practical.

The government announced a fiscal package on November 10 that was expected to yield an equivalent of over 2.5 percent of GDP in net saving to the public sector in 1998. In addition, Brazil, in November, obtained approval from the IMF for a $41.5 billion financial assistance package. The crisis began to fade, leaving the real plan badly shaken but standing.

How had Brazil successfully defended its foreign exchange regime when Thailand earlier had failed? Both countries relied heavily on intervention. The answer has to do with a subtlety in foreign exchange trading that was noted in Chapter 4.

The Bank of Thailand had decided to defend by buying hundreds of billions of bahts in the forward market. But at what forward exchange rate? The bank went into the market announcing that it would buy bahts at a higher rate than where bahts were being offered forward. In effect, the Bank of Thailand was simultaneously trying to support the baht and depress interest rates, two mutually exclusive acts. It was apparently acting out of concern that any upward movement in the baht interest rate would have disastrous effects on Thailand's fragile financial sector. But the net effect was that Thailand's central bank created a speculator's subsidy, in effect a one-way foreign exchange bet, for anyone who wanted to sell the baht. It had handed speculators a subsidized, massive short position in its own currency.

In the case of Brazil, the central bank intervened at the same time that it put short-term interest rates up to levels above 40 percent. Hiking the interest rate accomplished just the opposite of what Thailand did because the new higher interest rates on the real imposed a great cost on anyone trying to sell short the currency. The ploy worked; the Bank psyched out the traders. The real was anything but a one-way bet.

This is very tricky business, of course. What worked once in October 1997 might easily fail at another time. The Banco Central do Brazil could have overplayed its hand and wound up in the same sad position as did the Hong Kong Monetary Authority. The latter let interest rates rise to nearly 300 percent, almost by accident, with adverse implications for the local stock market. Brazil got away with its ploy because it didn't allow the interest rate to stay too high for too long, and because it had managed to convince the market that a fall in interest rates was imminent.

A second and more serious crisis occurred in Brazil in January 1998. This time it was unambiguous that all of the trouble was homegrown. The episode was triggered by the state of Minas Gerais's refusal to honor debts owed to various parts of the federal government. The confrontation originated in a bitter political feud between President Fernando Henrique Cardoso and his predecessor and political rival, former president Itamar Franco. Franco had become the governor of the Brazilian state of Minas Gerais after his presidency. He had the wherewithal to make good on Minas Gerais's debts but refused to pay because he decided to keep the money home, at the local level, to be spent on social programs. Franco didn't pay Cardoso so Cardoso couldn't service Brazil's staggering debt load. Brazil was effectively bankrupt.

Thus it was that Franco single-handedly brought the government of Brazil to the edge of financial ruin for personal political gain. All of this seemed to catch Cardoso by surprise while he was vacationing at a beach resort in the northern state of Sergipe. Before boarding his helicopter to make an emergency return to the capital Cardoso told reporters "Calm down, calm down. There is no crisis. Everything is calm." Cardoso was playing poker this time with no aces in his hand. His central bank was dangerously low on foreign reserves and was still trying to maintain its fixed exchange rate.

The Banco Central do Brazil found it impossible to hold the currency peg in an environment where it was about to default on its international bond debt. On January 13, 1999, the Bank attempted to devalue the real by 9 percent (from 1.21 to 1.32 to the dollar) under the hope that it would be allowed to keep the real pegged but at a lower rate. Two days later the Bank announced that it would no longer intervene in the foreign exchange market and the currency traded above 2.0 to the dollar within two weeks. The real plan ceased to exist.

Once again a call went to the IMF for help. A new head of the central bank, Arminio Fraga, was installed in February. Fraga's previous claim to fame was as one of George Soros's portfolio managers. Itamar Franco, the instigator of the crisis, quipped that Brazil now effectively had Stanley Fischer for its minister of finance (because of the involvement of the IMF in Brazil) and George Soros for its central banker (as Fraga's former employer). In actual fact, Fraga proved himself an effective central banker and there was no malfeasance concerning his Soros connection, contrary to Franco's suggestions.

Korea Learns Finance the Hard Way

TO THE OUTSIDE WORLD, South Korea was the least well understood of the Asian tiger nations in 1997. The inverse was also true. South Korea had a very poor understanding of the rest of the world, and in particular, of the workings of the international financial markets.

For all appearances, South Korea looked to be the very model of a modern Asian economy that was on the move. Korea, more than any other tiger country, had demonstrated that it could give Japan serious competition in basic industry. By the middle of the 1990s, South Korea had established a serious competitive foothold against Japan's export-oriented industries, examples being steel milling, shipbuilding, automobile manufacturing, and consumer electronics. South Korean construction companies had a presence everywhere that development was taking place; somehow it seemed that South Korean companies always managed to be the winning bidder for the big projects like airports, hospitals, and public housing. South Korea was beating Japan and the rest of the industrialized countries at their own game.

So much for appearances, as the world found out in 1998.

What stands out among the headline macroeconomic statistics for South Korea is how deeply indebted the nation as a whole was prior to 1998. South Korea's main problem was its private sector debt. Over the course of two years, from 1994 to 1996, short-term external liabilities of South Korean corporations and finance companies rose from $53.7 billion to $93 billion.[12] Financial corporations issued most of the debt. On top of the external debt there was a far deeper layer of debt owed to domestic banks.

Between 1994 and 1996, the total stock of external liabilities of Korean financial institutions and business corporations rose from $89.9 billion to $158.3 billion, a change of 76 percent.[13] Of this debt, 58 percent was short term in nature. Korean financial institutions and the companies seem in retrospect to have been oblivious to the risks of leverage. The IMF Staff Country Report in February 2000 described South Korea accordingly:

> Korea's impressive macroeconomic performance up to 1997 served to mask fundamental structural problems, notably a weak financial sector and an over-leveraged corporate sector. Korea conglomerates, known as chaebols, had invested excessively and were focused primarily on gaining market share. The resulting excess capacity depressed the profitability of companies and the financial institutions from which they had borrowed. Financial institutions traditionally lacked independence and were encouraged to channel credit to preferred sectors. Consequently, credit analysis and risk management techniques remained undeveloped. The misallocation of credit was facilitated by a weak system of prudential controls and forbearance by the supervisory authorities. The result was a banking system with little commercial orientation, limited ability to price risk, and excessive exposure to large corporations. Bank financing for large

investment projects was made available, even when such investment added to overcapacity. When export prices weakened and a number of chaebol went bankrupt in 1997, there was a commensurate deterioration in the asset quality of financial institutions.[14]

That much of the domestic debt was negotiated on the basis of arm's length negotiations is doubtful. Major decisions were triangular, passed on by a corporation, a bank, and the government. South Korea's business universe consisted of this domestic process on one hand and the external markets on the other hand. The purpose of the latter was to supply raw materials and absorb the production of the export industries. The process to some extent worked well in terms of the reconstruction of the country after the Korean War, in an analogous way to Japan's recovery from the Second World War. But as time passed, South Korea emerged as a modern industrial economy without having matured as a financial center.

This is backed up by the fact that Korean finance and insurance companies appear to have been under the illusion that they could borrow in foreign currencies at cheap interest rates and invest in other currencies that had high interest rates with no consideration of hedging foreign exchange risk.[15]

But the Koreans also plunged into all manner of carry trades, ranging from the Thai baht basket trade, trades involving taking leveraged positions in the Indonesian rupiah, and still other trades that amounted to leveraged positions in Brazilian Brady bonds. Most of these trades had to be done in the form of specialized derivative structures, something that the Korean institutions had little familiarity with, so as to avoid the restrictive Korean foreign exchange laws. According to an IMF report:

Increases in outflows were to be expected following liberalization, as Korean entities attempted to diversify their assets. The high returns available in Korea relative to world capital markets meant, however, the Korean capital outflows systematically sought out high-yield high-risk investments. On the emerging debt markets, the investments ran the gamut from Latin American Brady bonds, Russian GKOs, and a variety of emerging market Eurobonds that included especially regional credits and Korean offshore issue to Indonesian high-yield domestic debt instruments… In order to enhance yield, Korean entities also engaged in a variety of structured notes and other derivative products, including repos and swaps of securities, and total rate of return swaps on a variety of instruments such as the equity and debts of Indonesian corporates. Some of the products reportedly involved leverage ratios of 5 to 10."[16]

South Korean authorities had managed to keep the won as a partially floating currency. Capital account restrictions had been gradually lifted in the period of the 1990s. Nonetheless, a distinctive feature of the market for the won was that the onshore forward market for won was in a stage of developmental infancy. Hence, the means to speculate against the won was extremely limited in the late 1990s. The fact that there was any forward market at all can be attributed to a series of steps taken in the mid-1990s to liberalize the capital market. There was, and is still, a small forward market for offshore dealing in nondeliverable small forward contracts in won.

South Korea began to slip when Hong Kong experienced its troubles in October 1997. In response to the emerging North Asian crisis, Standard and Poor's downgraded South Korea's sovereign debt on October 23, 1997. Selling of the won immediately ensued. The Bank of Korea tried to support the won but was forced to surrender control of the currency to the market on November 17. On November 21 South Korea made its first call to the IMF for emergency assistance. By December 3, the IMF and South Korea had come to preliminary terms on a $57 billion package. Still, by December 23, international bond rating agencies downgraded South Korea's sovereign debt again, this time to speculative grade.

On December 19, voters in South Korea elected Kim Dae-Jung, a 73-year-old former dissident, as president. Mr. Kim had never held high elected office before, despite having spent most of his life trying to attain that goal. A few days after his election Kim was given a briefing on the actual state of the economy whereupon he said: "We don't know whether we would go bankrupt tomorrow or the day after tomorrow. I can't sleep since I was briefed. I am totally flabbergasted.... This is the bottom. It's a matter of one month, no, even one day. I just can't understand how the situation came to this."[17] An unnamed senior U.S. Treasury official was quoted the next day in the *New York Times* deadpanning "Somebody is going to have to teach the President-elect how to talk to the markets. He doesn't quite have the language down yet."

The actual start of the South Korean crisis could be marked with the sudden bankruptcy of Hanbo Steel in January 1997. This was the first large bankruptcy in South Korea in modern memory. A few of the large corporate groups (called *chaebols*) either went bankrupt or experienced near collapse in the following months. Pressure began to build on the banks and financial companies that were known to have lent to domestic corporations. Foreign lending institutions, all that had been happy to lend to the South Korean financial sector in previous years, began to ask probing questions for the first time. As the severity of the crisis advanced, they simply refused to roll short-term funding facilities.

Much has been made of the fact that South Korea was heavily financed by short-term debt, and a lot of that came from offshore sources. The buildup of the short-term debt came in large part from the way the government regulated the Korean financial system. In the accepted framework, banks, but not corporations, had the government's approval to borrow in foreign capital markets. Moreover, in what became known as *window guidance*, the authorities drove the banks to rely heavily on short-term financing by limiting the amounts that it was permissible to borrow on a medium- and long-term basis from international sources.[18]

Eventually, after much arm-twisting, the group of international banks agreed to roll over the South Korean loans on January 16, 1998. Nevertheless, the South Korean economy was in horrible shape, as Mr. Kim had earlier described.

The South Korean crisis had another special feature that is

worth understanding. As the economy began to collapse, the response of the central bank was particularly self-destructive in that it ordered local commercial banks to come to the aid of the corporate sector with fresh loans. That act guaranteed that the debt crisis of the corporate sector would thoroughly and lethally infect the banking and financial system. Second, as the banks in turn ran out of capital, the central bank began to lend to them its reserves. This went so far as to extend to the merchant banks and the overseas branches of South Korean commercial banks.

What was happening was that the Bank of Korea was moving its vital assets into the hands of failing financial institutions. At the same time, at least until November 17, the bank was trying to prevent the won from going into a total free-fall. Soon, the Bank of Korea was effectively out of usable reserves because what assets it hadn't lost in the unsuccessful defense of the currency were inaccessible, bound to the masts of sinking financial institutions. This dynamic is unique to South Korea, at least on the scale of the crises studied in this book.

Put another way, the South Korean authorities failed to keep a firewall between the central bank and the private sector. The more the Bank of Korea tried to extinguish the crisis, the deeper it itself became enmeshed in it. The crisis effectively ate the whole country alive, corporations, the financial sector, and even the government.

How much of the South Korean experience was due to contagion? One could say that the Hong Kong panic of October 1997 started the world thinking about the risk of South Korea. But the storm might have bounced off of South Korea, as it did off of Singapore, had the former not been so enfeebled by its crushing debt load. In another sense, South Korea was damaged when a great number of derivative securities with exposure to Southeast Asian currencies and debt markets owned by its financial sector and corporations became worthless, or even in some cases became negative in value. But the bulk of the collapse was due to the homegrown factors described above, namely, too much debt and a lack of insulation between the public and private sectors.

C h a p t e r   S i x

Exploding
Hedge Funds

B Y 1998, THE RUSSIAN Federation had shriveled to an economic dwarf, accounting for no more than 1 percent of the
world's gross output. Yet in August 1998, when Russia
defaulted on its maturing treasury debt and devalued the ruble, a
fresh round of financial crises was launched. It afflicted the whole
world. By some measures, the financial catastrophe ignited by
Russia was more extreme than what originated in Asia in 1997.

Russian Default Spawns a New Crisis

NOT TOO MANY RUSSIANS could have been nostalgic about the passing of the twentieth century. Russia, first as a member nation of the
former Soviet Union and later as an independent state, had the
misfortune of being a laboratory rat in the most grandiose political
and economic experimental failures of the twentieth century.
Russia was subject to monarchy, communism, dictatorship, and
finally a desperate and mismanaged rush to become a free-market
economy, all in the course of 100 years. These eras and the transi-
tions between them took their toll. The last years of communism, in
particular, stripped the country of much of its economic vitality.

Soon after the disintegration of the Soviet Union on December
25, 1991, a group of American economists, Professor Jeffrey Sachs
being notable among them, became advisers to Russian President

Boris Yeltsin with the backing of U.S. Deputy Secretary of the Treasury Larry Summers. They convinced Yeltsin that Russia needed to abandon its superstructure of price controls and subsidies at once. This harsh medicine, popularly called "shock therapy," was supposed to jolt the old communist economy into a market-driven recovery.

Shock therapy was never fully applied to Russia. Some prices were adjusted, but others, such as oil, domestic natural gas, and utility rates, were never brought up to market levels. Nonetheless, what shock therapy was administered has since come under enormous criticism. It has been asserted that the reforms triggered broad-based economic suffering, and this may be true. By 1998, Russian real gross national had declined 40 percent from the start of Russian independence in 1991.[1]

In fairness to Sachs and Summers, one has to ask if there was any alternative, because the prices of basic commodities in Russia had to be made congruent with world market prices. It was Russia's misfortune that these adjustments came at a time when national income was dropping precipitously.

The transformation of Russia to a capitalistic economy also required a massive privatization program to distribute state-owned assets to the private sector. Many Russians simply had no way of knowing what privatization was all about, and their limited participation brought them no tangible results. Most were effectively excluded from the important elements of the process, and the feeling of having been left out, on top of shock therapy, engendered a feeling of bitterness and dissatisfaction with Yeltsin.

Making things worse, and maybe making reforms impossible, was that Russia, as a former communist country, did not have a viable legal and social system that could function as the backbone for the new market economy. Adam Smith recognized the importance of having a legal infrastructure nearly two hundred years ago in the *Wealth of Nations:*

> Commerce and manufactures can seldom flourish long in any state which does not enjoy a regular administration of justice, in which the people do not feel themselves secure in

the possession of their property, in which the faith of contracts is not supported by law, and in which the authority of
the state is not supposed to be regularly employed in en-
forcing the payment of debts from all those who are able to
pay. Commerce and manufactures, in short, can seldom
flourish in any state in which there is not a certain degree of
confidence in the justice of government.[2]

Smith's insight into the importance of sound jurisprudence to a
market economy identifies what was missing in Russia's surge
toward becoming a market economy. Additionally, there were discouraging, if not astounding, inequities in the privatization program. In the mid-1990s, a group of highly placed Russian business-
men and politicians were able to acquire a substantial portion of
the state's productive assets and natural resources under grossly
favorable terms, and in some cases, practically for free. The prime
beneficiaries became known as *oligarchs*, when another term,
kleptocrats, would have been more appropriate.

Not only select Russians got rich, as Wayne Merry, a former
State Department official who had been stationed during his government career in Moscow, testified before the U.S. Senate:

Robbing Russia is a global activity, with lots of foreign participants. How else could Baltic states become major exporters of commodities they do not produce; how else did
Switzerland, Singapore and Caribbean islands become centers of Russian finance; how else could Russians transform
the real estate market in Southern Europe; and why else are
automatic teller machines in posh sections of Manhattan
programmed in Russian? I suspect that much of the loot is
already in non-Russian hands. The looting of Nigeria, Zaire,
Mexico, the Philippines, and Indonesia all enriched the
West. Why should Russia be different?[3]

Ultimately, the Russian state, stripped of much of its assets, bat-
tered by the low price for its principal export commodity, crude oil,
and suffering from acute tax collection problems, became utterly

dependent on external financing. A good deal of money came from the IMF. To its chagrin, the Fund later learned that Russia's central bank had exaggerated the amount of foreign reserves that it held in 1996, a fact confirmed by independent audit.[4] Other cash came directly from wealthy Western nations, from banks, and from private investors. The remainder of the funds needed to keep Russia as a going concern came from debt issuance.

Russian short-term treasury debt fell into two categories: "Gosudarstveni Kratkosrochnii Obligatsii" (GKOs), which were ruble-denominated couponless short-term instruments of 3 months and 6 months term at issue, and "Obligatsii Federal novo Zaima" (OFZs), which were medium-term notes of one or two years in term with quarterly coupon payments.

In retrospect, one wonders what foreign investors were thinking when they took positions in GKOs and OFZs and lent money to Russia. Russia did not come close to conforming to what a prudent investor would have judged to be a sound credit risk. But Russia was believed to be special. Investors thought that it was "too big to fail" financially. They were reassured that the industrialized nations had resumed treating Russia with some modicum of respect, even extending from time to time invitations for it to attend expanded G8 economic summits. Moreover, Russia was seen as being too nuclear to fail as well, meaning that the possibility of Russia's nuclear weapons arsenal falling into the wrong hands would keep Western money flowing.

Investors were also optimistic about Russia because it had the support of the IMF going into 1998. Stanley Fischer, first deputy managing director of the IMF, was sanguine about Russia, as can be seen in one of his speeches, this one given on January 9, 1998:

> Nineteen ninety seven was a year of achievement for the Russian economy. For the first time since 1992, the economy grew, albeit barely. The current account of the balance of payments was in surplus. The Central Bank of Russia once again proved its professionalism, as inflation continued to decline, and as late in the year it successfully fought off contagion effects from East Asia and maintained the

currency band.... In 1997, as in 1996, central government revenue shortfalls constituted the major failure of macro-economic policy.[5]

Fischer's remarks proved uncharacteristically wrong, except for the warning on the government's revenue shortfall which became the source of the country's undoing eight months later.

In a larger sense, the IMF's support of Russia may well have been a case of moral hazard. Stanley Fischer acknowledged this in a speech on December 9, 1999:

It seems highly implausible that Asia was a moral hazard play. It is more likely that lenders could not imagine that the miracle economies of the region could get into such serious trouble after decades of outstanding economic performance. But moral hazard exists, and for a clear example of the dangers that it poses, look no further than Russia. Many investors thought Russia was too big to fail. They were wrong, and the consequences for them and for other countries were severe.[6]

Western economists were not able to convince the Russians that the ruble should be turned into a freely convertible currency when shock therapy was being considered. Instead, the ruble was allowed to float within a fixed bandwidth. On January 1, 1996, the Russian central bank established a corridor within which the ruble was allowed to trade to 4.550-5.150 to the dollar.

With the ruble "stabilized," the Russian treasury debt market began to be perceived as a carry trade par excellence. Restrictions on foreign ownership of ruble-denominated debt meant that Russian banks were in control of the treasury debt market. Nevertheless, foreign investors were able to synthesize participation in GKOs and OFZs with the help of Russian and international banks. To guard against adverse changes in the ruble, a substantial amount of these positions was hedged with currency forward contracts. In other cases, investors bought derivative securities that were tied to the currency-hedged total return on GKOs in the form of structured notes and total-return swap transactions.

One such investor was George Soros, who stunned the world with a letter published in the *Financial Times* on August 13, 1998:

> The best solution would be to introduce a currency board after a modest devaluation of 15 to 25 percent. The deflation is necessary to correct for the decline in oil prices and to reduce the amount of reserves needed for a currency board. It would also penalize the holders of ruble-denominated government debt, rebutting the charges of a bailout.[7]

Soros was later blamed for having starting a panic in the Russian market—the thinking being that if Soros, the dean of currency speculators, thought that the ruble had to be devalued, then what else did anyone need to know? This was an instance in which his reputation worked against his own interests. It would soon be learned that the Soros organization had been holding a huge position in Russian securities at the time that the letter was published. Stanley Druckenmiller, Soros's chief portfolio manager, subsequently revealed in a television interview that their hedge funds had lost $2 billion in the Russian fiasco.

In fact, the ruble was about to collapse with or without commentary from Soros, based on the state of government finances in the summer of 1998. Tax collections were faltering, oil was down at $15 a barrel, and the IMF became reluctant to advance new funds without guarantees of reforms that the lower house of parliament, the Duma, blocked. On August 17, 1998 the government defaulted on the maturing GKOs and OFZs, instituted a ninety-day freeze on external foreign exchange transfers to meet debt payments, and unpegged the ruble.[8] The predefault face value of the debt thus voided on August 17 was approximately $40 billion.[9] By the end of 1999 the ruble was trading above 21, representing a 75 percent collapse since early 1996.

The Central Bank of Russia in the days leading up to August 17 expended a good portion of its foreign reserves defending the fixed exchange rate regime, as described by William H. Cooper in a report for the Congressional Research Service:

Until August 1998, the Russian government tried to maintain a stable exchange rate for the ruble. But to do so required the Russian Central Bank to sell foreign exchange for rubles when the ruble was facing downward pressure. At the end of May 1998, the level of foreign reserves stood at around $11 billion. The foreign reserves were augmented by a $4.8 billion loan from the International Monetary Fund but have dropped since then. On August 26, the RCB [Russian Central Bank] announced that it had expended $8.8 billion over the last two months, $1.9 billion alone from August 7 to August 14, in foreign reserves to defend the ruble.[10]

The defense of the ruble in August is a topic surrounded by accusations of gross misconduct by the Russian Central Bank. One's suspicions have to be raised by the fact that the intervention to support the ruble was conducted through the oligarch banks at exchange rates that were never publicly revealed. At best the ruble defense was an honest failure. On the other hand, although it failed to save the ruble, it may have succeeded in handing billions of dollars of IMF money to the oligarch banks at what are suspected to be off-market exchange rates.

What made things materially worse and undoubtedly caused the Russian crisis to echo across international capital markets was the fact that several Russian banks chose to default as counterparties to forward currency transactions that foreign investors were using to hedge the ruble. Some banks declared insolvency while others invoked force majeure provisions to cancel foreign exchange deals. When investors were able to enter into negotiations to settle their damages, they found their Russian counterparties insisting on the use of unrealistic, unfair exchange rates for the ruble.

The perennial question of debate in the years that have followed the Russian default has been "who lost Russia?" Few have suggested that Russia was a victim of foreign contagion or of speculative forces. The most common answer given is that Russia imploded of its own accord, as Secretary of the Treasury Robert Rubin implied in a *New York Times* interview on October 2, 1998: "I don't think it's the activities of the international community that have failed in Russia. I think what failed in Russia was Russian."[11]

Russia was indeed a financial accident waiting to happen. Still, the fact is that the United States intervened heavily into the political and economic affairs of Russia. The financial collapse of Russia in the summer of 1998 was an undeniable failure of financial policy, not just of Russian government but also of advice proffered by the Western economists. It was also a failure of the policies of the United States Departments of Treasury and State, and indeed the IMF. And the Russians all know this. The pity is that the United States missed a once-in-a-century opportunity to turn Russia, its one-time sworn enemy throughout most of the second half of the last century, into a permanent friend.

In the last analysis, George Soros was correct when in 1988 he said: "Stalin has been dead some thirty-five years; but so great has been the devastation wrought by his reign of terror that the country has not been able to rid itself of the structures that he left behind."[12]

The goal of turning Russia into a modern economy, given all that happened in the twentieth century, is nothing short of a Herculean task. What was amazing is not that Russia went broke but that when it did, the reverberations shocked markets around the world in such disproportion to the size of its economy.

Hong Kong's Fall
from Free-Market Grace

HONG KONG IMMEDIATELY felt the heat from Russia's default, and its authorities reacted as though a carefully orchestrated attack by speculative forces was underway. Hong Kong Monetary Authority Chief Executive Joseph Yam later described the events:

> In August we faced a much more complicated situation, in which speculators launched coordinated and well planned attacks across our financial markets. Speculators had discovered that by intensively selling Hong Kong dollars over a short period they could temporarily drive up interest rates

under the currency board system, which would exert downward pressure on stock prices. By pressuring the currency and selling stocks short, they could realize a profit on stock index futures contracts, even if they could not break the exchange rate link. This double play strategy, backed by massive pre-funding offshore (which protected the speculators against the interest rate volatility in Hong Kong) occurred with increasing intensity and formed the background to our controversial operations in the equity markets in late August.[13]

Yam saw as evidence of a premeditated attack the fact that there had been what he called "prefunding" of short Hong Kong dollar positions. As near as can be understood, what Yam was talking about was that traders who either wanted to construct currency hedges or go outright short the Hong Kong dollar had sold forward as opposed to spot. But of course they did, because it was already established in the marketplace that when the Hong Kong dollar comes under attack, short-term interest rates can rise to astonishing levels. As such, it is normal practice in trading currencies, especially fixed exchange rate currencies, to trade in the forward market, with terms of up to six months or even one year. This is normal trading practice regardless of whether someone is selling the currency short or simply executing a currency hedging transaction.

Yet there is a clue as to what happened in Hong Kong in Yam's remarks. Ten months earlier, in October 1997, the Hong Kong dollar had been subject to selling pressure in the midst of the Southeast Asian crisis, as was described in the previous chapter. At that time, Hong Kong residents rushed to sell Hong Kong dollars in order to hedge their local holdings in stocks, bonds, and real estate. The authorities chose not to accommodate an associated surge in demand for short-term liquidity. Interest rates soared to nearly 300 percent, with deleterious effects on the stock market.

If there was a speculative play in Hong Kong triggered by the Russian default, it was based on the idea that Authorities might make the same mistake twice. In fact, they did just that. In an attempt to preserve their currency board, they let interest rates again rocket up to ruinous levels and at least initially sat back and watched as their stock market began to melt down.

On August 14, Hong Kong decided to meet fire with fire by making massive purchases of shares in the local market using the assets of the currency board. The government over a two-week period spent upward of $15 billion, absorbing an estimated 5 percent of the entire stock market float. The government also intervened in the stock index futures markets by buying selected futures contracts to further frustrate short sellers. In the midst of the intervention, Hong Kong's financial secretary, Donald Tsang, told market participants that the intervention into the stock market would continue "for as long as it takes...at all reasonable costs."[14]

What impressed market participants more than Tsang's rhetoric was the intervention's demonstration that Hong Kong's stash of close to $100 billion in foreign exchange reserves might not be a sufficient bulwark against a larger, more serious episode of exchange rate instability. At the end of June, the board had $96.5 billion in assets. If a whopping 15 percent of foreign reserves could be used up in the stock market support program in only two weeks, how well fortified could the exchange rate regime truly be?

The intervention was widely condemned in financial circles. The reaction of the economics profession to the stock market intervention was more or less one of complete horror, as was somewhat predictable. Economists saw the Hong Kong act as anathema, especially considering the former colony's status as an icon of free-market economics. Milton Friedman, following a lifetime of lauding Hong Kong's free-markets orientation, branded the move as crazy, in so many words. On September 16, Alan Greenspan gave a definitive answer to the House Banking Committee when asked his opinion about the Hong Kong government's stock market incursion: "They won't succeed. And it erodes some of the extraordinary credibility the Hong Kong Monetary Authority achieved over the years."[15]

The Hong Kong stock market did recover in the subsequent months, giving the authorities cause to crow about their victory over the speculators. What was missing in their account of the episode is the recognition that many other countries were hit with extreme market turbulence at the same time as was Hong Kong, including the U.S. market. Virtually all of them managed to recover at about the same time. Yet only in Hong Kong did the authorities try to directly stabilize the stock market with government purchase of shares, a fact that puts in question the magnitude of the claimed victory over the so-called speculators.

The LTCM Fiasco and
Market Turbulence in Autumn 1998

IN SEPTEMBER 1998, THE investment firm of Long-Term Capital Management was at the center of one of the largest trading debacles in the history of U.S. capital markets. The incident has profoundly colored the way people think about trading, hedge funds, and financial markets.

LTCM's principals rose out of the ashes of the Salomon Brothers government bond scandal that had erupted in 1991. LTCM's chairman, John Meriwether, had been the vice chairman of Salomon Brothers, having worked his way to the top by dint of his talent for complex and arcane bond and derivative arbitrage trading.

Meriwether himself was tainted by the Salomon scandal in the sense that he had failed to supervise the activities of the errant government bond desk. Salomon Brothers, the best known and most powerful bond dealer in the world, was charged with using falsified customer orders to submit improper bids at the U.S. Treasury auctions in 1990 and 1991. The Federal Reserve, and later the U.S. Securities and Exchange Commission (SEC), treated this as a hanging offense. John Gutfreund, the chairman, was ousted. The affair shook Salomon Brothers to its foundations; the firm never got out of the shadow of this scandal.

Meriwether resigned from Salomon and settled with the SEC by accepting a three-month ban from the securities industry and paying a $50,000 fine. He was widely believed by Wall Street insiders never to have been part of any malfeasance. After he left Salomon, Meriwether was transformed into something of a trader's folk hero, if not martyr. So it is no surprise that when he announced that he was starting an investment company in 1994, meaning LTCM, investors greeted him with open arms and pocketbooks.

Meriwether hired the core trading personnel of his old Salomon bond arbitrage unit plus some other renowned Salomon trading alumni. As if that weren't enough, two the firm's partners were among the most respected finance professors in the world, Myron Scholes and Robert Merton. Scholes, Merton, and the late Fischer Black were codevelopers of the celebrated Black-Scholes option-pricing model for which the former two would be awarded the 1997 Nobel Prize in economics.

Investors committed $1.2 billion to the initial offering of the LTCM partnership, undeterred by the fact that the firm required a three-year commitment. LTCM's fee structure was 2 percent of assets per annum plus 25 percent of new profits, an arrangement not unusual but at the high end of fees for the hedge fund industry. In the world of hedge funds, raising such a staggering sum of capital for a start-up operation was unheard of. The partners contributed $100 million of their own money to LTCM.

The excitement over LTCM is hard to describe. It was the dream of virtually every Wall Street trader to get a job, or better yet, a partnership, with the Meriwether group. Institutional investors regarded placing funds with LTCM as a privilege. Many of LTCM's banking counterparties were no more circumspect when it came to extending loans and trading lines to the group.

Nor did LTCM disappoint, at least in its first few years. From the beginning, LTCM's performance was brilliant. Performance after fees was 19.9 percent, 42.8 percent, 40.8 percent, and 17.1 percent in the respective years between 1994 and 1997.[16] No matter that no one outside of the firm knew exactly what it was that Meriwether's traders were doing, beyond the vague concept that LTCM was continuing and expanding the activities of the old Salomon bond arbitrage unit. As long as the returns came in, nobody thought to ask the tough questions.

Much has been made of the fact that LTCM divulged so little about its trading activities to its bankers and its investors. But LTCM's policy of not disclosing its portfolio in its entirety was not much different from that of any other large investment pool or hedge fund. In all likelihood most of the same investors and bankers would have been chasing LTCM to invest and extend credit even if they had been given a look at its complex portfolio.

In December 1997, LTCM stunned the investment world by returning $2.7 billion of its total capital of $7.5 billion to investors.[17] Curiously, LTCM did not reduce the size of its investment portfolio at that time, meaning that the reduction in the capital base translated into an increase in the firm's balance sheet leverage.[18] Some investors, the "lucky ones," were allowed to stay in the firm along with the partner's money, the latter having grown to $1.6 billion. The investors who were asked to withdraw from LTCM were outraged at being deprived of future participation, but they did not feel that way for long. Basically, LTCM's partners had decided to keep all of the "good trades" for the remaining investors and for themselves, which was their right, of course. By declining customer funds, a rare phenomenon on Wall Street, LTCM enshrined its reputation for investment genius.

After the fact, it is now known that what LTCM was doing was making highly levered trades designed to exploit what were believed to be temporary anomalies in the pricing of interest rate swaps, government bonds, equities, and option markets. Eighty percent of the portfolio was invested in the government bonds of the G7 nations. The President's Working Group described LTCM's trading as being comprised of a variety of convergence trades and dynamic hedging strategies.[19]

The firm employed its enormous capital to pounce on any pricing anomalies in virtually any capital market anywhere in the world. Because its funds had been secured for a period of years, LTCM could afford to hold positions until markets reverted to what it considered to be the normal constellation of prices. As for the sheer size of the portfolio and its leverage, the president's commission reported:

Overall, the distinguishing features of the LTCM Fund were the sale of its activities, the large size of its positions in certain markets, and the extent of its leverage, both in terms of balance-sheet measures and on the basis of more meaningful measures of risk exposure in relation to capital. The Fund reportedly had over 60,000 trades on its books, including long securities positions of over $50 billion and short positions of an equivalent magnitude. At the end of August, 1998, the gross notional amounts of the Fund's contracts on futures exchanges exceeded $500 billion, swaps contracts more than $750 billion, and options and other OTC [over-the counter] derivatives over $150 billion.... With regard to leverage, the LTCM's Fund's balance sheet on August 31, 1998 included over $125 billion in assets. Even using the January 1, 1998 equity capital figure of $4.8 billion, this level of assets still implied a balance-sheet ratio of more than 25-to-1.[20]

The first sign that something might be wrong with LTCM surfaced in the summer of 1998, before the Russian default. The company lost 6.7 percent in May and 10.7 percent in June. July started out as a positive month but finished only up 0.48 percent.[21] The catalyst for the incipient disaster may have been none other than Salomon Brothers itself, now merged with Smith Barney as part of the Travelers Group insurance conglomerate.

Sometime in summer of 1998, Travelers decided to disband the Salomon Smith Barney (SSB) bond arbitrage trading operation. Accordingly, on July 6 a press release was issued to that effect. But therein lies a trading room mystery because Michael Lewis, in an article featuring an interview with Meriwether that was published six months afterward in the *New York Times Magazine*, reported that the trouble came on July 17, when Salomon Smith Barney announced that it was liquidating all of its red dollar–blue dollar trades, which turned out to have been the same trades Long-Term had made. For the rest of that month, the fund dropped about 10 percent because Salomon Brothers was selling all the things that Long-Term owned.[22]

Lewis had drawn on an analogy of red and blue dollar trades to explain LTCM's sophisticated arbitrage trading operations. For example, red dollar securities might have been Swedish govern-

ment bonds while the blue dollar items would be German government bonds if the idea was to catch Sweden's interest rates in the
process of converging on to those of Germany.

What no competent trader can understand is that it appears
that Salomon Smith Barney issued the press release of July 6
before it had completely unwound its huge bond arbitrage portfolio. The fact that SSB had tipped its hand was not lost on the trading community. By 1998, Wall Street was rife with traders who had
either trained at Salomon Brothers or had spent their careers trying to become John Meriwether clones. A lot of people were famil-
iar with the trading patterns of the old Meriwether unit. In the
feeding frenzy that ensued, normal capital market relationships
that LTCM regarded as being the equilibrium became severely
distorted, thereby creating the huge losses. The importance of the
July episode is that it revealed to the trading community that
LTCM was vulnerable.

The same thing happened to LTCM again but in larger proportions and with dire consequences in August and September,
when capital markets severely warped out of shape after Russia
defaulted on its debt. That proved to be the undoing of LTCM.

Franklin Edwards, a Columbia University professor of finance,
summarized the condition of the market at that time:

> By September 10th, 1998, yields on emerging market debt
> as shown by the J.P. Morgan emerging market bond index
> had risen to a spread of 17.05 percentage points above the
> return on comparable U.S. Treasury bonds, up from a 6 per-
> centage point spread in July and a 3.3 percentage point
> spread in October 1997. Similarly, yields of U.S. B-rated
> bonds rose to almost 11 percent, a spread of 5.7 percentage
> points above high-rated corporate bonds, up from a spread
> of about 2 percentage points. This sharp widening of yield
> spreads caused by a stampede to liquidity and quality was
> just the opposite of what LTCM was betting on. By mid-
> September 1998, LTCM's equity had dropped to $600 mil-
> lion, a loss of more than $4 billion.[23]

The phenomenon seen in the October 1998 market was eerily reminiscent of what John Kenneth Galbraith described as having occurred in the 1929 stock market crash:

> Never was there a time when more people wanted more money more urgently than in those days. The word that a man had "got caught" by the market was the signal for his creditors to descend on him like locusts. Many who were having trouble meeting their margin calls wanted to sell some stocks so they could hold the rest and thus salvage something from their misfortunes. But such people now found that their investment trust securities could not be sold for any appreciable sum and perhaps not at all. They were forced, as a result to realize on their good securities. Standard stocks like Steel, General Motors, Tel and Tel were thus dumped on the market in abnormal volume, with the effect on prices that had already been fully revealed. The great investment trust boom had ended in a unique manifestation of Gresham's Law in which the bad stocks were driving out the good.[24]

In the case of October 1998, normal relationships between classes of securities became skewed as investors scrambled to raise cash to meet margin calls and collateral top-up needs. As was the case in Galbraith's account of 1929, lack of liquidity in lower-credit-quality assets, especially in emerging market securities, led to selling of higher-quality assets, the phenomenon which Galbraith referred to as Gresham's law.

Lewis's *New York Times Magazine* article provides a take on what the LTCM traders were experiencing in these short quotes from LTCM partners:

> It was as if there was someone out there with our exact portfolio only it was three times as large as ours, and they were liquidating all at once... The hurricane is not more or less likely to hit because more hurricane insurance has been written. In financial markets this is not true. The more peo-

ple write financial insurance, the more likely it is that the disaster will happen because the people who know you have sold the insurance can make it happen.[25]

and

It ceased to feel like people were liquidating positions similar to ours. All of a sudden they were liquidating our positions.[26]

LTCM was on the ropes and the market was dispassionate in driving Meriwether, his partners, and their funds into the ground. Later, as reported in the Lewis article, Meriwether would reflect on the trading practices that ruined him. Meriwether was quoted in the Lewis article as saying:

The few things we had on that the market didn't know about came back quickly. It is the trades that the market knew we had on that caused us trouble.[27]

This is somewhat ironic talk from the former Salomon star trader who cut his teeth at a firm that was reputed to be knowledgeable about sharp-elbowed market tactics.

What killed LTCM? Some have said that it was the hubris of the firm's managers. Henry Kaufman, the former head of research at Salomon, and no apparent fan of Meriwether, said of LTCM's failure: "There are two kinds of people who lose money. Those who know nothing and those who know everything."[28]

LTCM's partners were on the joyride of a lifetime. They had accumulated over $1.6 billion dollars in profits, resurrected their reputations for having superhuman trading abilities, put together stunning performance, won Nobel Prizes in the cases of Scholes and Merton, and, maybe most of all for Meriwether, achieved if not vindication then certainly rehabilitation from the Salomon auction scandal. What more could they expect out of life in the way of material success and recognition?

In this atmosphere, it is no wonder that they were emboldened to take overreaching risks. The fact that they turned out customer funds to focus on their own money is further indication that LTCM was on the path to a fate of almost biblical proportions. The most important lesson for investors from the LTCM fiasco is that leverage can make holding massive trading positions untenable.

Lesson number two is that there is no such thing as a sure profit from a trade that is based on historical statistical relationships, especially when there is the possibility for macroeconomic instability. There is even greater danger if other like-minded traders decide to participate in the same trades. In fact, several funds with similarities to LTCM were distressed or became insolvent in October 1998. If everybody gets in for the same reason, and if everybody is using leverage, then it is a sure bet that everybody will be forced to make an exit simultaneously to meet margin and collateral calls.

Did the Federal Reserve Overreact to LTCM?

OFFICIALS AT THE FEDERAL Reserve wasted little time in responding to LTCM's situation. The New York Federal Reserve Bank convened meetings among LTCM's creditors and counterparties aimed at preventing the possibility of a forced wholesale liquidation of the fund's immense trading positions. Edwards writes:

> On the evening of September 22, the president of the New York Federal Reserve Bank summoned more than a dozen top executives of firms which had loaned money to LTCM to an 8 P.M. meeting and warned them that "the systemic risk posed by LTCM going into default was very real [Siconolfi, 1998]". The next day, a 16-member consortium agreed to put in additional capital of $3.625 billion in exchange for 90 percent of the remaining equity in LTCM. By the end of September 1998, the stakes of the 16 general LTCM partners were reportedly worth about $30 million down from $1.6 billion earlier in the year.[29]

In other words, the value of the partners' stakes was down to less than two cents on the dollar.

In the public's eye, the New York Fed had arranged for some sort of bailout of LTCM. This is not true, because no public funds were used to rescue LTCM. But what was the proper role of the Federal Reserve, and was it justified in intervening in a private dispute between LTCM and its creditors and counterparties? Did the Fed cross the line between prudent, necessary management of the nation's banking system and improper interference into the private sector?

Greenspan would later defend the New York Fed's actions:

> It was the judgment of officials at the Federal Reserve Bank of New York, who were monitoring the situation on an ongoing basis, that the act of unwinding LTCM's portfolio in a forced liquidation would not only have a significant distorting impact on market prices but also in the process could produce large losses, or worse, for a number of creditors and counterparties, and for other market participants not directly involved with LTCM.... This agreement was not a government bailout in that Federal Reserve funds were neither provided nor suggested. Agreement was not forced upon unwilling market participants. Creditors and counterparties calculated that LTCM and, accordingly their claims would be worth more over time if the liquidation of LTCM's portfolio was orderly as opposed to being subject to a fire sale."[30]

LTCM was unique among investment company failures in commanding this level of attention from the Federal Reserve. The Federal Reserve has enormous implied powers of coercion over banks. Summoning dozens of bankers to the "good offices" of the New York Fed at night recalls another incident in American financial history. It was when J. Pierpont Morgan, who had made up his mind to function as though he were the nation's central bank, locked fifty bankers in his library, forcing them to advance a $50 million loan package to the U.S. Treasury to avert a panic in

1907. Morgan, pointing to the loan agreement that he had draft-
ed, allegedly told the bankers to sign by saying "there's the place
and here's the pen."

Former *Wall Street Journal* reporter Roger Lowenstein's book
*When Genius Failed: The Rise and Fall of Long-Term Capital
Management* contains extensive first-person accounts of the
LTCM meetings at the New York Federal Reserve. Clearly, not all
of the bankers relished the idea of participating in the rescue of
the fund. The question is what would have the banks done about
LTCM absent the call from the New York Federal Reserve Bank?
In the worst case the banks would have liquidated LTCM's massive
and complex portfolio at once, taking any prices they could get. No
doubt this would have created a great deal of market volatility. It
is possible that a lot of damage could have been done to all manner of other parties. This was the testimony before Congress of
William J. McDonough, the president of the New York Federal
Reserve: "Had Long-Term Capital been suddenly put into default,
its counterparties would have immediately closed-out their positions.... Markets would have moved sharply and losses would have
been exaggerated."[31]

McDonough presumed a lot. The fact of the matter is that the
Fed's rescue of LTCM neither stopped the market's gyrations nor
did it insulate the financial community, as Lowenstein describes:

> Recapitalized with a fresh $3.65 billion, Long-Term contin-
> ued to plummet, like a parachutist who yanks the ripcord
> but keeps falling anyway. In its first two weeks, the consor-
> tium lost $750 million...by mid-October, all of Wall Street
> seemed to have caught Long-Term's disease. One by one,
> Merrill Lynch, Bankers Trust, UBS, Credit Suisse First
> Boston, Goldman Sachs, and Salomon Smith Barney—the
> linchpins of the new consortium—divulged large losses that
> in sum matched those of Greenwich [LTCM].[32]

McDonough's argument is further challenged by the fact that
the very bankers who were called to the Fed's nighttime emergency meeting operated some of the most sophisticated trading

operations on Wall Street. What is more likely than his fire-sale scenario is that these institutions would have absorbed LTCM's trading positions onto their own proprietary trading books with no help or prodding from the Fed. The banks' traders would have managed the risk of the LTCM positions, that were now their positions, as part of the total risk book. Over time, they would have decided whether to keep or liquidate the LTCM trades by applying the same market judgments as in all of their regular trading.

More in line with the way that it had worked to calm financial markets during other periods of crisis, notably in the October 1987 stock market free-fall, the Federal Reserve took emergency action to cut the interest rate. The Fed cut rates by 25 basis points on September 29, October 15, and November 17, 1998. Seven months later, stating that the fast-growing economy was at risk to a buildup of inflationary pressure, the Fed embarked on a program to raise interest rates.

Earlier in this chapter Federal Reserve Chairman Alan Greenspan was quoted sharply criticizing the Hong Kong Monetary Authority for having conducted its intervention into the stock market. Yet within a mere few months, the Federal Reserve itself took its action on LTCM and may have stepped over the line that normally separates a central bank from the private sector.

Worse yet is that both in the case of the Federal Reserve and the Hong Kong Monetary Authority, it was made to look as if the world's financial system would collapse without periodic guidance and extraordinary intervention of the government.

Chapter 7 *Seven*

Fast Fixes and Alternative Exchange Rate Regimes

THE ECONOMIC TURMOIL of the 1990s raised awareness of how the choice of its foreign exchange regime can be paramount to the future of a nation. The debate is as to what choice is the best. If nothing else, the experience of the decade ought to highlight how dangerous fixed exchange rates can be. With few exceptions, every crisis of the 1990s can be traced to a breakdown in a pegged exchange rate regime. What then of the remaining choices? Is one system preferable to all others?

Peg Hard or Float

CONSIDER THE REMARKS OF Stanley Fischer, first deputy director of the International Monetary Fund and former Professor of Economics at MIT:

> It turns out that in every one of the major crises of the last five years, Mexico '94, and Thailand, Indonesia and Korea, Russia and Brazil, the country had a fixed or pegged exchange rate in place prior to the crisis. That is a weighty piece of evidence suggesting that fixed exchange rate systems are crisis prone. There's another piece of evidence that I find equally persuasive: Some countries that might well

have had crises but had floating rates—I'm thinking of
Turkey, South Africa, Israel, Mexico in 1998—were badly
affected, but suffered much smaller crises. These facts take
you in the direction of the bipolar approach to exchange
rate systems for countries integrated into the international
capital markets, namely either peg hard, or float.[1]

Fischer's term *peg hard* could include cases where a currency
board is used to maintain a fixed exchange rate regime. Currency
boards have attracted a great deal of popular attention, even from
economists who normally would be thought to be supporters of
floating exchange rates. In concept, a currency board might be an
exception to the rule that fixed exchange rate systems are inherently prone to crisis.

Fischer's term peg hard could also include *dollarization*, an
idea that is getting more than casual attention among Latin American countries. When a country dollarizes, it eliminates its own
currency in favor of adopting the U.S. dollar as legal tender. The
dollar also becomes the currency that the government uses in official transactions. Panama has been dollarized for decades, and
Ecuador is in the process of dollarizing at the time of the writing
of this book.

On the opposite side of the field are economists who believe
that floating exchange rate regimes are best. But some of them,
while advocating in favor of floating exchange rate regimes, believe that measures must be taken to control the volatility of exchange rate fluctuations. Two ideas have been advanced on this
count. One is to establish an international superstructure for exchange rates with target zones. The *Tobin tax* is the other, which is
a proposal to impose a tax on foreign exchange trading for the purpose of discouraging what is seen as overtrading. This chapter
takes issue with these proposals, by way of returning to the central
question. What is so dreadfully wrong with a country having a
completely floating exchange rate regime?

Currency Boards

THE FUNCTIONING OF a currency board exchange rate regime has already been discussed in Chapter 5 in the material concerning the Hong Kong Monetary Authority. Besides Hong Kong, Argentina is another nation that operates a fixed exchange regime under the auspices of a currency board. Both countries regard their currency board experiments as successes.

A government that has decided to establish a currency board needs to have on hand a sufficient amount of a reserve foreign currency or assets denominated in the reserve foreign currency to match the outstanding monetary base. The monetary base, which in some circles is called *high-powered money*, is equal to domestic currency in circulation plus commercial bank deposits held at the central bank. The essence of the currency board is contained in its promise to buy or sell its domestic currency in exchange for the reserve currency without limit at the pegged exchange rate. A currency board offers a seemingly bulletproof fixed exchange rate regime.

Domestic interest rates will mechanically follow the dictates of the reserve currency's central bank, in most cases. Moreover, the domestic money supply will be controlled not by the local central bank but rather by the public's demand for holding the domestic currency. When the board is called on to buy domestic currency the base money supply diminishes because money is sucked out of the banking system. Likewise, when the public approaches the currency board with the intent to buy domestic currency for foreign currency, the domestic base money supply expands (Box 7.1). The higher-ordered monetary aggregates, like M2 (currency in circulation plus checking accounts plus time deposits), are determined by the outstanding monetary base, by the statutory reserve requirements, and by the willingness and ability of commercial banks to make loans.

Currency boards flourished in the days of colonial empire (see Schwartz[2] for a comprehensive history). Their function was to afford colonies the right to have their own currency while keeping their pro forma central banks on a tight leash to ensure automatic

BOX 7.1

More on the Operation of a Currency Board

A CURRENCY BOARD STANDS ready to buy or sell the domestic currency in exchange for the reserve currency at the pegged exchange rate. The board is established with a stock of reserve currency and assets denominated in the reserve currency (usually the government bonds of reserve country currency) that is sufficiently large to cover the entire monetary base (currency in circulation plus commercial bank deposits held as reserves at the central bank). The currency board can be operated by the central bank or in parallel to the central bank. Once the board is established, the central bank relinquishes control over monetary policy but holds on to some other functions, like the supervision of commercial banks. In this capacity, it remains as the custodian of the aforementioned commercial bank deposits held as reserves.

When the currency board sells reserve currency to the general public, the domestic money supply is reduced; when the board buys reserve currency from the public, the domestic money supply increases. Changes in the money supply, if sufficient in magnitude, can have profound effects on national income, the consumer price level, asset markets, and the value of country's currency, with no better illustration being the case of Japan in the 1980s and 1990s that was the subject of Chapter 2. Hence any country considering

monetary stability. With the collapse of colonialism following the end of the Second World War, the newly independent countries abandoned their currency boards in favor of establishing full-fledged central banks of their own.

The idea of the currency board was resurrected amidst the Mexican peso crisis of 1994–1995. Some economists thought that Mexico needed to consider adopting a currency board. This met with immediate opposition from the U.S. Treasury and from high installing a currency board should be aware of the fact that the cost of exchange rate stability could be subjecting the country to potentially gruesome macroeconomic adjustments.

One interesting, theoretical question is whether a currency board could ever run out of foreign reserves. In principle, it could never happen. Suppose citizens go to the currency board wanting to get rid of their domestic currency. The board would have to accommodate their demands by buying their domestic currency and surrendering an equivalent amount, at the pegged exchange rate, of its foreign reserve currency. This would make the domestic money supply fall. If the selling of domestic currency continued, the money supply would drop further. But at some point the demand for the domestic currency would have to return, simply because there would be so little of it in circulation.

Likewise, the domestic money supply under a currency board could not increase without limit. Money supply increases when the board is asked to supply more domestic currency in exchange for the reserve currency. At some point there would be so much domestic currency in circulation that its value would have to deteriorate and the demand for the currency board to supply more of it would shut down.

levels at the International Monetary Fund, whereupon the idea died, at least for Mexico.

Two years later, as was described in Chapter 4, Indonesia began to entertain the idea of a currency board under the tutelage of Professor Steven Hanke but the project was abandoned before it could be put into practice. Culp, Hanke, and Miller defend the concept of the Indonesian currency board with conviction. As they describe it, the Indonesian currency board was not able to overcome the objection of the Clinton administration and the IMF. More importantly, the Indonesian currency board never passed the acid test with many private sector investors, economists, and currency traders because of the suspicion that the board would enable a massive central bank fraud.

Still the idea of having a currency board appeals to many respected economists (Friedman[3], Miller[4], Hanke[5], and Schuler,[6] to name a few), all of whom feel that it would be an improvement over having an independent central bank and discretionary monetary policy. There is a natural alignment to the monetarist school associated with the University of Chicago and Milton Friedman. Friedman repeatedly has made a public case against having a central bank with discretionary control over monetary policy. With a currency board, money supply is demand driven, which means that the central bank has surrendered control of monetary policy.

Yet there are practical problems associated with having a currency board. For one thing, the local country is effectively tied to the monetary policy of the reserve currency country. There is no reason to believe that the monetary policy of the reserve currency country is appropriate for the local economy.

For another thing, regardless of the size of the reserves held by the currency board, external shocks may be big enough to damage confidence in the currency board. This happened to Hong Kong in October 1997 (Chapter 5) and again in August 1998 (Chapter 6), despite there being a massive stock of foreign reserves.

A practical problem occurs at the onset when the board must fix the permanent exchange rate for its currency against the reserve currency. Culp, Hanke, and Miller recommend that there be an initial period wherein the currency be allowed to float to find its own level. The advantage of this is that the market would in effect determine where the exchange rate should be fixed. But this defies practical sense. Countries that have stable floating exchange rates do not look to establish currency boards. A country comes to consider setting up a currency board when it is desperate to achieve exchange rate stability, usually in the midst of a currency crisis. The correct permanent rate of exchange is not knowable under these circumstances. Economist David Hale supported a currency board for Mexico in a January 19, 1995 article in the *Wall Street Journal:*

> At what rate should Mexico peg the peso to the dollar? Since the goal of the currency board would be to establish a fixed exchange rate capable of enduring for several years, it might be useful to launch it with an exchange rate that was clearly undervalued in the short-term, such as the current market rate of 5.25. At such a rate, no one would doubt Mexico's trade competitiveness or the potential attractiveness of Mexican assets if the government moves decisively to restrain the inflationary pressures resulting from the devaluation.[7]

The difficulty with Hale's approach is illustrated by the fact that in the five years since the crisis the peso has never been near the 5.25 to the dollar level. Within one month's time, the dollar/-peso exchange rate was above 6.00 and at the time of this writing it is above 9.00. It is hard to imagine that the currency board could have withstood the selling pressure on the peso without a serious depletion of its foreign reserves.

Indonesia is another case in point. As Culp, Hanke, and Miller point out, the rupiah was trading around 10,500 to the dollar when President Suharto was considering the currency board proposal. Had the board been established and the peg set at 10,500, there would have been, over the course of the next months, substantial excess demand for rupiah. This is evidenced by the fact that the postcrisis level for the rupiah was around 7,000, which is a 30 percent improvement. In the context of the suggested currency board, the excess demand for rupiahs would have brought about an automatic excess supply of money and a potentially severe future inflation problem.

The Achilles heel of a currency board is that the public's perception of its permanence can vanish in a moment. If the integrity of the board or the intention of the government to maintain the board comes into doubt, then something akin to a bank panic can ensue when local citizens, foreign investors, and foreign exchange traders try to sell the local currency. In the course of a crisis of confidence, it becomes obvious that the government is forced to consider whether to devalue the currency or even give up the peg altogether to preserve its hoard of foreign reserves. Friedman speaks directly to that point:

> Hong Kong and Argentina retain the option of terminating their currency boards, changing the pegged rate, or introducing central bank features, as the Hong Kong Monetary Authority has done in a limited way. As a result, they are not immune to infection from foreign exchange crises originating elsewhere. Nonetheless, currency boards have a good record of surviving such crises intact.[8]

Culp, Hanke, and Miller propose the extreme step of locating the currency board in a neutral country (they chose Switzerland) and appointing an independent board of directors. However, what a damning statement! Who would invest in a country that was so corrupt that it could not be trusted to run its own currency board?

In previous chapters it was shown that Hong Kong was not immune to currency crisis despite its operation of its currency board. Zarazaga discusses a similar incident that took place in 1995 when the Argentine currency board was caught up in the Mexican peso crisis:

> Argentina's problem started with a liquidity squeeze in Bank Extrader, a small bank that held barely 0.2 percent of all the deposits of Argentina's financial system. Extrader was heavily exposed in Mexican bonds and securities. When the value of those assets fell dramatically in the aftermath of Mexico's December 20 1994 peso devaluation, the bank could no longer cover its short-term liabilities, particularly time deposits. This shortage triggered a bank run, making matters even worse. On January 18 [1995] the central bank was forced to liquidate Extrader. Suddenly, the effect seen elsewhere in Latin America spilled into Argentina's domestic financial markets. Fear that other banks were also heav-

ily exposed to the collapsing Latin American capital markets led depositors to withdraw their money from banks for the security of their mattresses or accounts abroad. By April 30 [1995], the financial system had lost 18 percent of the deposits it had had before the Mexican peso devaluation. To cover the withdrawals, the banks were forced to liquidate assets. One liquidation method was not to renew lines of credit to consumer and businesses.[9]

The Argentine currency board operated throughout the crisis and Argentina nonetheless suffered a severe macroeconomic contraction, according to Zarazaga.

Despite the practical obstacles, the concept of the currency board has to be measured against what alternatives are available. If the alternative is having a hopelessly corrupt, politically compromised, or just plain incompetent central bank then the currency board concept may have something to offer, despite its logistical problems.

On the other hand, one has to come back to the question of whether there is anything wrong with having a freely floating exchange rate regime that is backed by a prudent central bank. But first, if absolute exchange rate stability is a prerequisite, there is one more alternative.

Dollarization

IF A HARD PEG TO ANOTHER country's currency is such a worthy idea, then why not take the extra step of adopting the reserve currency outright to replace the domestic currency? Why bother at all with having to operate a currency board? Why not dollarize? Any major currency could be adopted, for that matter, so "dollarize" could mean "euroize," or "yenize." Schuler reports that some twenty-nine-odd countries today use the U.S. dollar or some other foreign currency as their official currency. Panama is by far the largest independent country to be dollarized.

Unofficial dollarization, meaning cases where non-U.S. citizens hold wealth denominated in the U.S. currency that is not the legal tender of their country, has always been widespread. Schuler[10] reports that researchers at the Federal Reserve estimate that foreigners hold 55 to 70 percent of U.S. dollar notes, mainly as $100 bills.[11]

Official dollarization is a different matter. Politically speaking, official dollarization is a big step for any country to take, as Alan Greenspan has said: "To make another country's currency one's own is a momentous decision for any country."[12]

The idea of dollarization was made more palatable by the introduction of the euro, the single currency adopted by eleven European nations, that was introduced in January 1999. The euro project is too new to judge whether it is a success, but it has spawned some thought of trying a similar project in the Western Hemisphere. Instead of inventing a new currency, the prevailing thought is that countries in the hemisphere would adopt the U.S. dollar.

One country that did just that was Ecuador, a small South American nation, that unilaterally dollarized in January 2000. This decision came after a virtual collapse of the Ecuadorian economy in 1999. The Ecuadorian sucre had been pegged to the dollar. When adverse economic conditions forced the central bank to abandon the peg, the currency suffered a massive loss in value, depreciating from 7,000 to 25,000 to the dollar. The concept of dollarization invoked a violent reaction from the poor. President Jamil Mahuad was literally run out of office on January 21, 2000 by an armed uprising of angry citizens. Mahuad's successor, Gustavo Noboa, has decided to go ahead with dollarization nonetheless.

For as long as the U.S. dollar remains the principal reserve country of the world, the advantage that dollarization affords to a country like Panama or Ecuador is never having to worry about having a currency crisis like the one that affected the Mexican peso in 1994. The disadvantage is that the dollarized country loses its ability to determine its own monetary policy. The U.S. Federal Reserve would replace the local central bank insofar as determining monetary policy.

The question then is whether the Federal Reserve would take

into account economic conditions in dollarized countries when it makes policy decisions. The answer that Chairman Greenspan has given to date is that Federal Reserve policy addresses issues that end at U.S. political borders, and only those issues.

The circumstances under which Ecuador elected to dollarize is a perfect case in point. At the same time that Ecuador was trying to get out from under a near total collapse of its economy, the Federal Reserve was raising interest rates to ward off incipient inflationary pressures in the United States. How could anyone sustain the thought that the Federal Reserve's policy in 2000 was appropriate for both the United States and Ecuador?

There is a practical issue as to whether the dollarized economy can negotiate a participation in its own country's seigniorage. *Seigniorage* is the value to a central bank from not having to pay interest on the outstanding monetary base. The balance sheet of the Federal Reserve consists in large part of interest-bearing government securities (as assets) and currency and commercial bank reserve deposits (as liabilities). The latter, being non–interest-bearing liabilities, create seigniorage. Ecuador, for example, in adopting the dollar as its currency will forgo the seigniorage associated with its own currency. Additional seigniorage will come to the U.S. Federal Reserve from the new dollars in circulation in Ecuador. Whether or not Ecuador will share in the Federal Reserve's windfall seigniorage depends on its arrangement with the Federal Reserve.

On the other hand, it is not without possible cost to the United States to have another country use the dollar as its currency. Financial and political trouble in the dollarized country could have a negative effect on the value of the dollar. The question also arises as to whether the U.S. Federal Reserve would become compelled to play a role in inspecting and regulating banks in dollarized countries. There also is the larger issue of whether the distress, or even a collapse of financial institutions in dollarized countries, would complicate U.S. monetary policy.

Stanley Fischer compared having a currency board to dollarizing as follows:

Once a country has decided to peg hard, the main benefits of retaining its own currency are seigniorage, and the option to unpeg at some future date. Retention of the option to unpeg is likely to be quite costly in terms of interest rates, and so if some solution to the seigniorage problem can be found, countries may well want to dollarize or euro-ize or join some other bloc. I believe the example of the euro will be a powerful force pushing toward the creation of currency blocs.[13]

It is important to note that a currency board nation has the option of threatening to dollarize, which can be useful if the country is in a period of financial duress. Argentina experienced rapid increases in its local currency interest rates over and above the reserve currency interest rate when its currency boards came under pressure. The cheap, temporary fix was not lost on former President Carlos Menem who announced his intention to dollarize Argentina. Had his elected term not expired he might have carried it out, but his successor has shown little interest in the idea.

Hong Kong is a more complex case, as was described in Chapter 6. While it is true that Joseph Yam, the chief executive of the Hong Kong Monetary Authority, once did mention his interest in exploring dollarization, such a threat upon reflection would hold little water. Consider that Hong Kong was a British crown colony for 150 years before it became a special administrative region of the People's Republic of China. How enthusiastic could Beijing be about adopting a Western currency, let alone the U.S. dollar, for its newly reunited territory, Hong Kong?

Foreign Exchange Target Zones
and the Tobin Tax

IN THE WAKE OF THE FOREIGN exchange turbulence of the 1990s, a number of quick solutions have been put forward to stabilize floating exchange rate regimes without resorting to pegged exchange rates.

In 1998 and 1999 the idea that foreign exchange rate trading should be governed by fixed trading target zones became popular in some circles. The most vocal advocate of target trading zones for the major currencies, namely the dollar, the mark (later for the euro), and the yen, was Oskar Lafontaine, the minister of finance of Germany in the first year of Chancellor Gerhard Schröder's administration. Lafontaine preferred to refer to his idea as his "castle in the air," a term that his opponents found amusing.[14]

Gerhard Schröder himself supported Lafontaine on this. On January 20, 1999, while looking forward to his hosting the G7 summit of the Group of Seven (G7) industrialized countries in Cologne in June, Schröder stated: "We are on the eve of a new financial architecture" and put forward the notion of instituting "fixed fluctuation zones."[15] Days earlier, on June 14, 1999, Schröder had been positively gushing in his praise of Lafontaine and his trading zone initiative:

> The fundamental view that laissez-faire is no longer the right policy has won the argument.... When Oskar Lafontaine advocated such proposals three or five years ago, he was condemned as a dreadful economic fantasist. It just goes to show that determination sometimes pays off.[16]

When Lafontaine abruptly resigned from the Schröder government in March 1999, support in Europe for his target zones faded. But on the other side of the Atlantic, Lafontaine's trading zone initiative picked up support from C. Fred Bergsten, the director of the Institute for International Economics. Bergsten testified as follows before the U.S. House Committee on Banking and Financial Services:

> G7 currency gyrations in recent years have far exceeded any conceivable shifts in economic fundamentals. The dollar rose by 80 percent against the yen and 40 percent against the D-Mark from early 1996 to mid-1998 and late 1997, respectively. One result is that trade deficits in the US are at record levels, retarding our income levels and generating

strong protectionist pressures despite a 25-year low in the US unemployment rate (and probably setting us up for a very sharp, and possibly very disruptive, fall in the dollar at some early point).[17]

Bergsten in the same testimony advocated: "A better approach would be to announce limits on the extent of permissible swings starting perhaps as much as 15 percent on either side of agreed currency midpoints (as in the European Monetary System since 1993)."[18]

Every episode of financial crisis covered in this book, starting with the European Exchange Rate Mechanism (ERM) experience, argues that Bergsten's plan for 15 percent target zones is a blueprint for financial disaster. The same mechanisms that brought about the spectacular currency crises of the 1990s would come into play if target zones were established for major currencies. Target zones failed for ERM currencies. They also failed in the case of Bretton Woods.

The proposals for foreign exchange trading target zones were effectively shot down by the U.S. Treasury and the Federal Reserve. As Greenspan remarked: "One might argue that it's [achieving exchange rate stability] but [it is] neither credible nor feasible."[19]

Wim Duisenberg, the president of the European Central Bank, shared Greenspan's skepticism:

In a world characterized by highly integrated and sophisticated international financial markets, there is serious doubt whether target zones for exchange rates are feasible. Apart from the obvious risks of undermining price stability, such exchange rate targets, would, in essence imply that domestic policy objectives would have to be subordinated to external requirements.[20]

Economics Nobel Prize laureate James Tobin of Yale University put forth a different idea for controlling floating exchange rate volatility as early as 1971. Tobin is clear in his preference of floating exchange rates over pegged exchange rates, but he wants to put "some sand in the market's gears" of foreign exchange trading by imposing a transaction tax. Tobin wrote on December 17, 1997:

> The lesson of the Asian meltdown ought to be that the leaders of the global economy need to find ways to make the currency exchange system less volatile, so as to protect innocent bystanders from sudden economic crashes that destroy jobs and incomes. A global tax on currency transactions is one possible solution.... the tax would have to be the same wherever a transaction takes place, so it would have to be agreed upon internationally.... Because this tax would be the same whether funds are moving on a round trip of hours or years, it would be a significant deterrent to short-horizon speculation but a negligible factor in commodity trade and long-run investment.[21]

Eichengreen describes the support that the Tobin tax has received:

> Each episode of turbulence in international financial markets prompts calls for taxing foreign-exchange transactions. Some proponents of this tax question the rationality and efficiency of the market. They suggest that currency traders buy and sell in disregard of fundamentals, which introduces unnecessary volatility into foreign-exchange markets and capital flows [see, e.g., Felix]. Others acknowledge the rationality of currency traders but characterize their activities as socially counterproductive, invoking second-generation models of currency crises and arguing that unregulated financial markets make it too easy for speculators to shift the economy from the good to the bad equilibrium. It follows that a tax on foreign-exchange transactions that makes it more difficult for investors to speculate against currencies could in principle reduce the incidence of crises and enhance the social welfare.[22]

Eichengreen points to the logistical improbability of the Tobin tax ever coming into being. The likelihood such a law would be passed everywhere in the world is slim, and foreign exchange trading naturally would migrate to tax-free zones. Moreover, as Eichengreen describes it, the tax could be avoided by relabeling of transactions.

Beyond the issues of practicality, the basic presumption of the Tobin tax, as Eichengreen writes, is that foreign exchange trading is a hazard to global economic welfare. This kind of thought was also in evidence with Bergsten, as quoted above, in his support for target zones, when he made the case that the magnitude of fluctuations in exchange rates sometimes defies analysis. Yet who is to say that large swings in any price are sometimes not needed to bring markets into equilibrium? Furthermore, the period that Bergsten spoke about, 1996–1997, was a time of extreme central bank intervention into the foreign exchange market, a fact that might account for part of the observed volatility.

The Tobin tax turns out to have attracted more support from political activists groups than from economists and foreign exchange professionals. The former, while being quick to endorse a measure against what they see as speculation, are keenly interested in using the proceeds of the tax to finance their wide-reaching social causes. The concept of a tax on foreign exchange trading did actually pass the Canadian Parliament on March 23, 1999 by a vote of 164 to 83. The wording of Motion M-239 was: "That in the opinion of the House, the government should enact a tax on financial transactions in concert with the international community."[23]

The loose wording of the Canadian motion suggests that it was largely a symbolic gesture by the legislators. Little has come of it since its passage.

The Case for Freely Floating
Exchange Rates

COMPARE THE FOLLOWING two views on floating exchange rate regimes, the first from Tobin and the second from Krugman:

What can be done to make the world system of exchange rates and financial markets less prone to these sorts of crises? First of all, let the currency—won or baht or ringgit—depreciate and "float" in the market to its own level. Don't invite another crisis by pegging again. Floating is a preferable permanent policy. After all, the big three currencies—dollar, yen, and deutsche mark—have not been pegged to one another since 1971. The advantage of floating is illustrated by the recent appreciation of the dollar and the depreciation of the yen—no crisis, no headlines, no bailouts.[24]

and

When Bretton Woods system of fixed exchange rates broke up in the early 1970s, most international economists were not dismayed. Not only did they believe that greater flexibility of exchange rates was a good thing; they also believed that they understood reasonably well how the new system would work. They were wrong. The last 20 years of the international monetary system have involved one surprise after another, most of them unpleasant, all of them forcing economists to scramble to keep up with new issues and unexpected turns in old ones.[25]

If both Tobin and Krugman are right then the world is in a sorry fix. Floating exchange rates, the only system that will not blow up, according to Tobin, is fraught with economic peril, according to Krugman.

Other economists believe that floating exchange rate regimes are prone to overshooting. The term *overshooting* means that exchange rates can experience exaggerated reactions to changes in economic fundamentals. A famous example was the so-called "dollar bubble" in the winter of 1985, which occurred near the end of a long secular upward movement in the dollar against other major currencies. Some economists believe that the dollar's final upward movement overshot the equilibrium market-clearing exchange rate before it peaked in February 1985. Indeed, the rationale given for the Plaza intervention in the following September was that action was needed to correct the dollar back to realistic levels.

One possible theoretical explanation for the phenomenon of overshooting comes from economist Rudiger Dornbusch (1976). His model, called the "sticky-price" adjustment mechanism, posits that rigidity of prices in the goods market can force exchange rates to temporarily overshoot in order to achieve a global equilibrium across all macroeconomic markets. This would mean that what some people refer to as overshooting is actually part of a rational economic adjustment process; hence there would be no reason to regulate foreign exchange fluctuations.

Milton Friedman in 1953 published a classical defense of floating exchange rates, some twenty-three years before the breakdown in the fixed exchange rate Bretton Woods system. Friedman argued:

> The ultimate objective is a world in which exchange rates, while free to vary, are in fact highly stable. Instability of exchange rates is a symptom of instability in the underlying economic structure. Elimination of this symptom by administrative freezing of exchange rates cures none of the underlying difficulties and only makes adjustment to them more painful.[26]

Yet many central bankers and finance ministers are reluctant to let their currencies float. Some have positively visceral reactions to the foreign exchange market, perhaps because finance ministers and central bankers who have tried to tangle with the foreign exchange market have ended being bloodied by the experience. Some of them must have wished that the whole thing, meaning the foreign exchange market, would just disappear. This sentiment is usually amplified after a financial crisis, especially when it is suspected that the foreign exchange market is the genesis of the economic disaster.

In many circles there is a presumption that the only good exchange rate is a stable one, if not a completely rigid one. Part of the distrust of floating rates is the erroneous belief that having an absolutely stable exchange rate, or a least one that has a controlled and predictable rate of depreciation, is a prerequisite for attracting foreign investors. That view is wrong and dangerous as well.

To a market-oriented economist, these sentiments are ludicrous. Exchange rates are prices and as such play a vital role in achieving equilibrium balances in the world economy. If they fluctuate, then it is for a purpose. Artificial constraints on the movement in exchange rates distract from the proper workings of the world economy.

Even over short periods of time, government intervention into floating or what has been termed "managed" floating regimes can be disruptive. DeRosa wrote:

> The problem is that intervention can change the nature of the market itself in subtle ways that diminish the efficiency of the price formation process. For example, the focus of market participants can switch away from assessing the impact of natural economic forces to watching for signs of impending government action. In a market that has become nothing more than a guessing game about the next round of policy, the cost of hedging foreign exchange risk is likely to be erratic and arbitrarily exorbitant.[27]

As for investors, sophisticated ones do not care much whether an exchange rate goes up or goes down as long as they can freely transact in the currency and execute currency hedges.

Whatever disappointments Krugman was thinking about in 1995 with reference to floating rates have to be dwarfed today by the chaos of exploding fixed exchange rate regimes that was experienced the decade of the 1990s. All things considered, Fischer's advice (cited at the beginning of this chapter) to governments as to what were the best foreign exchange regimes would be better reworded to read "float—and if you can't float, then peg hard."

Chapter Eight

The Quest for a New Financial Architecture

C RISIS IS THE MOTHER of regulatory invention. Witness the formation of a number of study groups and task forces charged with determining what can be done to prevent episodes like those that happened in the 1990s from reoccurring. There has been a bull market in blue-ribbon committees all considering how to create what has been dubbed the *new international financial architecture.*

Reform Is in the Air

DISCUSSIONS OF REFORM of the financial architecture usually involve consideration of how to control the magnitude of fluctuations in exchange rates, as was covered in the previous chapter. Another topic concerns how to make the system more robust so as to prevent future failures of financial institutions. New capital requirements are under review for banks that deal in foreign exchange and derivatives products. Much attention has been given to new statistical risk models that provide quantitative measures of financial risk. The hope is that these models will have applications to capital adequacy determination. The fear is that model-determined capital requirements will underestimate the need for reserves in a real meltdown. Conversely, the models might overestimate the needs for reserves, a condition that would restrict capital flows.

Ideas have also been put forward for how the free flow of capital in and out of countries should be diminished. These include measures to regulate hedge funds and other "highly levered financial institutions" as well as the banks that supply them with trading facilities and loans. At the extreme is the issue of whether outright capital controls, once thought to be the equivalent of national financial suicide, have any medicinal value in fighting a financial crisis.

Intertwined through all of this is the question of what should be done, if anything, to alter the mission of the International Monetary Fund. The IMF has come under enormous scrutiny for its role in providing emergency assistance and forcing its ideas of reforms on Thailand, Korea, Russia and, most of all, Indonesia in the 1990s. The IMF's policies in these countries, as well as some others, bifurcated public opinion. Some believe that the IMF is needed now more than ever because future crises might strike. Others believe that the IMF should not have gotten involved in these countries and what role it had not only made local conditions worse but made future crises more likely to occur. Indeed, some very well-respected economists and public figures have stated categorically that the IMF should be abolished.

Statistical Risk Models and the Peso Problem

IN THE EARLY 1990s, a generic approach to risk modeling, called *value at risk* (VaR), began to gain acceptance as the industry standard of risk measurement (Jorion). As mathematical models in finance go, VaR is relatively simple. The objective is to quantify the risk embedded in a portfolio or trading position. The methodology rests on relatively basic statistical methods and formulas adapted from portfolio theory that were discovered a half-century ago.

VaR analysis begins by estimating historical statistics on the behavior of rates of return on currencies, stocks, bonds, and money market instruments. It then calculates probabilistic measures of the future profits and losses from portfolios or trading positions. The underlying hypothesis is that the portfolio or trading position is composed of assets whose future rates of return conform to a normal probability distribution. As such, VaR analysis can produce a report that tells a portfolio manager or trader the levels of loss that might be sustained over one day, or over a longer period of time, along with the associated probabilities.

VaR at one point in the 1990s had accumulated a degree of intellectual acceptance that approached a state of suspension of disbelief. A number of banks, hedge funds, and financial regulators placed their faith in it. New consulting firms specializing in risk analysis have sprung up left and right, most being advocates of VaR. A great deal of money and trust is based on the hope that VaR can predict whether or not a bad roll of the dice will turn into a nonsurvivable event.

For some healthy perspective, consider that the noted econometrician Henri Theil once wrote and often told his students, "I suppose that it takes maturity to know that models are to be used but never believed."[1]

VaR has validity and a degree of accuracy in the analysis of portfolios and trading positions that are comprised of currencies, bonds, and stocks of the major economies. It can be totally unreliable, if not outright dangerous when applied to other types of assets. Nassim Nicholas Taleb, a trader-mathematician, is a powerfully outspoken critic of VaR. Taleb was once asked by the magazine *Derivatives Strategy* why he distrusted VaR. His answer is worth considering: "VaR made us replace 2,500 years of market wisdom with a covariance matrix still in its infancy so a management consultant or an unemployed electrical engineer can claim to understand financial market risks."[2]

The broad application of VaR methodology is suspect for a number of reasons. Important factors like market liquidity and the size of a position relative to the depth of the market are not considered. The risks associated with movements in implied volatility for put and call options are neglected.

The most obvious problem with VaR starts with its proposition that historical estimates of standard deviations and correlations can be used in stress testing financial systems and portfolios. Historical risk measures, like all sample statistics, are founded on a maintained hypothesis of a constant population. The problem is that the behavior of financial markets can be notoriously intractable. Bubbles, exchange rate crises, and stock market crashes are all part of the investment landscape. These events may not be captured at the 95 percent or 99 percent confidence level. That's where most VaR analyses end. It is also where financial crises begin. Crises live in the extreme tails of return distributions. Perhaps it isn't even correct to view them as part of the same experience, so to speak, as normal market history. The important large-scale disruptions are more usefully understood as paradigm shifts rather than as rare events.

Nothing in the time series history of stock prices, interest rates, or exchange rates could have predicted any of the financial crises of the 1990s. Moreover, VaR was oblivious to the reality that the Asian tiger nations all had common preconditions, rooted in common policy errors, that made them jointly susceptible to catastrophe.

For example, the crash of the Thai stock market in July 1997 wasn't simply a bad day at the bourse. It signaled the beginning of a period of disintegration for the Asian tiger economies. A VaR report on Asian currencies and financial markets prepared before July 1997 would have been totally blind to how the whole region could crash at more or less the same time. Worse still, VaR analysis would have shown these countries to have been enormously attractive as places to invest because it bought into the illusion of stability created by the fixed exchange rate regimes throughout the region.

A concept often used in conjunction with VaR is the *Sharpe ratio*. This ratio is equal to the historical investment performance, adjusted for the risk-free interest rate, divided by the standard deviation of the investment portfolio returns. It is one of the most widely used measures of investment performance, particularly in the evaluation of hedge fund performance.

In popular usage, the higher the Sharpe ratio, the better the performance record. But this interpretation can be extremely perilous. A large Sharpe ratio would seem to point to consistent, positive performance. Yet a simple thought experiment can debunk this: what would have been the Sharpe ratio of a portfolio of

Mexican government peso Cetes prior to December 20, 1994? It would have had to have been a big number. Mexico would have appeared to be an incredible investment opportunity right up to the end. Then, when the government abandoned its fixed foreign exchange rate regime, the value of the portfolio would have been obliterated.

Cases like Mexico aren't hard to find in recent times. In fact, they are so prevalent that they now have been given the generic name *peso problem*. As it was originally observed, the Mexican peso appeared to be a currency that offered continuous superior returns with no appreciable risk for protracted periods of time. This was a problem for economists to explain, since high, steady returns without appreciable risk is a theoretical anomaly. But the 1990s showed that peso problems are plentiful. The Thai baht, Indonesian rupiah, Russian ruble, and Brazilian real were all peso problems, as were some of the European currencies that participated in the Exchange Rate Mechanism before the September 1992 crisis.

The lesson to be learned is that mechanical reliance on tools like the Sharpe ratio and VaR is tantamount to courting disaster. Both VaR and the Sharpe ratio, put into naive hands, become lighthouses for the soon-to-be shipwrecked. In its most abstract formulation, what the peso problem currencies and their associated crises reveal is that models that do not include consideration of important macroeconomic disequilibrium structures, like fixed exchange rates, are dangerously incomplete.

Arbitrageurs, especially ones that use large amounts of leverage, for example, Long-Term Capital Management, are also right to be hesitant to trust VaR-type models. Here too, an important element of risk is ignored by the models, as Taleb correctly anticipated:

Many forms of arbitrage often carry a higher variance of return than outright directional trading. This is partly due to the fact that the average arbitrageur carries larger amounts on his books than the average speculative trader. It is also due to the accumulation of positions by like minded arbitrageurs.... As the arbitrage community reaches its saturation level, pressure on the relationships will cause severe marks-to-market losses.[3]

First-generation VaR models were pretty much discredited by the end of the 1990s, as the Bank for International Settlements found out when it set to interview practitioners in 1999:

> There was a range of responses among the interviewees as to whether the magnitude of mature market turbulence was within or above their VaR limits. A large majority of interviewees admitted that last autumn's [1998] events were in the "tails" of distribution and that therefore their VaR models were useless for measuring and monitoring market risk. On the other hand, other respondents (though a very small number) judged that their VaR models remained adequate.... The deficiencies of the VaR methodology in conditions of contagion were unanimously emphasized by market participants. The surge in VaR levels above predefined limits during the crisis compelled market participants to unwind positions in the assets for which VaR limits were exceeded. Because of the widespread use of similar models, similar behavior was adopted by numerous investors. The resulting simultaneous pressure to unwind positions dried up the liquidity of markets and therefore exacerbated price volatility.[4]

Stanley Druckenmiller, head portfolio manager for the Soros Fund Management group, gave his professional opinion on VaR models on the occasion of his retirement in May 2000: "VaR is extremely dangerous. People look at their computer models and think they are safe. Much better to have no models and watch your own net worth every day."[5]

Clearly the world has a pressing need for a robust new model that can produce dependable estimates of portfolio risk. What is also clear is that simplistic models of risk that depend naively on historical estimates of variance and correlation are flawed in this application. What was missing in the first generation of risk models was an appreciation of the nature of the risks associated with macroeconomic dislocations.

Capital Controls and Malaysia's Legacy

THE MOST RADICAL DEPARTURE from either a floating exchange rate or fixed exchange rate system comes when a government imposes some form of capital controls to limit trading and block the free international flow of funds. Several of the episodes that have been discussed in this book involved the imposition of capital controls, including Thailand in 1997 and Russia in 1998. But the most notorious case is that of Malaysia in 1998. In some circles, Malaysia is lauded for having fixed its exchange rate and installed capital controls in bold defiance of international pressure. Closer inspection puts into question both the success and advisability of the Malaysian experiment.

Malaysia's gambit began on September 1, 1998 largely at the whim of its irascible prime minister, Mahathir Mohamad. As was described in earlier chapters this was not the first time that controls were imposed in Malaysia. Mahathir himself reveled in the plan, declaring that there "would be no more foreign exchange trading." A variety of measures were introduced by the government that were aimed at restricting capital flows out of the country, banning offshore trading in the ringgit, and fixing the exchange rate to the dollar at 3.800.

It is interesting to note that Malaysia was already one year and two months into the initial crisis that began in Thailand when Mahathir settled on instituting capital controls. The ringgit had fallen by 34 percent against the dollar since Malaysia's neighbor Thailand had let the baht float on July 2, 1997. It is not hard to understand that substantial capital took flight from Malaysia well before the controls were imposed.

Economists have always had mixed feeling about capital controls. Japan's Sakakibara supported them before and after the fact: "Malaysia's regulation was the right choice under the circumstances."[6]

Capital controls are not new, of course. The debate over controls was pertinent to the construction of the Bretton Woods system of fixed exchange rates in 1944. John Maynard Keynes, himself a delegate to the Bretton Woods conference in 1944, once proclaimed the virtues of the new system, including that it would be "not merely as a feature of the transition but as a permanent arrangement, the plan accords every member government the explicit right to control all capital movements. What used to be heresy is now endorsed as orthodoxy."[7]

There are any number of conservative, market-oriented economists who regard capital controls as unacceptable and dangerous. Merton Miller commented directly on Malaysia:

> For countries like Malaysia, moreover, and much of East Asia as well, convertibility restrictions run the very real danger of inhibiting the inflow of foreign investment funds. Those foreign inflows supplement internal sources of savings and capital, not sufficient by themselves, to sustain rapid growth. Why then did Malaysia take those risks, I asked an old friend of mine, a distinguished Malaysian economist who, for obvious reasons, prefers to remain anonymous.... Malaysia's policy, I teased him, reminded me of the lobster traps in New England, where I grew up. The trap entices lobsters to swim in; but once in, they cannot swim out. People are smarter than lobsters, however, I warned my friend. If you tell them they can't get out, they won't swim in.[8]

Great attention focused on Malaysia at the approach of the one-year anniversary of its capital controls because Mahathir had promised to lift the restrictions on that day. Japan had been persuaded to come to Malaysia's aid by advancing a billion-dollar swaps facility designed to meet any hemorrhaging of capital once the controls were lifted.

The big day, September 1, 1999, came and went with no apparent meltdown or capital flight from Malaysia. Malaysia claimed that it had been vindicated and Mahathir began to brag that he had found "a kinder, gentler way" by comparison to what the IMF had proposed for his country. A few days later, the *New York Times* went to press with a headline: "Malaysia Wins Its Economic Gamble."[9]

The concept began to gain acceptance that capital controls had been a success in Malaysia because they granted the beleaguered economy with "breathing room," meaning a chance to catch its breath and restructure before it had to face the economic realities that international markets were waiting to impose. But how successful were capital controls in Malaysia? Had Mahathir demonstrated that selective use of capital controls were a worthwhile policy tool?

What the *New York Times* and a good many others failed to understand were the implications of Malaysia's having retained its fixed exchange rate for the ringgit at the old rate of 3.800 to the dollar. Meanwhile, all the nations in the region that were competing with Malaysia, the same ones that had collapsed in the summer of 1997, had witnessed their exchange rates swing into dramatic recovery against the dollar in the course of the same one-year period (Thai baht +9 percent, Indonesian rupiah +45 percent, Korea won +14 percent). Most important of all was the Japanese yen that appreciated by 27 percent against the dollar in the period.

Thus it was that Malaysia, through this sleight of hand, effectively devalued against its primary Asian trading partners. Not surprisingly, Malaysia experienced an export boom, which is the primary reason why that country looked good to the rest of the world before and after the controls were lifted. Moreover, anyone who wanted to take money out of Malaysia had to convert ringgits at an artificially low exchange rate; this foreign exchange "tax" is the surviving component of the Malaysian capital controls.

The IMF was badly abused over the apparent success of the Malaysian capital controls. In response, the Fund wrote

[We have examined] the differences in Malaysia's policy approach and in the macroeconomic outcomes to date. [We] conclude that, with the exception of the capital controls, the policies implemented in Malaysia were broadly similar to those in the other crisis countries. Likewise, while yield spreads for Malaysia have remained higher, relative to Korea and Thailand, than before the imposition of controls, and capital inflows have been relatively subdued, macro-economic developments to date in Malaysia and other crisis countries have been broadly similar, making it difficult to identify, at least in the short time that has elapsed since the imposition of the controls, to identify any effects that they may have had. This may be considered not altogether surprising, both because capital outflows had abated markedly by the time the controls were imposed, and because the effects of such controls can usually be judged only over a longer period.[10]

For as long as Mahathir is remembered, the controls, along with his ranting at imaginary currency speculators whom he accused of bringing his country down, will be brought to mind.

But with Mahathir or without him, the debate on capital controls can dependably be expected to rage on into the future.

The dangerous part of the Malaysian experiment is that other nations might someday attempt to follow what Mahathir did. As Miller wrote, investors are not going to commit capital if there is a possibility that they will get trapped with no exit. There are profound implications for all emerging market countries. If investors begin to build the possibility of the imposition of capital controls into their financial calculations, these nations will become saddled with paying a risk premium to attract development capital.

Paul Krugman gave an objective account of the Asian situation a few days before the controls were lifted in September 1999:

> To the extent that Asia is recovering, no one can claim the credit. The amazing thing to me—if you leave Indonesia out—is how similar the performances are, regardless of the policies. Korea took the IMF's advice and it's bouncing back, Thailand took the IMF's advice and it starting to come back, Malaysia defied the IMF and did everything the IMF

told it not to—it's coming back fast. Everybody's contemplating success for their polices: Mahathir said he did it, the IMF said they did it. The truth is the natural resilience of the economies did it.[11]

What to Do about the IMF

THE INTERNATIONAL MONETARY Fund was created by the Allied countries at the end of the Second World War for the purpose of enabling participating Bretton Woods nations to maintain the newly created system of fixed exchange rates. When Bretton Woods collapsed in 1973, the IMF was deprived of its *raison d'être* because the dollar became a floating currency. By all rights, the IMF ought to have been abolished. Instead, the Fund managed to reinvent itself as a lender of last resort to nations and the fixer of financial breakdowns. It is endowed with a prodigious balance sheet and gargantuan staff (it had approximately 1,000 economists on the payroll in the year 2000). In its new role, the Fund found itself at the crux of every crisis that plagued the 1990s starting with the Mexican crisis of 1994–95.

The mere existence of an international body engaged in such efforts raised the possibility that the Fund was engendering moral hazard. As Milton Friedman wrote, "The IMF has been a destabilizing factor in East Asia, not so much because of the conditions it imposed on clients, whether good or bad, as by sheltering private financial institutions from the consequences of bad investments. It is not too much to say that had there been no IMF, there would have been no East Asia crisis, though countries might have had internal crises—as with Japan, whose troubles cannot be blamed on the IMF."[12]

Two views emerged in the 1990s in the United States concerning the IMF. By one, the IMF had been acting like a good samaritan to countries that had suddenly found themselves engulfed in financial crisis. Reason alone would suggest that some of its programs would be successful but others not. The situations that the IMF had chosen to confront were of exceeding difficulty. Having to deal with financial crisis is like trying to combat a rapidly spreading natural disaster. That mistakes are made in the heat of the moment is understandable. Moreover, in the words of Lawrence Summers, then deputy secretary of the treasury, "The IMF is indispensable and cheap at the price. Every dollar the United States puts into the IMF leverages four of five dollars from the rest of the world. Yet it does not cost the taxpayer once cent. And it does not add to the federal deficit."[13]

The Clinton treasury officials publicly exhibited complete faith in the IMF throughout the crises of the 1990s. The U.S. Treasury supported, if not directed, the Fund's efforts in Southeast Asia, Brazil, and Russia. Yet the Administration routinely encountered hostility from the Congress for what was seen as its unofficial partnership with the IMF. In response, Rubin and Summers advanced the absurd argument cited above, that the IMF had not cost the taxpayers "one cent."

The other view of the IMF was equally dogmatic. Summers's remarks cited earlier actually were in rebuttal to former Secretary of State George Shultz's congressional testimony the preceding day that the IMF should be abolished. Shultz and two other like-minded public figures solemnly decreed in a *Wall Street Journal* essay that "The IMF is ineffective, unnecessary, and obsolete. We do not need another IMF, as Mr. Soros recommends. Once the Asian crisis is over, we should abolish the one we have."[14] To appreciate the gravity of these remarks consider who the authors were. George Shultz was secretary of state under President Ronald Reagan and secretary of the treasury under President Richard Nixon; William E. Simon was secretary of the treasury under Presidents Richard Nixon and Gerald Ford; Walter B. Wriston is the retired chairman and CEO of Citicorp/Citibank. Soros's suggestion is contained in a letter that will be addressed below.

The first large-scale instance of its metamorphosis was when newly appointed Treasury Secretary Robert Rubin involved the IMF in a $17.5 billion dollar assistance program for Mexico in 1995. To conservatives like Shultz, the Mexican package was an example of runaway government:

I use the recent Mexican crisis as an example. The administration, you recall, proposed a very large-scale bailout. And they took that to Congress, and that proposal was debated around for several weeks and it became apparent that Congress would not act on it. It was not in favor of it. So the Administration then took that proposal off the table, and in an unprecedented, let me underline unprecedented move, used the Exchange Stabilization Fund that the Secretary of the Treasury has at his disposal. It had never been used like this before. And then with I think a $17.5 billion IMF commitment—the IMF had never operated on that scale before—put forward this very large Mexican bailout. Now aside from a legitimate debate about what that bailout did or did not do, it seems to me that there is a question of governance here: money that the Congress decided it did not wish to authorize and appropriate for an identified purpose was, through the IMF and through this funding by the Treasury, used in an unprecedented way by the Administration. I was always taught that the Constitution said something like you cannot spend money unless it is authorized and appropriated. So there are some real issues of governance here.[15]

A visibly frustrated George Shultz asked rhetorically, before Congress: "I personally wonder where it is going, where does Mr. Camdessus think he is taking us."[16]

Conservative ire reached its boiling point when the IMF, after having become so deeply involved in mopping up the Asian crisis, began to advance what seemed like endless amounts of dollars to Russia. The worst suspicions were confirmed when billions of dollars of IMF funds supplied to the Russian Central Bank vanished from sight in 1998. The IMF looked negligent, if not out of control.

Perhaps even more troubling was the question of who exactly was the IMF assisting, as Anna Schwartz would ask:

For whose benefit was the Mexican rescue arranged? Is there any doubt that the loan package was designed to pay dollars to Americans and other nationals who invested in

Tesobonos and Cetes and dollar-denominated loans to Mexican nonfinancial firms? Is that the reason emergency loans are needed? To eliminate risk from investment in high-yielding foreign assets? [17]

To the great aggravation of its client states, the IMF's special funding to meet the crises of the 1990s was accompanied by demands for reforms that often cut right through the economy if not the society. It began to be questioned just how good a job the IMF was doing for the countries that it was assisting. One critic was Japan's Eisuke Sakakibara who asserted in 1999 that IMF policy in Southeast Asia had been incorrectly focused toward solving the immediate balance of payments crisis by advocating tight monetary policy without considering the consequences to the internal economy. Also, Sakakibara was critical of the IMF's having been too ambitious with demands for reforms on the local levels.[18]

Joseph Stiglitz, a respected economics professor at Stanford University who served as chief economist at the World Bank from 1997 to 2000, has made some of the most stinging comments about the IMF's crisis management policies: "Every recession eventually ends. All the IMF did was make East Asia's recessions deeper, longer, and harder."[19]

Stiglitz wrote that the principal failings of the IMF in Asia was that it viewed that the crisis should be handled the same way as the 1980s financial panic in Latin America, when "bloated public deficits and loose monetary policies led to runaway inflation. There, the IMF had correctly imposed fiscal austerity (balanced budgets) and tighter monetary policies, demanding that governments pursue those policies as a precondition for receiving aid. So, in 1997, the IMF imposed the same demands on Thailand."[20]

However, as Stiglitz pointed out, the Asian nations were not running budget deficits at the time of the crisis and some of them were already running tight monetary policy.

Conservatives worry that the IMF's role as the world's crisis manager is showing signs of becoming permanent. One sign was a proposal made by Rubin advocating private sector burden sharing.

Rubin may have been responding to charges like those quoted above from Schwartz that Wall Street was getting bailed out, not the poor of Mexico or of Asia. His concept would require that trust indentures of emerging market bond issues contain contractual obligations binding the owner of the instrument to participate financially in any restructuring programs for the issuer country if the need ever came.

Rubin's idea got backing from a task force at the Council on Foreign Relations. The council was motivated from the standpoint of how future bailouts, or debt restructuring programs, could be more efficiently arranged:

> To increase the orderliness and timeliness of debt rescheduling, all countries—including the G-7 countries—should commit to including "collective actions clauses" in their sovereign bond contracts and to requiring that such clauses be present in all new sovereign bonds issued and traded in their markets.[21]

In effect, Rubin and the council proposed their own variety of what in the mergers and acquisitions field is called a *poison pill* for insertion into sovereign debt instruments. Yet the obvious questions were never addressed, such as by how much that would constrict the flow of funds to those nations or by how much their cost of financing would rise.

George Soros shocked conservatives with his own idea on how IMF-like crisis management ought to be expanded:

> I propose setting up an International Credit Insurance Corporation as a sister institution to the IMF. This new authority would guarantee international loans for a modest fee. The borrowing countries would be obliged to provide data on all borrowings, public or private, insured or not. This would enable the authority to set a ceiling on the amounts it is willing to insure.... The authority would base its judgment not only on the amount of credit outstanding, but also on the macroeconomic conditions in the countries concerned.[22]

As for who would run such an organization, Soros went on to write:

> How can bureaucrats know better than those who take risks for their own account? The answer is that the technocrats running the proposed international authority would be charged with maintaining macroeconomic balance, while the technocrats in charge of the banks are guided by profit considerations.[23]

It didn't take long for this idea to attract some fairly heavy fire. Shultz, Simon, and Wriston attacked it thus:

> What should we do about the problem? We certainly shouldn't follow the advice of George Soros, a well-known figure in the international currency markets, who has called for the creation of a new international credit insurance corporation to be underwritten by taxpayers of member countries. The new institution, which would operate in tandem with the IMF, would guarantee international loans up to a point deemed safe by the bureaucrats running the organization. "The private sector is ill-suited to allocate international credit," Mr. Soros writes in *The Financial Times*. "It provides either too little or too much. It does not have the information with which to form a balanced judgment." When will we ever learn? This appalling comment is exactly the opposite of the truth. The protected markets, not the open ones, are in trouble. Only the market, with its millions of interested participants, is capable of generating the information needed to make sound financial decisions and to allocate credit (or any other resource) efficiently and rationally.[24]

Despite so much flak being directed at the IMF, it would be a mistake to underestimate the strength of its incumbency. That was learned the hard way by the bipartisan International Financial Institutions Advisory Commission, coheaded by Carnegie Mellon

University economist Allan Meltzer, that was highly critical of the IMF. The commission's report, which was approved by a majority vote of its members with some dissension, contained this language:

> There is little evidence that the IMF efforts have prevent-
> ed the periodic financial crises that can set back growth for
> many years. IMF programs and prescriptions frequently
> delay necessary adjustments to emerging problems, result-
> ing in a protracted period of growth suppression. Reform
> of this system is essential not only for growth and improved
> living standards in developing countries, but also to avoid
> the periodic crises that can threaten worldwide financial
> stability.[25]

In other places, the commission appeared to be pulling its punches:

> Nor do we mean to suggest that the IMF always fails in it
> mission.... The Commission also recognizes many examples
> of the IMF's success in encouraging beneficial policies.[26]

But the commission was flying its true colors when it advocat-ed drastic reductions in the powers of the IMF, as well as for other supranational institutions like the World Bank. The stripped-down IMF, according to the commission, would have three functions, the first being "to act as a quasi-lender of last resort to solvent emerging economies providing short-term liquidity assistance to countries in need."[27] The IMF's lending would be restricted to short-term loans of 120 days with only one allowable rollover. Borrowing countries would have to pay "penalty rates" of interest. The other two, less controversial IMF activities would be to collect and publish financial data from member countries and to provide advice, but not impose conditions.

In spite of all of the criticism that the Meltzer Commission heaped on the IMF, and nobody has ever done that better, it stopped short of calling for abolition of the institution. Perhaps the commission had a practical insight. Why not keep the IMF in a reduced, if not hobbled form, because if the IMF were completely disbanded, its likeness would surely be reinvented on the occasion of the next financial crisis.

Meltzer and his Commission received immediate criticism, rejection, and ridicule.[28] Treasury Secretary Summers implicitly appeared to flatly reject the Commission's recommendations. On April 15, 2000, the IMF received a vote of confidence from the Group of Seven Industrialized Countries (G7) finance ministers and central bankers: "Preventing crises and supporting the establishment of a solid foundation for sustainable growth are at the core of the IMF's work."[29]

Shultz may have been right in principle, that the IMF should be abolished, and Meltzer may have been right in practice, that the IMF should be stripped down. Either way, it is going to take a colossal effort to convince Washington to yield to the basic thesis, no matter how worthy, that crisis nations should look after themselves and that the private sector should be free to settle its own disputes with distressed and indebted nations.

Chapter Nine

Conclusions

ADVOCATES OF FINANCIAL reform say that the 1990s and earlier periods teach that the foreign exchange market is episodically out of control and that capital flows can destabilize world markets, behaving more like wrecking balls than pendulums, in Soros's words. Consequently, the whole international monetary system needs redesign and supranational institutions like the IMF must be permanently and deeply involved with running the world economy.

These positions must be tempered by the study of the countries that have suffered the sharpest reversals of fortune in the 1990s. These same nations had dangerous domestic financial policies in place for a significant time before they descended into crisis. Moreover, when crisis did erupt, the government's response often exacerbated their problems.

The picture of history that is being told by most, but not all, of the would-be reformers lacks the essential recognition that financial crisis is mostly homegrown, not imported, and that it is usually preventable with modification of bad financial policies. By analogy, one could imagine a large, complex telephone network that is subject to intermittent failures. The reformers have concluded that the problem must be with the master switching circuitry, the analogue of the international capital market, before having taken a close look at the subscriber's kitchen wall phone, the parallel for domestic financial policies.

The common denominator in practically every crisis in the 1990s was an experiment with a fixed foreign exchange rate regime. Fixed foreign exchange regimes are founded on the promise of currency stability. Some of them have survived for years and have basked in their apparent success. Yet so many have ended in spectacular turmoil that one has to wonder if there isn't an inevitable day of reckoning for all pegged exchange rate currencies. What is often misunderstood is that fixed exchange rate systems, in and of themselves, have the power to attract foreign capital, provided that they reflect an appearance of permanence. They incubate the buildup of massive disequilibrium positions in the foreign exchange and fixed income markets. The famous carry trade, in which investors have taken leveraged positions in stabilized, high-yielding foreign currencies, is one example. Another is the phenomenon of foreign currency denominated debt accumulation in countries with fixed exchange rates. Both are motivated by the illusion that the fixed exchange rate regime will be permanent. If the day comes when the market suspects otherwise, a ferocious adjustment process can take place at a moment's notice when practically everyone inside and outside of the country tries to dump their exposure to the local currency.

The '90s, far from being an indictment of the international financial system, are a striking reminder of how potentially destructive fixed exchange rate regimes can be. Equally striking is the fact that once broken fixed exchange rate systems were replaced with floating regimes, no further disruptions occurred.

But while faulty exchange rate systems have proved to be financially explosive, other, deeper, and potentially more malignant factors can work to retard the natural growth of an economy. Chief among these are central planning and high degrees of government guidance of the private sector, both of which are prone to eventual economic disappointment. This was the root of the troubles in Japan, Malaysia, Indonesia, and South Korea, to mention a few examples.

Not exempt from this criticism is the IMF. If central planning at the local level is bound to fail, then why would central planning from an institution located in Washington, D.C. and funded from government sources do any better at trying to reform broken economies? The record of the IMF is mixed at best, at least at the time that this book is being written. Among the countries that received IMF aid and adopted IMF programs it appears that Russia and Indonesia are massive failures while Thailand and South Korea can say recovery is at hand.

As one studies these countries one appreciates how often investment spending is confused with true economic growth. Countries that have huge savings or large inflows of foreign investment capital are not necessarily marching toward prosperity. Instead, they may be courting economic disaster. Nobody would doubt that an individual could save income, borrow money from a bank, and then go broke by funneling all of that capital into a bad investment. The same thing can happen on the national level. National savings and foreign investment can be squandered on poorly conceived and inefficiently executed development projects, but the odds of that occurring are multiplied when central planners or ministry bureaucrats are active in the countrywide investment planning process.

Current account deficits by themselves have been blamed for a great deal of economic dislocation. But the exact mechanism by which a deficit can be dangerous is not always fully understood. A current account deficit means nothing more than that a country is importing more foreign goods and services than it is exporting. It is axiomatic that this country be the net importer of foreign capital, which it needs in order to bridge the aforementioned trade gap. For the most part, economists traditionally have had a prejudice against current account deficit economies. There is a general preconception that the value of a currency will be inversely related to the country's current account position. Yet there may be nothing wrong with the idea of a country importing capital, even massive amounts of capital, if the money is being put to good use. The key to whether or not a current account deficit is beneficial or pernicious is whether the associated investments being funded are economically worthwhile. A rapidly developing country where genuine wealth is being created through good investments in infrastructure, industry, and human capital can support a current account deficit indefinitely.

The reef that Mexico and developing Asia struck in the 1990s after periods of phenomenal economic growth is that they were running sizeable current account deficits at a time when their domestic investment opportunities were faltering. Some part of this has to be blamed on government planners who were steering their economies by the rear-view mirrors of former economic successes. Mexico could not sustain its economic boom and began to develop severe political problems. Asia became overinvested in heavy industry directed at export markets. Meanwhile the financial sectors in both Mexico and Asia, which had the appearance of thriving in former times, began to show signs of duress.

The final element in Mexico and Asia's combustible mixture was their fixed exchange rate and managed exchange rate systems. The rough picture of what took down Mexico, Southeast Asia, and South Korea can be assembled from the previous chapters. At the same time that growth prospects began to wane, capital flows associated with massive current account deficits started to reverse. Thereupon, massive portfolio positions in the local currency began to be liquidated, and local investors who had borrowed in foreign currencies—and this was mainly short-term borrowing—tried to hedge by selling the local currency.

In each case the government's actions immediately before and during the crisis made things worse. The Mexican government substituted dollar-linked tesobono bonds for its peso-denominated debt. This move temporarily mollified foreign investors but it created a leveraged position that was long the peso and short the dollar on the government's books. Two and a half years later, Thailand tried to avert its own currency crisis by buying its own currency in the forward foreign exchange market at prices that gave a heavy subsidy to anyone who wanted to express a negative view on the baht. Indonesia wasted precious time and money trying to halt the fall in the rupiah with intervention and by dallying over whether or not to accept the IMF's emergency packages. Malaysia panicked domestic and foreign investors who correctly feared the imposition of capital controls when they were confronted with the government's invective against the foreign exchange market. Finally, South Korea effectively looted its own central bank by placing official reserves in domestic banks for immediate relending to domestic corporations that were going to fail in any event.

Other major errors in macroeconomic policy led to economic reversals in this decade. Japan has been plagued by significant blunders in monetary policy starting with its ill-advised participation in the Plaza Accord dollar intervention in 1985. At that time, the Bank of Japan responded procyclically with expansionary monetary policy to the strengthening of the yen, which it, as a Plaza Accord participant, had partially caused. Hence the BOJ can be accused of having supplied excess liquidity in the early stages of the bubble economy. Later, after the bubble burst, the BOJ would spend the entire 1990s erring in the opposite direction by allowing monetary aggregates to fall to depression-inducing levels of growth.

The fact that exchange rates matter so much is an indication of the seriousness with which any nation should approach its choice of a foreign exchange regime. Some economists, politicians, and journalists have taken the bizarre stand that the currency crises of the 1990s invalidate the concept of having freely floating exchange rates. This could not be more erroneous because all of the crises occurred in exchange rate regimes that were either fixed, nearly fixed, or at least intensively managed.

Some economists argue that it does not make economic sense for very small countries to go to the trouble of maintaining a separate floating exchange rate, especially where there is a great degree of openness to world trade. For these countries, there appear to be only two systems that could withstand the test of time. One is the currency board system, and the other is outright dollarization. The common drawback is that the country that goes forward with either a currency board or dollarization has to live with another country's monetary policy. Whatever monetary policy the reserve currency's central banks sets for its own country applies directly to other countries that have dollarized and approximately to countries that operate currency boards. Also, experience with Hong Kong and Argentina shows that a country adopting a currency board is not as immune to crisis as they might hope.

The case has been made here that domestic financial policy is of paramount issue in understanding financial crisis. Still, consideration was given, and large nations should note, that some attribution could be made to the indirect consequences of large-scale macroeconomic policies. The U.S. strong-dollar policy orchestrated by U.S. Treasury Secretary Robert Rubin in the mid-1990s damaged the Asian nations that were highly indebted in dollar terms. Moreover, supporting a strong dollar meant trying to depress the Japanese yen, a factor that conferred an artificial trade advantage on Japan and contributed to the hollowing out of the export markets for the Asian tiger nations. Going back further in time, the U.S. Federal Reserve also could be examined for the indirect damage that it did to the Mexican economy in 1994 and 1995 when it embarked on its anti-inflationary tight monetary policy. Mexico before December 1994 had the peso pegged to the dollar. The question for the large countries, the United States, core Europe under the European Monetary System, and Japan is whether they give sufficient consideration to what goes on outside their borders when they make policy.

It is hoped that the historical examination of the events of the '90s presented in this book debunks many accounts that constitute the popular legacy of the financial crises. For example, hedge funds and other speculators were shown not to have caused the Southeast Asian crisis of 1997. Nor did they coordinate attacks on Hong Kong in 1997 and 1998.

Another widely held piece of fiction is that Malaysia showed the world a "kinder, gentler" alternative to freely floating exchange rates, and to the IMF, with its celebrated imposition of capital controls. Yet the Malaysian capital controls were imposed fourteen months after the outbreak of the crisis, well after capital flight had taken place—Malaysia locked the barn door after the horses had bolted. Moreover, what rejuvenation of Malaysia took place since the crisis came from a surge in exports that can be attributed to the devaluation in the ringgit and revaluation in the yen and some other Southeast Asian currencies. Hence Malaysia is no exception to the general rule that capital controls are universally to be eschewed.

None of what has been written in this book should be seen as denying that there is an important role for wise and tempered leadership and even occasional national crisis management in special circumstances. Nations need good leaders. Some central banks and finance ministers have been successful in managing financial crises, though this is a relatively rare phenomenon. The highest degree of circumspection and restraint are required when intervention into a private sector crisis is being considered. It must be remembered too that the effects can be permanent because government actions can set precedents that later serve to justify future forays into the private sector's markets.

Overall, a great danger to the world's economic well-being is that the level of tolerance for short-term economic disappointment is too low and the expectation for how well adjustments to the market economy can perform is too high, if not outright unrealistic.

Notes

Chapter 1

1. Eisuke Sakakibara quoted in "What to Do about Asia," *BusinessWeek*, January 26, 1998, 28.

2. Krugman, "Asia's Miracle," 62–78.

3. Keynes, xvi–xvii.

4. The United Nations, Report of the Task Force of the Executive Committee on Economic and Social Affairs, "Towards a New International Financial Architecture," New York, January 21, 1999, 1.

5. Kim Dae-Jung quoted by AFX-Asia, November 28, 1999.

6. George Soros, excerpt from "The Crisis of Global Capitalism" adapted from Soros's prepared testimony to the U.S. House of Representatives Committee on Banking and Financial services on September 15, 1998, *Asian Wall Street Journal*, September 16, 1998.

7. Richard Wolfee, "Soros Warns of Risk to Free Trade," *Financial Times*, September 16, 1998.

8. Gerhard Schröder quoted in David DeRosa, "Germany's Schröder Is Dreaming of Bretton Woods," Bloomberg News, January 20, 1999.

9. Bill Clinton, excerpt from Steven K. Beckner, "Clinton: Prepares Way For Proposals For Financial Architecture Reforms," April 20, 1999, *Market News International*.

10. "Plain Talk About On-Line Investing," by Chairman Arthur Levitt U.S. Securities and Exchange Commission at the National Press Club, Washington, D.C., May 4, 1999.

11. Larry Summers, "In the Wake of Wall Street's Crash; Monday Wasn't So Black," *The New York Times*, October 21, 1987, A35.

12. Franklin D. Roosevelt, First Inaugural Address, March 4, 1933.

13. Michael Molinski, "Malaysian Leader Says World May Need Fixed Exchange," Bloomberg News, September 28, 1999.

14. Mahathir bin Mohamad, A22.

15. Henry Morgenthau, Closing address to the Bretton Woods Conference, Bretton Woods, New Hampshire, July 22, 1944.

16. Eisuke Sakakibara, excerpted from "Japan Calls for More Control Over Markets," *Asian Wall Street Journal*, January 25, 1999.

17. Alan Greenspan made some interesting remarks about volatility in exchange rates and its supposedly deleterious effects on the world economy in a speech "Remarks on the International Financial System" on November 5, 1998. The background is that dollar/yen had made a massive move downward in the previous month:

> Last month's unprecedented three-day weakening in the dollar, rela-
> tive to the yen, reportedly as a consequence of a large scale unwind-
> ing of the so-called yen carry trade, has not induced spasms in the
> U.S. financial markets, nor for that matter in Japan, despite its severe
> banking problems.

Chapter 2

1. Kahn may have been the coiner of the term *Asian century* although he had reservations about the term. Kahn, *Japanese Superstate*, 2.

2. Ibid., 101.

3. Ibid., 130.

4. Ibid., ix.

5. Ibid., 102-103.

6. Katz, 89-90.

7. Ibid., 3-4.

8. Kahn, *Japanese Superstate*, 86.

9. Ibid., 86.

10. According to the IMF publication *World Economic Outlook*, October 1998, there have been six major economic stimulus packages in the 1990s. Total spending was as follows:

	Yen (Trillions)	Percent of GDP
August 1992	10.7	2.3
April 1993	13.2	2.8
September 1993	6.2	1.3
February 1994	15.3	3.2
September 1995	14.2	3.0
April 1998	16.7	3.3

The largest portion of each package was direct public investment projects, but there was also money spent on land purchases, tax reductions, and increased lending to the Housing and Loan Corporation. International Monetary Fund, *World Economic Outlook* (October 1998), 115.

Mühleisen (2000) argues that the "real water" content, a phrase that refers to genuine new commitments for government spending, was considerable. However, he assigns more responsibility for the expansion in budget deficit to a drop in the tax elasticity than to the stimulus spending. Tax elasticity measures how tax revenue changes in response to changes in economic growth.

11. International Monetary Fund, *World Economic Outlook*, October 1999, 82.

12. Krugman, "Asia's Miracle," 73.

13. Ibid., 67.

14. Ibid., 74-75.

15. Kahn, *Japanese Superstate*, 80.

16. Miller, "Laws of Economics," 181.

17. Miller, "Laws of Economics," contains similar themes linking the Plaza intervention to the bubble economy.

18. Funabashi, 23 cites the Federal Reserve Bank of New York, *Quarterly Review*, no. 10 (Winter 1985–1986): 47.

19. See Funabashi, Dobson, Dominguez and Frankel, and Takagi.

20. Ramaswamy and Samiei (2000) find evidence that the Bank of Japan's interventions did have a small but persistent impact on dollar/yen in the period 1995–1999 despite the practice of sterilization: "The paper argues that sterilized interventions have been effective primarily because they influence market participants' expectations of economic fundamentals and the stance of monetary policy, and also erode bandwagon effects."

21. Milton Friedman in his December 17, 1997 editorial "R_x for Japan: Back to the Future," in the *Wall Street Journal* wrote:

> At the Louvre conference in February 1987, the assembled leaders agreed to stabilize the foreign exchange value of the dollar. Japan, as its part of the deal, bought dollars, in the process creating yen. The resulting acceleration in monetary growth led to higher inflation, and, initially, to higher real growth. The most notable result was the "bubble economy," an explosion in the prices of land, stocks and other assets; the Nikkei stock index more than doubled in three years. The Bank of Japan reacted belatedly in 1990, reducing monetary growth to less than 3% from 13% in the first year of the new policy, and to negative rates in the second—too much of a good thing. Tight money was spectacularly effective; the stock market, and also nominal income growth, plunged.

22. Cargill, Hutchison, and Ito, 77.

23. Bank of Japan, "On Current Monetary Policy," September 21, 1999.

24. International Monetary Fund, "Japan's Crisis," 119.

25. Friedman and Schwartz, 299, 300.

26. Friedman, "R_x for Japan."

27. Miller, "Laws of Economics," 180.

Chapter 3

1. International Monetary Fund, "The ERM Crisis," 49.

2. International Monetary Fund, "Prologue to the ERM Crisis," 10.

3. See David F. DeRosa (1996) *Managing Foreign Exchange Risk*, Chicago: Irwin, 1996 and David F. DeRosa (2000) *Options on Foreign Exchange, sec-*

ond edition, New York: Wiley, for discussions of forward swaps and interest parity theorem.

4. See DeRosa (1996) for discussion of the composition of the ECU and additional history of the Exchange Rate Mechanism.

5. George Soros, interview with Anatole Kaletsky, *The Times,* October 26, 1992.

6. Ibid.

7. International Monetary Fund, "Prologue to the ERM Crisis," 8, 10.

8. Ibid.

9. Temperton, 16.

10. Stephen Fidler, Ivo Dawnay, Peter March, Quentin Peel, James Blitz, Emma Tucker, David Marsh, and Tracy Corrigan, "Sterling Was Being Sold Like Water Running Out of a Tap," *Financial Times,* September 19, 1992.

11. Kathleen Morris, "Global 'Money Funds' Take a Fall," *Mutual Fund Watch,* October 27, 1992.

12. Gil-Díaz and Carstens, 189.

13. Froot and McBrady, 13.

14. Ibid., 14.

15. Measured in millions of U.S. dollars, Mexico's current account deficit was:

1987	+2.9	1991	-14.9
1988	-3.8	1992	-24.8
1989	-6.1	1993	-23.4
1990	-7.5	1994	-29.5

Source: Froot and McBrady, 16.

16. As quoted in Froot and McBrady, 3-4.

17. Dornbusch, "The Folly," 127-128.

18. It is the stated practice of the U.S. Federal Reserve Board to conduct monetary policy with an eye solely toward what it believes is in the best interest of the United States. Foreign concerns in and of themselves are irrelevant, as Alan Greenspan announced in a warning to countries considering dollarizing:

> Our basic policy—our basic monetary policy—does take into consideration what is gong on in the rest of the world largely because the rest of the world does affect us. But what we do not do is focus on the well-being of the rest of the world as a whole as distinct from the well-being of the United States.

Testimony before the Senate Banking International Trade Subcommittee, Washington, D.C., April 22, 1999.

19. International Monetary Fund, "Mexican Peso Crisis," 57.

20. Ibid., 64.

21. Ibid.

22. Ibid.

23. The lenders were as follows: $9 billion came from the United States, $1 billion from Canada, $5 billion from the Bank for International Settlements, and $3 billion from U.S. banks.

24. The International Financial Institutions Advisory Committee report of March 2000 (sometimes referred to as the Meltzer Commission) reports that Mexico eventually used $13 billion of IMF money and $13.5 billion of U.S. official funds, 19.

Chapter 4

1. International Monetary Fund, "From Crisis to Recovery," 64. The IMF assumed that "in a non-crisis scenario output would have slowed down from rates in the 7–8.5 percent range prior to the crisis to 4 percent a year from 1997 onward—a hypothetical 'soft-landing' scenario."

2. Martin Peretz, "Capitalists Tools; Jiang Zemin; George Soros; Cambridge Diarist," *New Republic,* November 24, 1997.

3. President Suharto as quoted in *The Age,* Melbourne Online, February 12, 1998.

4. Lee J. Miller, "Soros Led Attack on the Baht, Says Thai Central Banker," Bloomberg News, June 24, 1997.

5. International Monetary Fund, "Asian Crisis," 50.

6. Stephen Brown, William N. Goetzmann, and James M. Park. The study used data from Capital International's Emerging Markets Fund, Everest Capital International, Ltd., Haussman Holdings, NV, Tiger Management's Jaguar Fund, NV, Orbis Global Equity Fund, Orbis Optimal Equity Growth, the Quantum Fund, Quantum Emerging Growth, Quasar Fund, NV, Quota Fund, NV, and the Swiss Bank Corporation's Currency Portfolio, Ltd.

7. Ibid.

8. Eisuke Sakakibara, as quoted in the *Australian Financial Review,* May 26, 1999.

9. The IMF points this out in its *World Economic Outlook*, Interim Assessment, December, 1997, 7.

> In terms of the U.S. dollar, the unification of the official and swap exchange rates of the yuan implied a devaluation of the official rate by 50 percent.... However, since by late 1993 a large proportion estimated to be 80 percent of foreign exchange transactions was already essentially carried out at the swap market rate, the effective depreciation is estimated to have been less than 10 percent.... Structural reforms in China may have been a more important source of improvements in its international cost competitiveness in recent years.

10. Eisuke Sakakibara quoted in the *Australian Financial Review,* May 26, 1999.

11. Bank of Thailand, 26. The Bank of Thailand described the regime as follows:

On November 2, 1984, the exchange rate of the baht vis-a-vis the US dollar was announced daily by the EEF Exchange Equalization Fund, which stood ready to buy and sell US dollars with commercial banks at the pre-announced rates from 8:30 a.m. till noon. On November 5, 1984, the baht was devalued by 15 percent relative to the US dollar in order to reduce the problem of trade deficits.

12. Ibid., 24.

13. Ibid., 25.

14. Stanley Druckenmiller as quoted in Henderson, 105.

15. David DeRosa as quoted in Michael R. Sessit and Laura Jereski, "Traders Burnt in Thailand's Battle of the Baht," *Wall Street Journal,* May 22, 1997, C1.

16. Bank of Thailand, 25-27.

17. Paul Chertkow, "Outlook for the Thai baht Finance," Union Bank of Switzerland, April 3, 1997.

18. International Monetary Fund, "IMF Supported Programs," 21:

Short-term foreign borrowing was also encouraged by the governments through the provision of explicit or implicit guarantees, and in Thailand was even institutionalized and subsidized through the creation of the Bangkok International Bank Facility—a tax-exempt entity specialized in short-term borrowing from abroad and on-lending in the domestic market.

The Financial Stability Forum recognized this:

In Thailand, where the authorities adopted a more aggressive policy of attracting capital inflows and liberalized capital movements progressively during 1989–1992, the general thrust of the regulatory framework also did not differentiate between the maturity of capital flows per se. However, with the establishment of the Bangkok International Banking Facility (BIBF) in 1992 and the Provincial International Banking Facility (PIBF) in 1995, the government tried to improve the access of domestic entities to international capital markets through the banking system and gave BIBF banks tax incentives and preferential treatment in their operations. Some foreign banks saw the expansion of BIBF and PIBF as a step toward acquiring a full branch in Thailand, which may have also provided an incentive to build up business. Although a 7 percent cash reserve requirement was imposed on short-term nonresident baht accounts and new borrowing by commercial and BIBF banks in 1996 to limit short-term inflows, certain transactions were exempt (overdrafts and liabilities from currency trade, international trade financing, and nonresident deposits at BIBF banks). While it is difficult to quantify the magnitude of these exemptions, they may have served as potential channels for circumvention of the existing controls on short-term inflows. PIBF banks could obtain funding from overseas and extend credits both in baht and foreign currencies, while BIBF banks could take deposits or borrow from abroad and lend in foreign currencies in Thailand and abroad. (Financial Stability Forum, 53-54, footnote 21.)

19. David Gillen, Yoolim Lee, and Bill Austin, "How J.P. Morgan Got Tangled in a $500 Million Derivatives Debacle," Bloomberg News, January 24, 1999.

20. International Monetary Fund, "The Asian Crisis," 46:

Due to concerns about financial sector fragility, falling asset prices, and a slowing economy, the Bank of Thailand remained reluctant to raise interest rates, and the bulk of its interventions were carried out in the forward market. It is notable that during this period, three-and six-month interest differentials vis-à-vis the U.S. dollar rates were less than 3 percent so that, for example, the cost of taking a short position against the baht for three months was a mere three-quarters of 1 percentage point. In an environment of capital outflows, which made the possibility of an appreciation of the baht extremely remote, three-quarters of 1 percentage point represented the maximum perceived downside risk to an investor from taking such a position. The upside, on the other hand, in the event of a discrete devaluation was substantial. These contracts presented, therefore, very attractive one-way bets.

21. International Monetary Fund, "Asian Crisis," 46.

This point was also detected in a report issued by Morgan Stanley currency analyst Stephen Yung-li Jen entitled "An Agnostic View of the Baht," May 13, 1997:

I detect a major departure in the BOT's intervention strategy compared to the last episode. As we recall, the BOT opted to squeeze the interbank interest rates up to "punish" the speculators, and to disburse some of the burden to supply dollars to other players in the market who found the interest rate attractive. However, on Friday May 9, the BOT seemed to be the sole counterparty to most of the THB Thai baht offers. The decision to keep interest rates low may be an indication that the state of the financial sector is much more perilous than in February, and cannot withstand high interest rates, not even temporary spikes.

22. Bank of Thailand, 40.

23. International Monetary Fund, "Emerging Market Currency Crisis," 51.

24. Chuan Leekpai as quoted in the *Seattle Times*, November 24, 1997.

25. Keith B. Richburg, "Cashing In On Years in Power," *Washington Post*, May 22, 1998, A40.

26. Eisuke Sakakibara as quoted in "IMF's Indonesia Reforms Too Severe," special to *Yomiuri Shimbun*, December 10, 1999.

27. Ibid.

28. Ibid.

29. Dow Jones, "Suharto Considers Controversial Move to Peg Rupiah to Dollar," February 10, 1998.

30. Hanke, 30-33.

31. Michel Camdessus as quoted in David Sanger, "Longtime I.M.F. Director Resigns in Midterm," *New York Times*, November 10, 1999, C1.

32. Clifford and Engardio, 160.

33. Ibid.

34. Shalendra D. Sharma "Bitter Medicine for Sick Tigers: the IMF and Asia's Financial Crisis," *Pacific Rim Report* no. 8, April 1998, Center for the Pacific Rim, University of San Francisco.

35. David Clemens and Greg Feldberg, "Asia Economy: Bank Negara Not concerned About Account Deficit," Bloomberg News, February 23, 1995.

36. Bank Negara Malaysia, *Annual Report* 1996, 1, 3.

Chapter 5

1. Schwartz, "International Financial Crises."

2. HKMA Chief Executive Joseph Yam, speech given in Manila, January 5, 1999.

3. Schwartz, "International Financial Crises."

4. International Monetary Fund, "Fundamentals," 127.

5. International Monetary Fund, "Asian Crisis," 51.

6. The IMF had an interesting take on the "double play" in Hong Kong:
> An important point with regard to the logic of the strategy of simultaneously short selling the currency and equity markets that should be noted is that a foreign investor shorting the equity market needs to put up local currency carry that represents a long local currency position, which offsets any short foreign exchange position.
> Ibid.

7. Ibid.

8. The proper name for the currency of the People's Republic of China is the *renminbi*. The renminbi is divided into units of *yuan*, which is the term that market participants seem to prefer.

9. The drop in the S&P 500 contracts on October 27, 1997 exceeded that of the cash market. The former, as measured by the December front-month contract actually fell by 70 S&P 500 points.

10. Merton Miller as quoted in *USA Today*, October 28, 1997.

11. International Monetary Fund, "Asian Crisis," 51.

12. International Monetary Fund, "Republic of Korea," Statistical Appendix, Tables 23, 26.

13. Ibid.

14. International Monetary Fund, "Republic of Korea," 5-6.

15. See note 20, Chapter 4.

16. International Monetary Fund, "Asian Crisis," 55.

17. Kim Dae-Jung as quoted in *Chosun Ilbo*, December 23, 1997.

18. The Financial Stability Forum wrote the following about Korea's relaxation of its capital account regulations:

> In Korea the authorities followed a very gradual approach to capital account liberalization, beginning a cautious liberalization of capital inflows into the domestic securities market in the mid-1990s. Restrictions were removed on a range of transactions, including forwards, futures, currency options, and various forms of bonds and loans, but most transactions remained subject to prior approval. In 1992, non-residents were permitted limited access to the stock market, the types of securities that residents could issue abroad were expanded, and some forms of trade financing were deregulated, which led to a rapid growth in trade credits. The letter of the foreign exchange law did not entail a preferential treatment for short-term inflows, reflecting the authorities' view that short-term flows could hamper macroeconomic and financial market stability. However two aspects of the capital account regulations sought to control longer-term flows. First, the regulations favored foreign borrowing (and on-lending) by banks over direct access by corporations to international markets: foreign exchange banks were authorized to borrow abroad, but direct foreign borrowing by corporations (which would tend to be longer term) was controlled through prior approval requirements (with the exception of trade credits), which apparently discourage this kind of operation. Second, beginning in 1994, the ceiling on commercial banks' lending in foreign currency was lifted, but the Bank of Korea applied "window guidance" in the form of ceilings on commercials banks' medium and long-term borrowing from international markets. Those two regulations together, which encouraged greater intermediation through banks and forced banks seeking to borrow aboard to rely on short-term liabilities to finance long-term loans at home, indirectly encouraged recourse to short-term inflows.

Financial Stability Forum, 53 and footnote 20.

Chapter 6

1. Cooper.

2. Smith, vol. 2, 445.

3. Merry.

4. Jeremy Pelofsky, "IMF Lend To Russia, Even As It Fumes Over Central Bank Audit," Bloomberg News, July 29, 1999.

5. Stanley Fischer, "The Russian Economy at the Start of 1998," speech at the U.S.–Russian Symposium, Harvard University, January 9, 1998.

6. Stanley Fischer, "Learning the Lessons of Financial Crises: The roles of the Public and Private Sectors," Speech given before the Emerging Market Traders' Association, New York, December 9, 1999.

7. Letter from George Soros to the *Financial Times*, August 13, 1998.

8. In a statement dated August 17, 1998, the government of the Russian Federation declared that it was imposing temporary limitations on residents conducting foreign currency transactions that are capital in nature.

9. Laura Zelenko and Sabrina Tavernise, "Russia Delays Debt Swap As Foreigners Seen Most Hurt," Bloomberg News, August 19, 1998.

10. Cooper.

11. Robert Rubin quoted in David Sanger "Rubin Urges More Disclosure in Global Finance and Making Investors Pay Bailout Share," *New York Times*, October 2, 1998, A10.

12. George Soros "Joint Ventures, A Way to Make Perestroika Work," *Financial Times*, June 15, 1988.

13. Joseph Yam, Speech at A Symposium in Commemoration of 50 Years of Central Banking in the Philippines organised by the Bangko Sentral ng Pilipinas, "Causes of and Solutions to the Recent Financial Turmoil in the Asian Region," Manila, January 5, 1999.

14. Donald Tsang, as quoted in David Gillen and Jason Singer, "Betting Against the Hong Kong Dollar: A How-To Guide," Bloomberg News, August 17, 1998.

15. Alan Greenspan, testimony before the U.S. House Banking Committee, Washington, D.C., September 16, 1998.

16. Edwards, 197.

17. President's Working Group on Financial Markets, "Hedge Funds," 11.

18. Ibid.

19. Quoting from the President's Working Group on Financial Markets, "Hedge Funds," footnote 14, 10:

> Convergence trading also sometimes known as relative value arbitrage refers to the practice of taking offsetting positions in two related securities in the hopes that the price gap between the two securities will move in a more favorable direction. In some cases, there is an underlying reason why the favorable relative price changes are thought to be inevitable, while in others the trade is more purely speculative.

Dynamic hedging refers to the practice of managing nonlinear price risk exposure i.e. from options through active rebalancing of underlying positions, rather than by arranging offsetting hedges directly.

Loweinstein writes that LTCM's largest losses came from SWAPS trades and equity volatility positions, 234.

20. President's Working Group on Financial Markets, "Hedge Funds," 11-12.

21. Conversations with Roger Lowenstein, author of *When Genius Failed: The Rise and Fall of Long-Term Capital Management* (Random House, 2000).

22. Lewis, 42.

23. Edwards, 199.

24. Galbraith, 123-124.

25. Victor Haghani, Partner of LTCM, as quoted in Lewis, 42, 71.

26. Richard Leahy, Partner of LTCM, as quoted in Lewis, 42.

27. John Meriwether, as quoted in Lewis, 42.

28. Henry Kaufman, quoted in Robert Lenzner, "Archimedes on Wall Street," *Forbes* Magazine, October 19, 1998.

29. Edwards, 200.

30. Alan Greenspan, "Private-sector refinancing of the large hedge fund, Long-Term Capital Management," before the Committee on Banking and Financial Services, U.S. House of Representatives, Washington, D.C., October 1, 1998.

31. Statement by William J. McDonough, President Federal Reserve Bank of New York before the Committee on Banking and Financial Services, U.S. House of Representatives, Washington, D.C., October 1, 1998.

32. Lowenstein, 221.

Chapter 7

1. Federal Reserve Bank of Minneapolis.

2. Schwartz, "Currency Boards."

3. Friedman "How Asia Fell."

4. Culp, Hanke, and Miller.

5. Ibid.
   Hanke and Schuler.

6. Hanke and Schuler.

7. Hale.

8. Friedman, "How Asia Fell," 2.

9. Zarazaga.

10. Schuler makes the following distinctions as to the stages of dollarization: Unofficial dollarization often occurs in stages that correspond to the textbook functions of money as a store of value, means of payment, and unit of account. In the first stage, which economists sometimes call "asset substitution," people hold foreign bonds and deposits abroad as stores of value. They do so because they want to protect against losing wealth through inflation in the domestic currency or through outright confiscation that some countries have made. In the second stage of unofficial dollarization, which economists sometimes call "currency substitution," people hold large amounts of foreign-currency deposits in the domestic banking system if permitted, and later foreign notes, but as a means of payment and as stores of value. Wages, taxes, and everyday expenses such as groceries and electric bills continue to be

paid in domestic currency, but expensive items such as automobiles and houses are often paid in foreign currency. In the final stage of unofficial dollarization, people think in terms of foreign currency, and prices in domestic currency become indexed to the exchange rate.

11. See Porter and Judson.

12. Alan Greenspan, testimony before Senate Banking and International Trade Subcommittee, April 22, 1999.

13. Federal Reserve Bank of Minneapolis.

14. Catherine Hickley and Poilin Breathnach, Bloomberg News, "Germany Drops Call for Dollar, Euro, Yen Target Zones," January 27, 1999.

15. Schröder as quoted in David DeRosa, "Germany's Schroeder Is Dreaming of Bretton Woods," Bloomberg News, January 20, 1999. Schröder's remarks were given at a news conference in Berlin on January 14, 1999.

16. Poilin Breathnach, "Schröder Says G-7 Probing Cost of currency Bands," Bloomberg News, January 14, 1999.

17. Bergsten.

18. Ibid.

19. Alan Greenspan quoted in Judy Shelton, "Oskar Lafontaine: Off Target," Intellectualcapital.com, November 26, 1998.

20. Wim Duisenberg, "European Economic and Monetary Union—Latest Developments," Address to Second Asia-Europe Finance Ministers' Meeting, Frankfurt am Main, Germany, January 15, 1999.

21. Tobin.

22. Eichengreen, 88.

23. Canadian Parliament, Motion M-239, March 23, 1999.

24. Tobin.

25. Krugman, *Currencies and Crisis*, ix.

26. Friedman, "Flexible Exchange Rates," 158.

27. DeRosa, "Managing Foreign Exchange Risk," 43.

Chapter 8

1. Theil, vi.

2. Nassim Nicholas Taleb as quoted in *Derivatives Strategy*, January 1997.

3. Taleb, 87.

4. Bank for International Settlements, 41-42.

5. Stanley Druckenmiller as quoted in *The Economist*, May 6, 2000.

6. Sakakibara quoted in Keiko Kambara, "Keio's Sakakibara Says Global Markets Need Government 'Activation,'" Bloomberg News, October 1, 1999.

7. Attributed to John Maynard Keynes.

8. Miller, "Reflections."

9. Mark Landler, "Malaysia Wins Its Economic Gamble," was the headline on the *New York Times'* Web site but in the print edition the same story appeared

as "The Ostrich That Roared—Did Malaysia, Its Head in the Sand, Duck the Asian Crisis?" *New York Times*, September 4, 1999, C1.

10. International Monetary Fund, "Malaysia's Response," 54.

11. Alistair Hammond, "Krugman on Malaysian Capital Controls," Bloomberg News, August 25, 1999.

12. Milton Friedman, letter to the *Times*, London, October 12, 1998.

13. Lawrence Summers, Address to the Economic Strategy Institute, May 6, 1998.

14. George P. Shultz, William E. Simon, and Walter B. Wriston, "Who Needs the IMF?," *Wall Street Journal*, February 3, 1998.

15. Secretary George P. Shultz, Statement before the Joint Economic Committee, U.S. Congress, May 5, 1998.

16. Ibid.

17. Schwartz, "International Financial Crises."

18. Vivienne Stanton, "Sakakibara Says Currencies Should Be Pegged," Bloomberg News, March 26, 1999.

19. Joe Stiglitz, "What I Learned At the World Economic Crisis," *New Republic*, April 17, 2000.

20. Stiglitz, 60.

21. Council on Foreign Relations, 14.

22. George Soros, "Avoiding a Breakdown," *Financial Times*, December 30, 1997.

23. Ibid.

24. Shultz, Simon, and Wriston.

25. International Financial Institution Advisory Commission Report. The Commission balanced its criticism of the IMF with this: "A main reason for the IMF's modest success is that countries come to the IMF mainly when they have serious problems, often when they are in crisis."

26. Ibid.

27. Ibid.

28. Paul Krugman, "Errors of Commission," *New York Times*, March 8, 2000, A29.

29. G7 communiqué dated April 15, 2000.

References

Bank for International Settlements, *A Review of Financial Market Events in Autumn* 1998, Basel, Switzerland (October 1999).

Bank Negara Malaysia, *Annual Report*, Kuala Lumpur, Malaysia: 1998.

Bank of Thailand, "Focus on the Thai Crisis," *Quarterly Review* 2, No. 2 (April-June 1998).

Bergsten, C. Fred, "Alternative Exchange Rate Systems and Reform of the International Financial Architecture," Testimony before Committee on Banking and Financial Services, U.S. House of Representatives, May 21, 1999.

Brown, Stephen J., William N. Goetzmann, and James Park, *Hedge Funds and the Asian Currency Crisis of 1997*, Yale School of Management, International Center for Finance: May 1998.

Cargill, Thomas, Michael M. Hutchison, and Takatoshi Ito, *The Political Economy of Japanese Monetary Policy*. Cambridge, MA: MIT Press, 1997.

Clifford, Mark L. and Pete Engardio, *Meltdown: Asian's Boom, Bust, and Beyond*, Paramus, NJ: Prentice Hall, 2000.

Cooper, William H. "The Russian Financial Crisis: An Analysis of Trends, Causes, and Implications," *Congressional Research Service* (updated February 18, 1999).

Council on Foreign Relations, *Safeguarding Prosperity in a Global Financial System: The Future International Financial Architecture Report of an Independent Task Force Report*, New York: September 1999.

Culp, Christopher, L., Steve H. Hanke, and Merton Miller, "The Case for the Indonesian Currency Board," *Journal of Applied Corporate Finance* 11, No. 4 (Winter 1999).

DeRosa, David F. *Managing Foreign Exchange Risk*, Chicago: Irwin, 1996.

———, *Options on Foreign Exchange*, 2nd ed., New York: John Wiley & Sons, 2000.

Dobson, Wendy, *Economic Policy Coordination: Requiem or Prologue?* Washington, DC: Institute for International Economics, 1991.

Dominguez, Kathryn M. and Jeffrey A. Frankel, *Does Foreign Exchange Intervention Work?* Washington, DC: Institute for International

Economics, 1993.

Dornbusch, Rudiger, "Expectations and Exchange Rate Dynamics," *Journal of Political Economy* 84, No. 6 (December 1976): 1161-1176.

———, "The Folly, the Crash, and Beyond: Economic Policies and the Crisis," in *Mexico 1994: Anatomy of an Emerging Market Crash*, Washington, DC: Carnegie Endowment for International Peace, 1997.

Edwards, Franklin R., "Hedge Funds and the Collapse of Long-Term Capital Management," *Journal of Economic Prospectives* 13, no. 2 (Spring 1999).

Eichengreen, Barry, *Toward a New International Financial Architecture*, Washington, DC: Institute for International Economics, 1999.

Federal Reserve Bank of Minneapolis, "Interview with Stanley Fischer," *The Region*, 14, no. 4, December 1999.

Felix, David, "Financial Globalization vs. Free Trade: The Case for the Tobin Tax," UNCTAD discussion paper no. 108, New York: United Nations Conference on Trade and Development, 1995.

Financial Stability Forum, "Report of the Working Group on Capital Flows," April 5, 2000.

———, "Report of the Working Group on Highly Leveraged Institutions," April 5, 2000.

Friedman, Milton, "The Case for Flexible Exchange Rates," *Essays in Positive Economics*, Chicago: University of Chicago Press, 1953.

———, "How Asia Fell," *Hoover Digest*, no. 2, 1999.

———, "R_x for Japan: Back to the Future," *Wall Street Journal*, December 17, 1997: A22.

Friedman, Milton and Anna Schwartz, *A Monetary History of the United States*, 1867–1960, Princeton, NJ: Princeton University Press, 1963.

Froot, Kenneth A. and Mathew McBrady, "The 1994–95 Mexican Peso Crisis," Harvard Business School, 9-296-056, December 9, 1999.

Funabashi, Yoichi, *Managing the Dollar: From the Plaza to the Louvre*, Washington, DC: Institute for International Economics, 1988.

Galbraith, John Kenneth, *The Great Crash 1929*, Boston: Houghton Mifflin, 1954.

Gil-Díaz, Francisco and Agustín Carstens, "Pride and Prejudice: The Economics Profession and Mexico's Financial Crisis," in *Mexico 1994: Anatomy of an Emerging Market Crash,*" Washington, DC: Carnegie Endowment for International Peace, 1997. Sebastian Edwards and Moises Naím, editors.

Hale, David, "How to End Mexico's Meltdown," *Wall Street Journal*, January 19, 1995.

Hanke, Steve, "How I Spent My Summer," *International Economist,* July/August 1998: 30-33.

Hanke, Steve H. and Kurt Schuler, *Currency Boards for Developing Countries: A Handbook,* San Francisco, CA: Institute for Contemporary Studies Press, 1994.

Henderson, Callum, *Asia Falling,* New York: BusinessWeek Books–McGraw-Hill, 1998.

Hicks, J.R., "Mr. Keynes and the 'Classics'; A Suggested Interpretation," *Econometrica* 5 (April 1937): 147-159.

Institute of International Finance, Inc., *Comparative Statistics for Emerging Market Economies,* Washington, D.C., December 1998 and April 2000.

International Financial Institution Advisory Commission Report, March 2000.

International Monetary Fund, "The Asian Crisis: Capital Markets Dynamics and Spillover," *International Capital Markets,* Washington, DC: September 1998, 11–58.

———, "The ERM Crisis of September 1992," *International Capital Markets,* Washington, DC: April 1993.

———, "Emerging Market Currency Crisis of July 1997," *International Capital Markets,* Washington, DC: November 1997.

———, "Evolution of the Mexican Peso Crisis," *International Capital Markets, Developments, Prospects, and Policy Issues,* Washington, DC: August 1995, 53–79.

———, "From Crisis to Recovery in the Emerging Market Economies," *World Economic Outlook,* Washington, D.C.: October 1999.

———, "Fundamentals, Timely Policy Measures Help Singapore Weather the Asian Crisis," *IMF Survey* 28, no. 8, April 26, 1999.

———, "IMF Supported Programs in Indonesia, Korea, and Thailand; A Preliminary Assessment," Preliminary Copy, Washington, DC: January 1999.

———, "Japan's Crisis and Policy Options," *World Economic Outlook, Financial Turbulence and the World Economy*, Washington, D.C.: October 1998.

———, "Malaysia's Response to the Financial Crisis: How Unorthodox Was It?" *World Economic Outlook,* Washington, DC: October 1999.

———, "Prologue to the ERM Crisis: The Convergence Play," *International Capital Markets,* Washington, DC: April 1993.

———, "Republic of Korea: Economic and Policy Developments," IMF Staff Country Report no. 00/11, February 2000.

Jorion, Philippe, *Value at Risk,* Chicago: Irwin, 1997.

Kahn, Herman, *The Emerging Japanese Superstate: Challenge and Response,*

Englewood Cliffs, NJ: Prentice Hall, 1970.

————, *On Thermonuclear War,* Princeton, NJ: Princeton University Press, 1960.

————, *Thinking about the Unthinkable,* New York: Horizon Press, 1962.

Katz, Richard, *Japan: The System That Soured,* New York: East Gate, 1998.

Keynes, John Maynard, *Tract on Monetary Reform,* London: Macmillan, 1923.

Kindleberger, Charles P., *Manias, Panics, and Crashes: A History of Financial Crises,* New York: Wiley, 1996.

Krugman, Paul, "It's Baaack! Japan's Slump and the Return of the Liquidity Trap," *Brookings Papers on Economic Activity* 2 (1998): 137-205.

————, *Currencies and Crises,* Cambridge, MA: MIT Press, 1995.

————, "The Myth of Asia's Miracle," *Foreign Affairs,* November/December 1994: 62-78.

————, *The Return of Depression Economics,* New York: Norton, 1999.

Lewis, Michael, "How The Eggheads Cracked," *New York Times Magazine,* January 24, 1999.

Lowenstein, Roger, *When Genius Failed: The Rise and Fall of Long-Term Capital Management,* New York: Random House, 2000.

Mahathir bin Mohamad, "Highwaymen of the Global Economy," *Wall Street Journal,* September 23, 1997.

Merry, Wayne, "Corruption in Russia and Recent U.S. Policy," Testimony, before the Committee on Foreign Relations of the U.S. Senate, September 23, 1999.

Miller, Merton H. "Do the Laws of Economics Apply to Japan?" *Merton Miller on Derivatives,* New York: Wiley, 1997.

————, "Reflections of a Retiring Keynote Speaker," Address to 10th Annual Conference of PACAP/FMA, Singapore, July 8, 1999. Pacific-Basin Capital Market Research Center/Financial Management Association.

Mühleisen, Martin, "Too Much of a Good Thing? The Effectiveness of Fiscal Stimulus," *Post-Bubble Blues: How Japan Responded to Asset Price Collapse,* Washington, D.C.: The International Monetary Fund, 2000.

Mundell, Robert A., "Capital Mobility and Stabilization Policy under Fixed and Flexible Exchange Rates," *Canadian Journal of Economics and Political Science,* 29 (November 1963): 475–485.

Ouchi, William, *Theory Z,* New York: Avon, 1981.

President's Working Group on Financial Markets, "Hedge Funds, Leverage, and the Lessons of Long-Term Capital Management," April 1999.

————, "Over-the-Counter Derivatives Markets and the Commodity

Exchange Act," November 1999.

Porter, Richard and Ruth Judson, "The Location of the U.S. Currency: How Much is Abroad?" *Federal Reserve Bulletin* 82, no. 10, October 1996: 883-903.

Ramaswamy, Ramana, and Hossein Samiei, "The Yen-Dollar Rate: Have Interventions Mattered?" International Monetary Fund, Washington, D.C., Working Paper WP/00/95, 2000.

Sakakibara, Eisuke, *Beyond Capitalism,* Economic Strategy Institute, Lanham, MD: University Press of America, 1993.

Schuler, Kurt, "Basics of Dollarization," Testimony before U.S. Senate Joint Economic Committee, January 1999.

Schwartz, Anna J. "Currency Boards: Their Past, Present, and Possible Future Role," *Carnegie-Rochester Conference Series on Public Policy,* 1993: 147-193.

———, "International Financial Crises: Myths and Realities," *The Cato Journal* 17, no. 3 (Winter 1998).

Sharma, Shalendra D. "Bitter Medicine for Sick Tigers: The IMF and Asia's Financial Crisis," Center for the Pacific Rim, University of San Francisco, Pacific Rim Report no. 8, April 1998.

Sharpe, William F. "Asset Allocation: Management Style and Performance Measurement," *Journal of Portfolio Management* (Winter 1992): 7-19.

Shiller, Robert J., *Irrational Exuberance,* Princeton, NJ: Princeton University Press, 2000.

Siconolfi, Michael, Anita Raghavan, and Mitchell Pacelle, "How the Salesmanship and Brainpower Failed at Long-Term Capital," *Wall Street Journal,* November 16, 1998: 1.

Smith, Adam, *An Inquiry into the Nature and Causes of the Wealth of Nations,* reprinted Chicago: University of Chicago Press, 1976.

Stiglitz, Joe, "What I Learned At the World Economic Crisis: The Insider," *New Republic,* April 17, 2000.

Takagi, Shinji, "Foreign Exchange Market Intervention and Domestic Monetary Control in Japan, 1973–89," *Japan and the World Economy* 3 (1991): 147–180.

Taleb, Nassim, *Dynamic Hedging,* New York: Wiley, 1997.

Temperton, Paul, Editor, *The European Currency Crisis,* Cambridge, England: Probus Publishing Company, 1993.

Theil, Henri, *Econometrics,* New York: Wiley, 1971.

Tobin, James, "Why We Need Sand In the Market's Gears," *The Washington Post,* December 21, 1997.

United Nations, "Towards a New International Financial Architecture," *Report of Executive Committee on Economic and Social Affairs,* January 21, 1999.

United States General Accounting Office, "Long-Term Capital Management," Report to Congressional Requesters, October 1999.

Vogel, Eric F. *Japan as Number One: Lessons for America,* Cambridge, MA: Harvard University Press, 1979.

Williamson, John, Ed. "Fundamental Equilibrium Exchange Rates," Washington, D.C.: Institute for International Economics, 1994.

Zarazaga, Carlos M. "Argentina's Currency Board During a Financial Crisis," *Southwest Economy,* Federal Reserve Bank of Dallas, Issue 4, 1995.

I n d e x

About Bloomberg

Bloomberg L.P., founded in 1981, is a global information services, news, and media company. Headquartered in New York, the company has nine sales offices, two data centers, and 80 news bureaus worldwide.

Bloomberg, serving customers in 100 countries around the world, holds a unique position within the financial services industry by providing an unparalleled combination of news, information, and analytic tools in a single package known as the BLOOMBERG PROFESSIONAL™ service. Corporations, banks, money management firms, financial exchanges, insurance companies, and many other entities and organizations rely on Bloomberg as their primary source of information.

BLOOMBERG NEWS℠, founded in 1990, offers worldwide coverage of economies, companies, industries, governments, financial markets, politics, and sports. The news service is the main content provider for Bloomberg's broadcast media, which include BLOOMBERG TELEVISION®—the 24-hour cable and satellite television network available in ten languages worldwide—and BLOOMBERG RADIO™—an international radio network anchored by flagship station BLOOMBERG® WBBR AM1130 in New York.

In addition to the BLOOMBERG PRESS® line of books, Bloomberg publishes *BLOOMBERG® MARKETS, BLOOMBERG PERSONAL FINANCE™*, and *BLOOMBERG® WEALTH MANAGER*. To learn more about Bloomberg, call a sales representative at:

Frankfurt:	49-69-920-410	San Francisco:	1-415-912-2960
Hong Kong:	852-977-6000	São Paulo:	5511-3048-4500
London:	44-171-330-7500	Singapore:	65-438-8585
New York:	1-212-318-2000	Sydney:	61-29-777-8686
Princeton:	1-609-279-3000	Tokyo:	81-3-3201-8900

For in-depth market information and news, visit **BLOOMBERG.COM®**, which draws proprietary content from the BLOOMBERG PROFESSIONAL™ service and Bloomberg's host of media products to provide high-quality news and information in multiple languages on stocks, bonds, currencies, and commodities, at **www.bloomberg.com.**

About the Author

David F. DeRosa, Ph.D., is the president of DeRosa Research and Trading. He is an adjunct professor of finance and fellow of the Center for International Finance at the Yale School of Management. Before teaching at Yale, he taught at the Graduate School of Business of the University of Chicago.

DeRosa has had more than two decades of experience in international capital markets and in particular in foreign exchange trading. He writes a thrice-weekly column for Bloomberg News on international finance and politics. The DeRosa column has also appeared in newspapers all over the world. He is the author of *Options on Foreign Exchange* (Wiley 2000) and *Managing Foreign Exchange Risk* (Irwin 1996) and is the editor of *Currency Derivatives* (Wiley 1998). DeRosa received his A.B. in economics from the University of Chicago and his Ph.D. from the Graduate School of Business of the University of Chicago.